INDIAN DIASPORA

Economic, Political and Cultural Inquiry

INDIAN DIASPORA

Economic, Political and Cultural Inquiry

Dr. S.N. Yadav

ज्ञानम् ददाति ज्ञानदा

JNANADA PRAKASHAN (P&D)

NEW DELHI

Published by :
JNANADA PRAKASHAN (P&D)
4837/2, 24, Ansari Road, Daryaganj
New Delhi-110002
Phone : 011-23272047
Mobile : 9212137080
Email: jnanadabooksdelhi@yahoo.com
Website: www.jnanadabooks.com; text.ind.in

Assisted by :
TEXT BOOK PROMOTION SOCIETY OF INDIA
4837/2, 24, Ansari Road, Daryaganj
New Delhi-110002
Phone : 011-23272047
Mobile : 9212137080

Edition : 2011

Indian Diaspora: Economic, Political and Cultural Inquiry

ISBN: 978-81-7139-436-4

Typesetting by :
Vardhman Computers
New Delhi-110 017, India

Published by Mrs. S. Chowdhary for M/s. Jnanada Prakashan (P&D) Daryaganj, Ansari Road, New Delhi-110002, India and printed at Balaji Offset, Navin Shahdara, Delhi-110032, India.

PREFACE

Demographically speaking, Indian Diaspora is relatively smaller than the Chinese and Jewish. However, it is perhaps the oldest and most widespread all over the world. Not surprisingly, Indian Diaspora is found today in nearly one hundred and thirty-six countries, including both the developed as well as developing economy. More significantly, they are estimated over twenty million. Remarkably, in forty countries, the number of Indian immigrants exceeds 50,000.

Against this general background, the author has mode serious endeavor to examine closely the various issues associated with the Indian immigrant community especially since the beginning of the Europeans colonisation of India. The very first chapter presents an overview of Indian emigration during the colonial era. The concept of Indian Diaspora has been dealt with in the second chapter.

A comparative study of the economic role of Africans, Europeans and Indians is the part of the third chapter. The social and cultural profile of the Indian Diaspora has been critically evaluated in the fourth chapter. The economic contribution of Indian Diaspora has been analysed in the fifth chapter. Political and educational role of the Indian immigrants have been studied in the sixth and seventh chapters respectively.

The prevalence of caste and religion has been a unique feature of the Indian Diaspora. This aspect of the problem has been examined in the eight chapter. The Indian Diaspora has played a significant role is generating nationalism, especially in East Africa, which has been covered in the ninth chapter.

In the wake of decolonisation, the political role of the Indian Diaspora has been greatly marginalised. This aspect of the problem has been covered in the concluding chapter.

The author is convinced that the book entitled "Indian Diaspora: Economic, Political and Cultural Inquiry" would contribute significantly to understand properly their overall performance in the development of the countries of their adoption. Undoubtedly, it would be a great contribution to the literature on the Indian immigrants.

CONTENTS

ACRONYMS

ASP	Afro-Shirazi Party
DP	Democratic Party
ICDC	Industrial and Commercial Development Corporation
KADU	Kenya African Democratic Union
KANU	Kenya African National Union
KAU	Kenya African Union
KCCI	Kenya Chamber of Commerce and Industry
KFP	Kenya Freedom Party
KY	Kabaka Yekka
NCCCI	Nairobi Central Chamber of Commerce and Industry
NDC	National Development Corporation
NICC	Nairobi Indian Chamber of Commerce
NKP	New Kenya Party
TAFCO	Tanzanian African Finance Co. Ltd.
UAG	Uganda Action Group
UP	The United Party
UPC	Uganda Peoples' Congress
UTP	United Tanganyika Party
ZNP	Zanzibar Nationalist Party
ZPPP	Zanzibar and Pemba Peoples' Party

1

AN OVERVIEW OF INDIANS EMIGRATION DURING THE COLONIAL ERA

India–East Africa Economic Linkages

For over two thousand years, Indians were at the heart of the economic activity which brought the influences of a wider world to the East coast of Africa. Indians rarely controlled the great oceanic trade routes and never controlled politically or militarily the East African coast itself. But, throughout the period, whoever governed the coast and its hinterland and whoever dominated the Indian Ocean, India remained the most important market for East African goods and the most important source of the trade goods which were exchanged for them.

East African gold, ivory and slaves poured into India over the centuries; and into East Africa there poured in return Indian cloth and beads, Indian skill and capital. For, it was never merely a matter of others, acting as middlemen, exchanging goods between Africa and India; there were always Indian merchants, financiers, sailors, pilots.

Of all the peoples who were at one time or another involved in the East African trade, indeed, the Indians showed themselves the most persistent and the most resilient. In times of economic prosperity, when the whole Indian Ocean trade complex was booming, Indians throve in the East African trade.

But, in times of economic disruption, when old trading systems were being shattered by the advent of new political powers, whether Portuguese, German or British, Indians were still in demand for their skills and labour. Neutrals the great struggle between Christianity and Islam, the Hindu merchants and traders especially were able to continue their activities along the East African coast throughout the whole period.

The process was first recorded in the 'Periplus of the Erythrean Sea', a Greek guide for sailors compiled around A.D. 100. Marco Polo retailed stories about Indian links with Africa centuries later; later still the Portuguese, as they forced their way round Africa into the Indian Ocean, found the ancient Indian commerce with East Africa at one of its most prosperous peaks. They found ports crowded with Indian ships; a great East African demand for Indian goods which in the end forced the newcomers to deal in such goods themselves instead of attempting to compete with the products of Portugal: Indian settlements; Indian pilots. There is nothing, indeed, to indicate that Indians had penetrated into the interior or made contact with its Bantu state systems. But, on the coast they were playing a key economic role.

Economic Role of Indians in the Colonial East Africa

The Portuguese attack upon the Moslem controlled economic system of the Indian Ocean and the consequent disruption of the East coast trade was the first of the great crises faced by the Asians in East Africa. In the sixteenth and seventeenth centuries the prosperity of the whole coast was sapped and as opportunity declined, so too did Indian participation. But, the Indian link was not broken. Trading links with India continued to the north of Portuguese settlement, and within the area of Portuguese control Indian activity and influence even developed new forms. For the Portuguese, after all, their East African possessions and tributaries were part of a great Oceanic empire of which Goa was the economic, administrative and cultural centre. In a real sense, the East African coast became a province of an Indian administration and Indians, especially Goans, were soon actively involved in Portuguese penetration and development. Indian labour was used to construct forts along the coast. Indian traders and adventurers and junior administrators took part in the chequered process of penetration into the interior. By the nineteenth century, Asians were an informal advance guard of Portuguese influent in Central Africa; Asian traders operated every season in the gold areas of Mashonaland; Goan adventurers, of whom Gouveia was the best known, carved out virtual personal empires for themselves on the western borders of the Portuguese colony.

Something of the same pattern can be seen with the coming of German and British imperial rule in East Africa. In the first part of the nineteenth century the coast north of Mozambique experienced a striking revival of economic prosperity under the influence the Omani Arabs and particularly of Sultan Seyyid Said. Basing himself on Zanzibar, the shrewd merchant prince Built up a commercial empire and his subjects pushed deep into East Africa in the interests of a booming trade in ivory and slaves. European and North African markets were perhaps the key ones in this trade but Indian participation was as vital as ever. Seyyid Said made explicit and successful efforts to involve Indian traders, administrators and financiers in his ventures. They did not participate on any scale in the push into the interior any more than Indians had done before the arrival of the Portuguese but in Zanzibar itself and on the coast their numbers steadily grew.

In 1844, it was estimated that there were some 1,200 Asians resident in East Africa; by 1860 there were some 6,000. In Zanzibar the key post of Customs Master was almost always held by an Indian in this period, its holder acting as banker and financial adviser to the Sultan as well as being collector of customs revenue. Indians were the virtual monopolists of retail trade. In 1873, Sir Bartle Frere noted that 'throughout our whole circuit, from Zanzibar "round by Mozambique and Madagascar and up to Cape Guardafui, we did not, except at Johanne, meet half a dozen exceptions to the rule that every shopkeeper was an Indian." Above all, Indians financed and supplied the caravans to the interior.

The coming of the Germans and the British—and of the Free State in the Congo—opened the second instalment of

Christian–Muslim contest in East Africa. This time the economic and political interests of Islam suffered a massive overthrow. Zanzibar was cut off from its hinterland; the whole far-flung structure of Arab-Swahili trade was shattered; the caravans suppressed; and European political control established after fierce resistance by the old controllers of East Africa trade had been put down. Once again, an economic system in which Asians had been operating profitably was broken. But, once again the Asians survived.

As far as the British were concerned, it was even more true of them than it had been of the Portuguese that their East African territories were extensions of an Indian empire. The carry-over of ideas from the Indian administrative system to British East Africa was greater even than the old flow between Goa and Mozambique. The Indians, who had been participating in the Zanzibar–Swahili trade System had been, in fact, British subjects, and this had been itself a factor in British expansion on the mainland. The charter of 3 September, 1888, granted by Queen Victoria to the Imperial British East Africa Company, for instance, gave as one of the reasons for official backing of the Company that: 'the possession by a British Company of the coastline, as above defined, and which includes the port of Mombasa, would be advantageous to the commercial and other interests of our subjects in the Indian Ocean, who may otherwise be compelled to reside and trade under the government or protection of alien powers.'

Many of the British officers who came to East Africa during the early days, had served the Government of India. Burton and Speke were themselves officers of the Indian army and were provided with instruments and equipment by the Government of India. Indian coinage was made the official coinage in East Africa; Indian laws were extended them. Indian troops were imported from time to time to keep order. Just as the Portuguese had used Indian labour to build forts, so the British used Indian labour to build the railway systems of British East Africa. And just as the Portuguese penetration of Mozambique had been followed, or sometimes preceded, by Indian and Goan enterprise, so the establishment of British administration and the opening of the line of rail was followed by a large-scale movement of Indian traders into the interior, long before white settlers in any number arrived. It was little wonder that some Englishmen at least thought of East Africa in terms of an economic dependency of India; envisaged it being exploited through the immigration of Indian peasant farmers; and generally conceived of an Indian development of the area under British control.

In German East Africa, 'under the government or protection of an alien power', natives of British India were in a much less immediately strong position. The Germans made some effort in the early days to break the Indian monopoly of trading activity in their territory by encouraging African enterprise. But, the economic facts remained and had to be accepted; in Tanganyika Asians played only slightly less an important economic role than in Kenya.

Up to this point of their connection with East Africa, Indians had rarely taken part in explicitly political activity. Concentrating upon economic enterprise, they had adapted themselves in turn to the indigenous coastal chiefs to the Arabs to the Portuguese to the Arabs again, and now to the British and the Germans. To all these regimes, they had been, to a greater or less degree, economically indispensable. But, now a new factor began to operate. It was not long before the idea that East Africa was in some way an area providentially set aside for Asian economic enterprise was challenged by the idea that East Africa was white man's country.

The growth of white settler communities in East Africa for the first time offered a fundamental challenge to the economic position of Asians. Between these white settler communities and the Asians, there did not exist that alliance of mutual economic benefit which had been struck between the Swahili caravan leaders and the Indian financiers of the 19th century instead, a fierce economic rivalry sprang up, most obviously centring on access to land but flowing into many other fields.

It would be wrong, of course, to over-state this situation. Asians, white settlers and Africans managed to co-exist and co-operate economically and Asian attitudes have remained profoundly tinged by the old gospel of co-operation and survival, no matter what the regime. But, there were frequent enough threats to the whole economic position of the Asians to drive them into political activity, especially because they saw that the white settler element was using political pressure to achieve economic end twentieth century the Asian communities of East Africa, and of Kenya in particular, began to play a part in the political as well as the economic history of the area.

Once this development had begun, the old connection with mainland India began to take on a new significance. For not only were Indians in East Africa driven to political action but at the same time Indians in India itself were developing a newly articulate national sense and building up strong nationalist movements. The interconnections between the two developments were of the utmost importance to the course of East African politics, and just as Britain had been inclined to treat East Africa in the past as an economic dependent of India, so now she had to see East African politics in the context of Indian nationalism.

It will be best to take the Kenyan experience to illustrate these generalisations. In the first days very much use was made of Asians in Kenya; it was planned to introduce Indian peasant settlers; and official British opinion was favourable towards these industrious and valuable subjects. But, things soon began to change. From the Governorship of Elliott onwards a policy of discrimination in favour of the white settler came to be adopted. The settlers themselves developed with skill and energy the arts of political pressure; to a varying degree they succeeded in influencing both local administrative officials and British politicians. And it was the aim of the settlers to achieve both political and economic dominance.

As fanning developed in Kenya, access to land became one of the main points of controversy. As early as 1902, the Indian Association of Mombasa was protesting about discrimination in land grants, and then received an assurance that there was 'no intention of drawing a distinction between Europeans and Indians as far as rights of mining, settling and acquiring land' were concerned. This official policy came under heavy pressure, however. In 1905, a Commission on land allocation, under the Chairmanship of the settler leader. Lord Delamere, reported that while there was 'no objection to the general proposition that Indians should hold land in the Protectorate... considering only a small area of the Protectorate is suitable for European settlement and colonisation, it is desirable that land within that area should be reserved for the support and management of a white population.' In July 1906, this pressure was successful; Lord Elgin, Secretary of State for the Colonies, approved the practice of granting land in the so-called White Highlands only to European settlers.

This initial settler success was followed up by attempts to deny Asians the right to own land anywhere in Kenya. In 1907 the Land Board passed a resolution to that effect; but it proved impossible to carry British opinion to this extent. In 1915, however, the reservation of land in the Highlands for whites was embodied in law And in practice the principle of segregation was also applied in urban areas through the imposition of racial covenants.

It soon became apparent to the Asian community of Kenya that if they were to protect themselves against this sort of discriminatory economic competition they must seek some rival source of local political power and pressure. Thus, not content with merely lobbying the Aga Khan and Winston Churchill over the land issue, they raised the issue of the non-European franchise long before it had become the target of African politicians. The struggle between the Asian and European communities over representation was of very considerable importance to Kenya, very possibly frustrating the white drive to self rule there, and stimulating African political thinking and activity.

Indian demands for political representation at first met with some success. Winston Churchill, as Under-Secretary at the Colonial Office, was an advocate—'There can be no reason for excluding this large and meritorious class', he minuted. After an Indian petition in April 1908 it was decided that a representative of that community should be nominated to the Legislative Council and in 1909 Mr. A. M. Jeevanjee was selected by Acting Governor Jackson. But, already the counter-tide was running strongly and the Kenyan Indian community began to appeal to wider audiences. As early as 1910, they demonstrated their ability to win the sympathies of the Indian national movement. In that year Jeevanjee took his case to London and achieved the support of the All-India Moslem League. Later, his statements were printed in India itself with an appeal for the support of Congress and a suggestion that East Africa be annexed formally to the Indian Empire.

So, it went on with each white initiative countered by an Asian reaction. War-time demands by whites provoked the founding of the East African Indian National Congress; the success of the whites in gaining a European-only franchise in 1917 provoked the great struggle between themselves and the Asian community in the years immediately following the First World War. These years were marked by white abuse and suspicion of Asians, even by white plans to arrest and deport the leaders of the Asian community. They were marked also by Indian appeals to Britain, to Indian nationalism, to the Government of India.

At this time also, there came into being the first contacts between Indian and African nationalism; the Indian editor, M. A. Desai, giving publicity in his paper to the grievances of the Kikuyu and allowing Harryj Thuku to use his office as a headquarters. At the time there was a tendency to see emergent African politics in the context of the struggle between whites and Asians and to judge the 'loyalty' of Africans in terms of their hostility to Indians. But, the links between early African nationalist leaders and Indian nationalism through Asians resident in East Africa, had a significance in the precocious emergence of radical African politics in Kenya which has not yet been fully explored.

Asian Politics and African Nationalism

Whatever positive contributions Asian politics made to emerging African nationalism in terms of objectives or methods, there is no doubt that negatively Asian activity was of very great importance to the long term results of the struggle between black and white. Because of the Asian community the question of the Justice or propriety of white political demands there received altogether wider debate than the similar white aspirations in Rhodesia.

While there was no articulate opponent of Southern Rhodesian white demands for self-government, the Government of India constituted itself the formidable advocate of the Kenyan Asian case, and argued point for point with the advocates of white advance. 'Would the settlers now succeed in making Kenya a typical British Colony?', asks George Bennett rhetorically in his *Kenya: A Political History*. 'In this objective they were under challenge from the Indians.

It may well be that it was only their rivalry which prevented the Europeans from establishing their position in Kenya as in places further south.' Or again, describing the rebuff delivered to white aspirations with the African paramountcy declaration of 1923. Bennett writes: 'The full weight of this rebuff may be measured against the grant of this same status to the Southern Rhodesian settlers in the same year—but they had no Indians to contend with.'

This was the most significant Asian contribution to the political history of East Africa but it was not the only one. The European rebuff certainly did not mean an Indian victory and the contest between the communities continued. Among the Indian politicians were a handful of radical nationalists of a political sophistication beyond anything possible for African politics at the same date and these men had a significant influence on developing African nationalism. There was Isher Dass, with his policy of boycott and ion-cooperation; his opposition to Closer Union moves; his links with the Indian nationalist movements. It was Dass who in the 1939 Legislative Council read into the record the petitions of the African organisations, the Kikuyu Central Association and the Kavirondo Taxpayers' Welfare Association against the Order in Council to define the Highlands. There was Makan Singh, the Sikh trade unionist, who organised the Labour Trade Union of East Africa, established contact with Kikuyu labour leaders, and played a key role in the Mombasa dock strike of 1939.

Economic and Political Rivalry between Asians and African

There is no point, of course, in attempting to over-state this Asian radicalism or their part in opposition politics. There was always an economic and incipient political rivalry between

Africans "and Asians; and that majority of the Asian community had no desire to associate itself with the radicalism of Makan Singh or V Isher Pass. Still, by virtue of the situation in which they found themselves. One can the links with Indian nationalism, the Asian did at times speak for the Africans as well as for themselves. One can quote African testimony to this, all the more effective for being obviously reluctant. In the Legislative Council in the late 1940s an African member admitted: 'I never thought that I would ever side with the Indian community as I now do, but I am forced by circumstances and cannot help it. I must, therefore, say that in this Council, the Indian members are more helpful to the African community than the Europeans because they think of what the African community desire.'

The other East African territories had a more peaceful political history than Kenya. Essentially, the Asian communities in these territories were faced with precisely the same problems as Kenyan Asians, but racial conflicts were not so acute or denned. In Tanganyika, indeed, with its Trust Territory status, Asians rose to the senior ranks of the civil service and there was less franchisal discrimination.

But, there comes out of the history of these other territories the second theme of Asian life in East Africa—a theme which is now the dominant one. We have already said that in Kenya especially the challenge of white economic enterprise "drove Asians into political activity. We have remarked also on the incipient political and actual economic competition of Asians and Africans there. In Uganda and Zanzibar this competition was already the major issue during the 1920s and 1930s.

In the long history of Asian economic enterprise in East Africa, there had been until the colonial era relatively little contact with the African peoples either in the form of economic collaboration or competition. Asians had mainly been dealing with the various powers who controlled the coast or the ocean trade routes. In particular, they had not been concerned with the production of goods, though they had financed their collection; it was their role to trade in the goods produced by others. As Indians went inland under the umbrella of the colonial power they came to play additional economic roles and to assume positions hitherto monopolised by Africans themselves.

As various African peoples responded to the new economic opportunities rivalry between them and the Asian businessman and trader was bound to develop. This happened most clearly in Uganda, where the traditional system managed to modify itself successfully; to retain its control of land and production; and to exclude white settlers. The highly material, competitive society of the Baganda entered into the world of modern economic opportunity with zeal. Asians played a significant role in assisting the development of agriculture in Uganda and were especially prominent in the early stages of the cotton industry. But, their participation brought them into repeated conflict with African farmers who resented the Asian monopoly of marketing and ginning; and gradually African co-operatives began to act effectively to break down that monopoly. This economic competition created much ill feeling and during the Kenya contest of the early 1920s, the whites were able to produce numerous anti-Asian statements from Uganda Africans to strengthen their case. Any Indian who rested his optimism about Asian relations with Africans on the growing co-operation between them in Kenyan politics would have been well advised to look at Uganda as a corrective. In Uganda, the Asians were also meeting with economic competition backed by use of political power; but there was little possibility of countering it.

Asian Investment in Zanzibar

In Zanzibar, a similarly instructive situation developed. Asians had for long occupied posts importance in the island's administration and continued to do so. Though the break-up of the old economic system reduced the importance of Zanzibar and led to a movement of Asians to the mainland, there still remained considerable Asian investment. Asians had, a virtual monopoly of the marketing and export of cloves, which were now the mainstay of the Zanzibar economy. During the 1930s, there was a very considerable reorganisation of the industry in order to increase the participation of the indigenous population. In this case the Asian merchants attempted to counter with political pressure; they protested to the Indian

Government and K.P.S. Menon was sent to examine the situation. But, the publication of his report had no impact on the policy of government in Zanzibar and the Indian merchants had to adapt themselves to the new situation.

In various ways, the events of the twentieth century, even before the independence revolution, had greatly changed the character of Asian activity in East Africa. With its emphasis upon Asian economic interests this study has not perhaps sufficiently brought out the extent to which Asians were steadily ceasing to play a dominant role in East African commerce or development. Significant though their skills and capital remained, more sophisticated skills and much greater capital resources were becoming available from other sources. And this is a picture which has certainly not been modified with independence; neither the Indian Government nor Asians generally now take an important place amongst the suppliers of skills and capital to the independent nations of East Africa. The old Indian Ocean trading complex is no longer an important element in their economic life.

Thus, Asians have lost their economic indispensability and they have also become involved in competition with Africans. To protect themselves in this vulnerable position the new tradition of political activity which they developed in Kenya as a retort to white pressures is of little avail to them. The techniques of appeal to India and to the British press cannot be used in the new circumstances. In fact, the old link with India which was for centuries of such vital economic and political significance, has little reality now.

It might be thought that there was little from their long history in East Africa likely to be of use to Asians today. Still, Asians can not unreasonably claim to have contributed something to development over hundreds of years; they can claim also to have shared the common disabilities of white racialism; they can claim to have helped to do something about them. To this extent, their history can be used; and of course, whether useful or not, it is still this history which continues to mould and to shape Asian attitudes and actions today.

2

INDIAN DIASPORA: A CONCEPTUAL FRAMEWORK

Concept of Community

To understand the significance of Hindu castes and religious cults and of Muslim sects in Uganda, clarification of certain terms is needed. In East African usage the English term community was considerably over-worked. It might, for example, signify people in 'racial' categories: the African, the Asian or the European communities. One also heard of the Arab community, which was not regarded as a part of the Asian community. The Goan community, whose members came from the former territory of Portuguese India, even more surprisingly was not always of the Asian community either.

Occasionally, though not often, a 'racial' category or a part of it, such as Indian Muslims, might be considered as a section of a larger religious grouping, the Muslim community which included Arabs, Africans, Indians, and others; or it might be divided into smaller categories such as the Hindu or the Sikh communities, which were neither castes *(varna)* nor sub-castes *(jati)*. Sometimes, too, the 'racial' categories were divided into communities of regional origin, as for example the Greek community among the Europeans or the Surti and Maharastra communities among the Indians. Finally, one also heard of such occupational categories as the 'trading community', the 'farming community', and so forth.

Indian Background of the Term Community

Among Indians the word 'community' usually in its English form, whatever the language actually being spoken) had a special connotation, and was used, as a rule, to refer to caste groups *(jati)*, caste categories or sects. Thus, in 1954 an article in a newspaper began: 'Today the Ismaili community the followers of the Aga Khan—celebrates the Imamat day....[1] The members of the Patidar sub-caste, who in Kampala had organised themselves into a caste association known as the *Patidar Samaj*, reserved membership to men and women belonging to the tatidar community whose original home was in Qujera or Saurashtra (Kathiawad)....' The association was formed 'to serve and advance generally the social, educational, economical, cultural and physical activities... of members of the Patidar caste settled in the town'.[2] Although, the founders of the association and most of its members belonged to the Gujarat proper, the terms of membership admitted men and women from the wider caste category, distributed over a large part of the Bombay Presidency.

The word community, as used in East Africa covered almost any category of people with an easily recognised common identity. Moreover, this lack of precision had value. Among Indians the question 'What is your community?' would normally be answered by the name of a Hindu sub-caste or a Muslim sect, unless there was a clear indication that some other group or category was meant. The Gujarati question *'tamari jati shu?'* (What is your *jati)* was a more limited enquiry and referred to a range of social ideas which was not always felt to be relevant in East Africa. A man was likely to ask the question in Gujarati if he wanted to know of some traditional aspect of the 'community', as, for example, marriage regulations.

A Muslim might misunderstand the question altogether. If his family's conversion to Islam was recent he would know his former Hindu *jati* and might answer 'potter' or some other sub-caste name rather than that of a religious sect. For Muslims who maintain that Islam is without caste or sect a neutral word like community is useful to indicate its divisions. The fundamental unit of their organisation is the mosque congregation, the *jamat,* and this term was occasionally used for all the members of a sect; but for Hindus it would have been wholly unacceptable. On the other hand, the Indian words *samaj, mandal* and *sabha* were either limited to voluntary associations or had overtones that made Muslims avoid them.

The word community is also technically used in sociological writing for the aggregates of people within which all an individual's social relationships may be found.[3] In this sense neither castes, nor sub-castes, nor sects, neither Hindus nor Muslims, nor the Indians as a whole constituted communities in East Africa; but as the term was so universally used there it is inconvenient to substitute another. In what follows, therefore, the term community refers to Hindu castes, both *varna* divisions, as in the *Brahmin community, smidjati* sub-caste categories and groups, as in *the Patidar* or *Lohana communities.* It also refers to Muslim sects and other groups based on religious or territorial affiliations, like the *Sikh* or *Goon communities.* If necessary the word will be preceded by an adjective to make the meaning clear.

Caste Structure of the Indian Immigrants

The failure of the Indian immigrants to transplant any cross-section of their traditional society in Africa was a fact of capital importance. As traders and settlers in British Protectorates and Colonies, they were subject to circumstances and laws that were often in direct conflict with Hindu and Muslim culture. It is hardly surprising that large numbers abandoned many traditional practices and began to model their behaviour not on the Brahminical or Islamic ideals which they had observed in India, but on those they believed to be held by Europeans or the Europeanised classes in the larger cities of India.

An outsider might have postulated that in these circumstances a single Indian community would emerge, stratified possibly in terms of social class, but not in terms of caste or sectarian differences. What in fact emerged was a number of separate caste and sectarian communities, each one of them more significant in the everyday lives of its members than the Indian community as a whole. The traditional hierarchy of the caste system in India and the relationships of dependence between one caste and another had disappeared, but caste exclusiveness still remained.

In 1955, these communities were still emerging in all parts of East Africa, but for Africans and Europeans it was usually less trouble to ignore the process and to speak of 'Indians' or 'Asians' than to make the distinctions that marked off one Indian from "' another. This fact had practical importance. In legislation, it was customary to refer to the 'Asian community'. Administratively there were special 'Indian' schools, and the categories Hindu and Muslim were frequently treated as if they were corporate groups with responsible leaders able to answer for their members, when in reality the effective organisations within the categories were those of the component caste or sectarian communities.

Nevertheless, the wiser administrators always knew that though they might speak of an Indian community, and in certain contexts treat Indians as if they all belonged to a homogeneous and united body, the facts did not really permit such a view. Whenever Indians were needed to sit on advisory committees, the divisions of caste and sect had in practice to be observed, and men selected accordingly. For most Indians in Uganda, the wider categories had an importance that was mainly ideological. It is true that organisations existed which purported to speak for all Indians, or Hindus, or Muslims, but their strength and usefulness did not compare with those of caste or sectarian bodies.

The terms 'Indian', 'Hindu' and 'Muslim' stood for categories of the population which, indeed, had the potentiality of being fully organised corporate groups, but which in 1955 were not such. Fifty years earlier when all settlements were small, the immigrants acquiesced in being treated as a united community, and frequently acted as one, for the hazards of the environment were normally enough to unite all Indians in their transactions with non-Indians. Their occupations, too, were sufficiently similar to produce a superficial unity; and their leaders, who, by and large, took their opinions from the educated classes in India, did not approve of caste and sectarian 'communalism'. At the same time the immigrants did not fundamentally alter the views which they had brought from the rural districts of India on proper social relationships towards one another and strangers, in which caste and sectarian exclusiveness was fundamental. If they were to return to India and take up their proper place there, then they could not afford to make inappropriate marriages for their children or damage their chances of being fully accepted at home. Consequently, it is not surprising to find that as soon as the numbers of any caste or sect grew large enough for the members to feel safe in negotiating separately with the administration, then that caste or sect tended to emerge as a distinct group out of the general category of the Indian community.

Emergence of Communities

In 1910, the Protectorate government of Uganda enacted the Registration of Associations Ordinance. By this Act any group of people who wished to collect subscriptions from the public or to hold property was required to incorporate itself by registration with the Land Office. The property of such an association could be legally vested only in trustees, of whom there were to be at least two. Members were obliged to deposit at the Land Office a copy of the association's aims and objects and of the rules and regulations governing it. In addition they were to elect annually a committee of management with a stipulated number of officers. By 1918, only six associations had registered their existence. Two of these were for the management of Muslim mosques; two were recreational clubs; another was for the supervision of a Hindu cremation ground; and the last was a Freemasons' lodge, mainly for Europeans.

There were, of course, other similar non-commercial associations. Most of those already registered had existed long before their legal incorporation; and the fact that the Indian section of society possessed important structural groups that were unknown to or ignored by the administration is not a feature peculiar to Uganda.[4] In the earlier days of settlement it was seldom necessary for such groups to make their existence officially known, and then only in special circumstances.

Sectarian Graveyards

One of the earliest of such circumstances arose in 1913, when the government initiated a policy to prevent the permanent alienation of land to non-Africans. Its application unexpectedly revealed the complexity of Indian social relationships and the administration's lack of information about them. In Kampala, a plot of land was set aside on leasehold as a burial ground for all members of the Indian community.

Both African and Indian Muslims at once sent deputations to the Land Office protesting that they could not possibly bury their dead in or build mosques on ground that was not absolutely and permanently dedicated to God. To do so 'was against the principles of their religion as directed by their Prophet Mohammed'.[5] Sunnis and Shias, Africans and Indians, all combined in demanding freehold land for burial grounds. Objections to a shared graveyard were familiar to the officials of the Protectorate from their experience with Christians, but the demand for freehold was new to them. They, therefore, consulted Sunni Arab theologians in Mombasa, who ruled that Muslims could bury their dead in leasehold land and did not require freehold plots for the worship of God. The Muslims consequently had to accept the decision, but rejected the principle; and in 1955 at least one sect, the Shia Daudi Bohora, had for this reason still built no mosques in Uganda.

By 1922, the cemetery in Kampala was too small, and the Land Officer proposed setting aside another piece of land for the Muslim community to divide among its members as they chose. On the instructions of the Aga Khan, his solicitors in Zanzibar sent a letter to the Protectorate government. In it they reminded the administration that there were important differences in the tenets of the Ismaili faith of his followers and those of other adherents to Islam. In consequence, Shia Imami Ismailis had always considered themselves as distinct from other Muslim communities. Following a judgment given in the High Court of Bombay in 1866, the Aga Khan, as Imam of the sect, absolutely owned all communal property; and any arrangement for sharing a graveyard, or even a discussion of dividing a commonly held piece of ground, could not be accepted, because it might derogate from his title. The matter was eventually settled. The administration made no concession in its policy of refusing freehold grants; but each Muslim division had its own cemetery, and the Aga Khan and his followers had successfully demonstrated the uniqueness and separateness of their community.

Sectarian Mosque and Temple Land

Another set of closely related circumstances which again demonstrated the strength of sectarian sentiment and indicated the lines of the later development of 'communities' arose from the government's handling of land for buildings of worship. The refusal to grant any but leasehold sites for mosques was a serious matter in the eyes of almost all Muslims. Before 1913, freehold grants at a nominal cost were readily made for religious and charitable purposes; but after that date only leases could be obtained, and then only if an application was signed by at least ten members of a congregation who lived within a mile of the site. Moreover, the land was granted on the understanding that 'a full-stand premium', based on the commercial value of the plot, and a full commercial rent were to be paid.

This rule was never rigorously applied. It aroused strong passions among the Indians and caused such disunity that it was quietly allowed to lapse; and by 1925 the Land Office would normally grant a leasehold plot in every township 'for a nominal consideration to each religion—Mohammedan and Hindu'. But, each sect if it wanted its own separate place of worship was still required to make its 'own arrangements or rent sites at the usual rents'.[6] However, if its members were willing to accept a 'temporary occupation licence', then the administration was ready to grant them land at a nominal rent on the assurance that they would not be asked to remove their buildings, except for very good reason. This arrangement satisfied nobody, and members of all sects continually applied for freehold or leasehold sites at nominal rents and maintained that they were the only true Hindus or real Muslims in Uganda. The officials at the Land Office were seldom sure that land which they granted was in fact used only for religious or charitable purposes as they understood these ideas, and suspected that they were being cheated of revenue. In 1923, the Protectorate government wrote to Kenya to find out how land was granted there for religious and charitable use. At the same time, they asked the Central Council of Indian Associations in Uganda to submit a memorandum on the views of the Indian community about land for mosques and temples, and in particular concerning which religious sects ought to be eligible for leases at a nominal rent.

The Central Council of Indian Associations had been founded during the First World War, but was not registered with the government until 1921. Most Indian associations in the country were affiliated to it, and the administration looked on it as representing all Indians. At that period the Indians in Kenya were involved in a prolonged quarrel with the Europeans about racial segregation and the purchase of land. In Uganda, the Indians were reluctant to take part in the dispute; but their leaders thought it wise to have a central organisation which could, if necessary, speak for the community as a whole and negotiate with the administration. The government for its part welcomed the Central Council as a convenient means of handling a small but influential section of the population, and hoped, in pursuit of the policies of indirect administration then current in most parts of the British Empire, that it might eventually be able to entrust minor powers of administration to the officers of the Council.

The request for a memorandum revealed the Association's essential weakness. It could obtain no general agreement at all, and was obliged to recommend that seven plots of land should be granted in Kampala for temples and mosques: three for Hindu sects; three for Muslim sects; and one for the Sikhs. Instead of one united Indian community, unfortunately divided into two major and often hostile religious factions—the Hindus and the Muslims the government was asked to recognise that a number of sects and cults (often hardly known by name to its officers) were significant elements of a permanently divided community. No sooner was the memorandum submitted than the leaders of the different sects and cults asked leave to send deputations to the governor.

The Shia Imami Ismaili Muslims were the first to visit the Land Office and formally ask for a reduction of the rent of the land on which their mosque stood. They were, they said, 'the principal exponents of the Mohammedan religion and were in the majority of the Indians in Kampala'. When asked if the Central Council would confirm the statement, they replied that they were not bound by any of its decisions, and that it did not properly represent Indian opinion, least of all their own. In his report the Land Officer wrote:

> The deputation practically expressed the opinion that they did not care what happened to the other sects, but they wished for the rent free [i.e. nominal rent] plot for themselves... they also seemed to consider that it would affect their prestige with the other sects if they paid anything—evidently in India the person who gets something for nothing is considered of more importance than those who pay their just dues. This is the Eastern point of view.[7]
>
> A visit from the Hindu Sanatan Dharma sect followed hard on the heels of the Ismailis. They say that they are the principal sect; they did not recognise the Central Association as having anything to say about it, and again it is to their prestige to get a plot rent free.[8]

The Land Officer asked if the deputation would agree to vest the site in the Hindu Union, an association formed in 1914 to manage the cremation ground. They refused and said that it was not their concern if other Hindus were dissatisfied.

In the end, the administration realised that a satisfactory solution was impossible, and in 1925 ruled that in future no land at all would be granted to religious bodies at nominal rents.[9] The lack of unity displayed within the Indian community and the bitter feelings so openly expressed had taken both the government and the Indian leaders by surprise, though neither was willing to accept the demonstration; the government because it could not afford to administer small numbers of disunited people, and the leaders because they feared the weakness of disunity.

Non-sectarian Religious 'Trusts'.

Until after the First World War the Protectorate government was principally concerned with the problems of establishing law and order and of raising a revenue. It had neither the officers not the resources to undertake other public services on a large scale, and it was, therefore, always anxious to encourage the growth of centralised organs of administration which would be cheap and simple to run. In 1924, after the Central Council of Indian Associations had failed to obtain any common policy on land for cemeteries and places of worship, the government, in consultation with the Executive Council (on which no Indian sat), informed the Indians that a multiplicity of small religious and charitable organisations was undesirable, and to avoid their further proliferation, both Hindus and Muslims were asked to consider plans for setting up a central trust for each religion to hold and administer the property of its constituent bodies.

In this way, a few reputable officers would be answerable to the public and the government. The arrangement, it was thought, would be familiar and acceptable to Muslims, at any rate, since mosques and other types of trust property are in most parts of Islam established as *waqf,* or property dedicated in perpetuity by single individuals or groups for charity, which in many parts of the British Empire were, under the supervision of a central *Waqf Board.*[10]

The followers of the Aga Khan immediately protested. All their mosques, schools, playing fields, clinics and hostels were in law the absolute property of the Imam. He had never in any way allowed his rights of managing communal affairs to be questioned, and had always successfully upheld these rights in the courts of India and East Africa. In 1905, he had appointed attorneys to manage some of his affairs in East Africa but by 1924 only one, a very old man, survived. Transactions between the administration of Uganda and the Shia Imami Ismaili community often took years to complete, and it was this which had prompted the government to suggest a central charitable organisation.

Other Muslim and Hindu groups also disliked the proposal, and it came to nothing; but it showed the Indians that the administration's policy was to unite their divergent interests whenever possible. In particular, it made the leading Ismailis and the Aga Khan realise that if they were to maintain the separateness of their community and have complete control over its internal affairs, they would need to alter certain of their administrative arrangements. A system of regional councils having authority to deal in the name of the Imam with the governments of East Africa was quickly developed; and one attorney, called the Estate Manager, was appointed by the Aga Khan to act in consultation with him and the appropriate local Ismaili councils in handling communal property. By 1926, this system was in full working order, and proved so successful in negotiating with governments and in training men and women in methods of Western administration that when other Muslim sects and Hindu castes observed how the Ismaili leaders gradually obtained complete recognition of the community in its own right and successfully defended its sectarian interests, they too were stimulated to follow the example.

Education

By organising themselves into a 'corporate community' the Shia Imami Ismaili sect acted as a kind of 'pace-making' group in the growth of other caste and sectarian communities. The process eventually undermined all the pretensions of the Central Council of Indian Associations for Uganda to represent one united Indian community. It also made it virtually impossible for anybody to establish united Muslim or Hindu organisations, because every sect or caste was anxious to obtain for itself advantages similar to those of the Ismailis. Once 'communal crystallisation' began, the process soon influenced almost all relationships with the administration and of one community with another.

Education System for the Indians

Schools always were essential to the Indians in East Africa. As traders they were the middlemen between the economy of the West and the illiterate African farmers, and as craftsmen, mechanics and clerks, they could not afford to let their children grow up uneducated. In the early days the government was unable to provide elaborate educational services, and most schools were run by Christian missionaries little interested in Indians, who were left to form and support their own schools.

As the population grew, the burden was too great for a few merchants or even a whole community to carry, and the government was obliged to help. In 1926, the Director of Education in Uganda reported that all Indian schools were practically government schools in that they received grants-in-aid and were regularly inspected.

Caste, Sect and Education

This situation inevitably produced disagreement and accelerated the emergence of separate caste and sect organisations. The Shia Imami Ismailis were more reluctant than most to send their children to 'mixed' schools where they might be given inadequate instruction and exposed to heresy. In addition the success of the recent reforms inaugurated by the Aga Khan and the modernisation of his followers' social life depended on his control of education. With the rapid growth in the Indian population, too, places in schools became scarce; and members of other larger castes and sects began to make provision for their own children and to seek assistance as separate communities.

Advisory Council for Indian Education

The government, on the other hand, was still determined to treat the Indians as one; and when in 1927, under a new Education Ordinance, the whole educational system was re-examined, an Advisory Council for Indian Education was set up. It was formed to hold school property, to manage the many private schools that relied on government support, and to consider applications for grants-in-aid and new schools. The proposal immediately raised the former controversy on 'free' sites. Only two' leasehold plots at nominal rents were to be granted for schools in any township—one for Muslims and one for Hindus. The Shia Imami Ismaili community once more was the main opponent. Its members had come to see that they could safeguard their interests and keep their identity separate from that of other Indians only by resisting every attempt to assimilate them in any way at all with non-Ismailis.

The objectives of the administration and of the Indians, especially the Ismailis, were, therefore, different in a number of important fields of education; and though the Advisory Council for Indian Education still survived in 1955, it had never taken on any of the more important functions for which it was designed. The Indians had seen in it an obstacle to their own separate communal aspirations; and by 1946 the crystallisation of the larger Hindu castes and the Muslim sects into corporate communities had reached a stage at which any reversal was unlikely. The organisation and wealth created by the Ismailis, to take the clearest example, would have made it almost impossible to submerge their interests in a larger Indian organisation.

Attempts were, in fact, made after the partition of India in 1947 when the Muslims tried to re-activate the Central Muslim Association. At the same time, the Hindus also tried to revive the importance of the Central Council of Indian Associations for Uganda as a representative body for all Indians. Both attempts failed. Caste and sectarian communities had emerged as the main structural units of Indian society and the political and social conditions in Uganda at 'that time did not make it necessary or advantageous for all the Indians to unite.

Emergence of Communities in Politics

The emergence of castes and sects as separate communities had largely been a reaction to special circumstances threatening particular interests. The members of a community might find themselves obliged to band together either to resist some measure being pushed by the administration or to obtain a special concession. Continuing interests like schools or hostels for children required a permanent organisation to deal with the different departments of government concerned with them; but the interest was usually a relatively narrow one; and in Uganda no community had felt it necessary to organise as an open political group with a programme covering its whole range of interests.

There were probably many reasons for the failure of castes and sects to emerge as small political parties or factions within them, but two would appear to be important. In the first place the Indians were a very small minority. Most were traders, and in Uganda they had always been careful not to raise the policies of segregation and restriction on immigration as open political issues. Moreover, the political system provided very little opportunity for direct action.

In 1903, Uganda was placed under the rule of the Colonial Office in London; and the mixed assemblage of African kingdoms, stateless tribes, Indian traders, and European settlers was governed by an oligarchy of civil servants, of whom the senior members were recruited in Britain. In 1955, a form of representative government with a legislative assembly and universal franchise was inaugurated. Indians and a small number of Africans had always been employed in the lower grades of the civil service; but the ordinary inhabitants of Uganda did not share, as of right, in political power. After the First World War, a few 'non-official' Indians and Europeans were asked to serve on technical and advisory bodies that were formed by the government for consultation, thus drawing ordinary members of the public into political life.

Executive and Legislative Councils

The most important of these advisory bodies were the Executive and the Legislative councils, They were formed in 1920 to help the governor and his senior officers rule the Protectorate; but they were purely advisory, and the administration of the country ultimately remained entirely in the hands of the civil service. Although, Buganda and areas of the Western Province were African kingdoms in treaty relations with Britain and were partly indirectly administered under Residents or Provincial Commissioners and District Commissioners aided by technical officers, nevertheless all matters of policy were the prerogative of the governor in consultation with his civil service, and not with the people of the country, whether African, Arab, European, or Indian.

The system of administration under District Officers was mainly designed to govern the rural African population; and Indians and Europeans living in the district raised special problems. Before the formation of the Legislative Council 'unofficial' Europeans (farmers and business men) had been demanding a direct influence on the decisions taken by the government. They had done this privately, and officially through the Uganda Chamber of Commerce, to which a few Indian merchants also belonged. When the Legislative Council first met in 1921, it consisted of the governor, four senior civil servants, and two nominated European members. The first meeting of the Executive Council, whose membership was the same as that of the Legislative Council without the unofficial members, had met two months earlier. No Indian sat on either body, though the local Indian Association of Kampala had been asked to send a member to the Legislative Council. On neither council were Africans then, or for twenty years to come, considered for membership.

The reason for the Indians' refusal to sit on the Legislative Council was that they were offered fewer seats than the Europeans. Their fear of policies of segregation and restriction were sufficient to unite them in expressing their misgivings in this way. A public meeting organised by the Indian Association of Kampala passed a resolution:

> This public meeting of the Indian community of Kampala urges the government of Uganda to admit the Indian claim for equal representation with non-official Europeans, and appoint an equal number of Indians as non-official Europeans on the Council.[12]

Similar meetings were held in other parts of Uganda; and in spite of a general reluctance to be closely connected with political bodies in Kenya, support was obtained from the Kenya branch of the East African National Congress, which was affiliated to the National Congress of India.

Indians Participation in the Legislative Council

By 1926, some of the Indian community's fears were allayed, and when a Hindu was nominated to the Legislative Council in that year he took his seat. Subsequently, the council was enlarged and more Indians were invited to sit on it, but it so happened that it was not until 1937 that a Muslim member was nominated. He was appointed not because he was a Muslim or a member of the Shia Ithnasheri sect, but because he was a business man with large cotton interests.

Right up to 1955, most of the Indians who sat on the council were nominated because they belonged to a small and capable group of highly Westernised business men, most of whom were engaged in the cotton or coffee trade. The Indians called them the 'upper classes'. Whatever their caste or sect they associated closely with one another in business and social life and were on friendly terms with Europeans and officers of the administration.

While the Indian community was still small in numbers, and when no serious interests were threatened, these men did on the whole represent a united community. They controlled the Central Council and the Indian trading associations; as a group they were well-qualified to discuss trade, housing and immigration with the government. As these were matters, which affected all Indians, individual traders and the various communities were content to allow these men to handle such matters on their behalf. But, this well-to-do official group, recruited from 'the upper classes', had relatively few members among the Ismaili Muslims and the Hindu Patidar and Lohana castes, so that when these groups emerged as communities, the associations which the older group of leaders had controlled were either taken over by 'new' men or allowed to fall into disuse.

Post-Second World War Position of Africans in the Legislative Council

After 1945, Africans were appointed to the Legislative Council and it was clear that when it became an elected body and primarily African in composition, then the privileged position of the Indian leaders would be very different. By their long service on advisory committees they had been favourably placed for safe-guarding Indian interests by their personal knowledge of the members of the civil service. As long as a caste or sectarian community had a man in one of these privileged positions, it did not as a rule much matter if the administration nominally insisted on treating all Indians as one group, and it was not too important for a caste or sectarian community to organise as a separate political group.

But, in an African state things might be different. Indians might find themselves under attack because they were foreigners and traders; and without constitutional protection for minorities the prospects of political rewards for small communities might be less, so that there would, therefore, be even less reason for castes and sects to emerge as parties in the political field. In certain circumstances, it might even be advantageous to submerge themselves once more in a united Indian community.

Indian Opinion on Communalism

Some Indians, especially among the richer Hindus, always deplored the emergence of separate small communities. Like the educated urban classes of India, they considered the traditional Hindu social system, in which caste was an indispensable element, to be old-fashioned and ill-adapted to modern circumstances. They noticed that the caste and caste category communities in Africa were different from the *jati* at home, and attributed the changes to ignorance. For many the persistence of caste ideals was a sign of a failure to understand the dangers of division in Africa. This point of view was very clearly expressed in a newspaper article in 1954:

> Indians constitute the largest, richest and in a way the most influential community in Kampala. They are wealthy and generous, and it is well-known that no appeal for funds in this country could have been successful but for the generosity of Indians. Yet, by a queer twist of fate Indian institutions in Kampala starve from want of money and have an appearance of neglect and poverty. At one time when the Indian population of Kampala was negligible in comparison with its present size, Indians founded a school, a Public Library, the first of its kind in the town, a Hindu Temple and later a club.... And these Indian institutions which at one time might be considered passable in the Kampala of old look more and more like poor relatives in the Kampala of today.... All round, we see public institutions belonging to different communities and sub-communities raising new buildings and adapting old buildings to their present needs.... The Ismailis have built a most imposing Mosque, and are building schools and a boarding house for the pupils. The Lohanas have built a club with a large hall and a large boarding house to meet the needs of up-country Lohana boys. The Arya Samaj has recently built a magnificent school-building. The Patels (Patidar) had their *samaj* and are now

> building a boarding house for their community. Only nobody cares for the institutions that are for all Indians.... Can't the Indian leaders divert some of their communal interests and constructive enthusiasm towards the rehabilitation of Indian institutions? Can't all these sub-communities think of their smaller interests and yet serve the Indian community at large? Will the Indians ever remain divided, even though the greater interests of the community suffer?[13]

The emergence of communities had always been an uneven one and was most complete in the larger towns; in some rural districts the process had hardly begun, even in 1955.

In one primarily Indian settlement in Uganda, the population in 1955 was about 250 people. Out of fifty families, thirteen were Shia Imami Ismailis who wanted to build a school and a social club for themselves and Ismailis in the district. They, therefore, applied for a plot of land adjacent to their mosque. The District Commissioner refused the application, saying that the school would not benefit the whole Indian community. After hearing the arguments of an Ismaili leader from Kampala, he changed his mind, and thus inaugurated the emergence of caste and sectarian communities in his district. Like the older leaders of the Indian community, he disapproved of the process but could not resist it.

Ordinary members of the Indian public had few political opinions on the affairs of the Protectorate or the place of the Indian community within it. They did, of course, object to regulations which prevented friends and relatives in India from joining them, and worried a great deal about education for their children. On matters such as these, they were willing to follow their leaders, and if ambitious men within their own community found it possible to get better treatment by organising them as a separate group, then they were willing to follow. But, for the most part the ordinary trader wanted to live quietly and get on with earning a living in ways that—kept him on good terms with other members of his caste or sect. It was their opinion which made his reputation, not only in Africa, but in India as well. The strength or weakness of the Indian community and its relations with the administration were the concerns of rich men rather than of ordinary traders.

Environment for the Emergence of Communities

In analysing the process by which caste and sectarian communities emerged from the Indian community, there are four sets of factors which need consideration. They are:

(a) The closeness of East Africa, to India and the relative ease of communications.
(b) The growth in numbers and the relatively favourable political atmosphere in East Africa.
(c) The existence of a 'pace-making' group.
(d) The ambitions of individuals.

All these factors are implicit in what has already been said and some have been partly discussed, but a closer examination of their significance is needed.

Ease of Communications

The Indians in East Africa were a commercial group of recent, spontaneous settlement, and not peasants recruited by indenture and settled on the land, as they were in Mauritius, Fiji, and British Guiana.[14] The relative ease of communications with India meant that social relationships with people at home were not broken off and individuals frequently went back on visits. Many East African Indians lived in two worlds and could neither maintain nor change their habits to be completely at home in either. If they did so in one world, they would not be easily able to perform their expected roles in the other. There is a junction on the railway from Bombay to Delhi which the women from that area, who lived in Africa, called 'Anand raise the veil' or 'Anand lower the veil', because passing through this station homewards they were expected to cover their faces.

Even if individuals did not often go backwards and forwards between Africa and India, gossip did, and its influence on a man's reputation and, therefore, on his status was important. It could affect him in two ways. In the first place, he would probably want to return to India and settle there in his old age; in the second he would be obliged at some stage to arrange marriages for his children. This latter duty raised one of the most formidable obstacles in Africa to the amalgamation of the immigrant communities with one another or with other sections of the population. Its significance was connected both with the relative ease of communications with India and with the numbers of Indians living in Africa at any one time.

The first immigrants were men, and for a long time the ratio between the sexes in Uganda remained seriously unbalanced. Because of the strength of traditional sentiments in favour of caste and sectarian endogamy, and because the Indian Ocean was a link rather than a barrier, this imbalance did not result to any marked extent in inter-marriage between Indian men and African women, or between Indians of different castes and sects. Instead, wives were brought from India or were visited there at intervals. Marriages were, therefore, carefully arranged according to the full details of local home tradition. Later, as girls of the new African-born generations began to grow up, husbands were also imported from India. It was indeed a recognised road to fortune for a young man in India to marry the daughter of an Indian established in Africa who, in return for the heavy dowry he might have to pay for a son-in-law of higher traditional status than his own, acquired prestige in both India and Africa. New legal restrictions placed on immigration in the 1950s made this recruitment of spouses from overseas more difficult; but communities which had been able to maintain their endogamy in the past despite a grossly unbalanced sex ratio were not likely, once a balance had been achieved in East Africa, to give up easily or soon the views which they had held so tenaciously.

From the very start, then, the communities maintained their exclusiveness as far as marriage was concerned. This remained a constant factor. Yet, in spite of communal exclusiveness, the traditional hierarchy did not appear in Africa. At the same time, most of the distinctive caste and sectarian behaviour patterns that were badges of rank, so to speak, in that hierarchy were abandoned too. These patterns could, of course, be taken up again whenever an individual returned home. The new behaviour patterns that were adopted instead were mostly male fashions of behaviour, of the—

European type, which had structural implications as marks of status in the quite different, non-traditional hierarchy of East Africa.

Now, it is not suggested that all or even most of the traditional behaviour patterns of Indian men in Africa were dropped and others adopted; but it is suggested that the widespread dropping of them was connected not with any relaxation of caste or sectarian exclusiveness—the continuance of endogamy took care of that—but with the disappearance in Africa of caste hierarchy, the failure, therefore, to establish traditional relationships between different castes, and the substitution of a different system of leadership and ranking.

Growth in Numbers

As long as the population in a trading settlement in Africa remained small and the men were engaged in occupations which necessarily meant that they shared common interests, the Indians-were willing, with some reservations as we have seen, to act and to be treated as a united community. It would, they felt, have been unwise in the face of the legal, cultural and physical uncertainties that confronted them to allow disunity to appear. Furthermore, the lack of choice of friends in a small settlement drove them to associate with one another; most spoke the same language and had many memories of India in common.

Whenever the numbers of a particular caste or sect grew large enough for its members to consort mainly with one another, it was not long before they began to emerge as a distinct communal group. The emergence of communities was also facilitated by the relatively favourable political atmosphere in which the Indians as a whole lived. In Uganda before 1955, what are usually called 'race relations' were superficially very cordial, and this state of affairs was warmly appreciated by the immigrants, who wanted above all else to be left alone to get on with trade. In Uganda, particularly, there were few occasions for them to close their ranks against a hostile world; and the tendencies towards separation inherent in the structure of Indian society in East Africa had not been seriously countered by the pressure of outside forces.

Existence of a 'Pace-making Group'

Closeness to India and the failure to reproduce traditional society in Africa were no more than pre-disposing factors in later developments. The separation of independently organised caste and sectarian communities could not safely take place until numbers were large enough; but in Uganda and most other parts of East Africa the forms assumed by the communities when they did emerge were deeply influenced by the example of the followers of the Aga Khan, who early and deliberately withdrew from close association with other sections of the Indian community, and whose success with the administration and in economic life compelled all other Indians to examine and in greater or lesser degree imitate their precedent. In this sense, one may refer to the Ismailis as a pace-making group.

The efficiency of the Ismaili organisation was displayed on many occasions. Their leaders, were especially concerned with matters of education, and their success in obtaining grants-in-aid for schools acted as a spur and model to other Indians who were facing the same problems. The leaders of the earlier united Indian associations were for a variety of reasons unable to attack the new problems with the same undivided enthusiasm brought by the Ismaili leaders to matters concerning their own community, with the result that members of other communities began to act on their own behalf rather than continue to rely on the Indian associations.

In Kenya, too, the early organisation of the Shia Imami Ismaili community had important consequences, for when Indians were granted a limited franchise the Ismailis were ready to act either as a political faction of great effectiveness within the larger Indian community or as a potentially separate political party representing its own ends completely. Whatever the situation, the Ismailis invariably set the pace.

Ambitions of Individual Leaders

The Ismailis, of course, had a supreme leader, the Aga Khan, who was not a local resident. No other community was in this somewhat peculiar position, at least not as regards secular affairs. The local Ismaili leaders were not themselves the nominal initiators of communal organisation: they were the agents who put it through. Individually, they had their followings within the community; but because in the last resort their status depended on the Aga Khan's favour, they were not as dependent upon their clienteles as were the leaders of other communities. Indeed, one of the most important men in the Ismaili structure had one of the smallest followings in the community and a large number of active enemies. He was, however, able to maintain his position because he was known to have the personal friendship and backing of the Imam.

These observations lead to a fourth set of factors in the emergence of caste and sectarian communities, namely the role of the leaders. Owing to the Ismailis' successful efforts to establish their distinctness, leadership in that community usually brought with it important position in the wider society—seats on educational and other committees, on the legislative councils of the territories, and so on. The same incentive drove other successful men to emphasise the separate interests of their own communities and thus to multiply the routes to power and prestige.

On the whole, it may be said that the structural changes which occurred in Indian society with the growth of population and wealth fell into two broad categories. First were the changes brought about by the government, intentionally or accidentally, in its pursuit of efficient and convenient administration. Second were the changes initiated by the Indians themselves, in response either to administrative requirements or, more generally, to their changed social environment.

NOTES AND REFERENCES

1. *Mombasa Times,* 14 August, 1954.

2. *Constitution of the Patidar Samaj Kampala,* Kampala, 1953, p. 1.

3. R.M. MacIver and C.H. Page, *Society,* London, 1955, p. 9.

4. Tien Ju-Kang, *The Chinese of Sarawak,* London, 1953, p. n.

5. Land Office, Entebbe, LOMP 2659.

6. *Ibid.* A sect's own arrangements meant that it had to share a common plot of land in the town. This plot could be leased for a nominal rent. If the sect did not choose to do this it could usually lease land at a full commercial rent and put up a place of worship.
7. Land Office, Entebbe, LOMP 2659.
8. *Ibid.*
9. *Uganda Protectorate Government Gazette,* 14 March 1925. Notice No. 136 1925, p. 87.
10. B. Benedict, *Indians in a Plural Society,* London, 1961, p. 139.
11. At this time the Central Council of Indian Associations for Uganda was not registered and the administration was officially not aware of its existence. In part it was this incident which led to the registration of the council.
12. *Uganda Herald,* Kampala, 25 March 1921.
13. *Ibid.*, 10 April 1954.
14. B. Benedict, *Indians in a Plural Society,* London, 1961; A.C. Mayer *Peasants in the Pacific,* London, 1961; C. Jayawardena, *Conflict and Solidarity in a Guianese Plantation,* London, 1963.

3

A COMPARATIVE STUDY OF THE ECONOMIC ROLE OF AFRICANS, EUROPEANS AND INDIANS

Pattern of Annual Income of the Indian Immigrants

In comparison to the other African countries in 1955, Uganda was rich. The annual income per person was about £25. The African share was not much more than £16 to £17 a head; the Indian share was higher, though, as with the Africans, there were wide differences between the rich and the poor; and the annual real income of the poorest Indians was probably not far from that of the rural Africans.[1] The total geographical income of the Protectorate in 1951 was estimated at about £98 million, to which the Indians (0-7 per cent of the population) contributed approximately £16 million.[2] In the same year the value of retail trade (most of which was handled by Indians) was about £39 million.[3] The following year the total revenue was just over £17 million, 47 per cent of which came from cotton and coffee export taxes.[4] These crops were mostly grown by small African farmers, but their processing and export was mainly an Indian occupation.

In 1948, 38 per cent of all Indians (10,029 individuals) were in gainful occupations.[5] Most were engaged in private industry (92-1 per cent), with 6.1 per cent in government employment, and 1.8 per cent in public transport.[6] Half the working population (50-4 per cent) was occupied in commerce,

29 per cent in manufacturing industries and 9-3 per cent in public services.[7] Information on the division between employers and employees was incomplete, but roughly 56 per cent were employees.[8]

The political and economic system of Uganda was, of course, Western in form. The principal contribution of the Indian immigrants to its evolution had been in the diffusion of a monetary economy, especially among the African population. To perform this task they had to alter many of their traditional institutions which had been appropriate to small-scale rural caste systems but which did not always fit conditions in East Africa. With the diminished importance of the ritual and jural aspects of caste, the economic aspects also ceased to be important. Occupations such as the meat trade and leather-working were still felt to be impure, and were, therefore, generally carried on either by Muslims or members of the shoemaker sub-caste. Most jewellers were members of the goldsmith *jati*. Large numbers of carpenters made a start in Africa in their traditional occupations, and though Barbers and Brahmins might exercise their special ritual roles on ceremonial occasions, they, and especially their sons, usually earned a living as traders or civil servants.

Division of Labour in East Africa

The division of labour in East Africa, as in the modern cities of India, was not consistent with that of a traditional caste system. Licensed traders in Uganda in 1952 numbered 16,908. Of these, 11,634 were African and 4,809 Indian. Although, there were more than twice as many African traders as Indian, the Department of Commerce estimated that non-African traders (most of whom were Indian) handled almost three times as much business as the Africans. Population was densest in the cotton and coffee growing areas of Buganda and the Eastern Province, where 83 per cent (14,129) of all the licensed traders and 81 per cent (3,913) of the Indian traders were registered.[9]

The density of Indian traders was, of course, connected with the wealth and the growing population in these two provinces, but the heavy concentration of Indians within the five principal towns was mainly due to administrative rules which prohibited any non-African or his agents from setting up shop outside specified centres.[10] This was re-enforced by other regulations which made it impossible (with a few exceptions) for non-Africans to acquire more than a leasehold interest in land anywhere in Uganda.[11] Indian merchants and hawkers were, therefore, unable to trade easily in African settlements and were confined to bazaars. A successful merchant in this situation was, thus, restricted in the investment of this profits.

A few Indians acquired estates on the relatively small amount of freehold land which had been alienated from African ownership earlier in the century and farmed them as sugar, coffee or tea plantations; but the law did not allow them to be managed as co-parcenary estates belonging to joint families. A merchant could invest his savings in a leasehold site in a trading settlement, but the longest period of tenure was ninety-nine years. If he were rich he might be able to buy an interest in a cotton ginnery, a cotton-seed oil-mill, or embark on some quite different type of business or manufacturer Although, money was remitted every year from East Africa to India, there was little evidence in 1955 that the Indian population, as a whole, transferred a substantial part of their profits abroad.

Usually a trader invested his savings in opening another shop. The history of all districts in Uganda shows how businesses spread from the earlier founded settlements to newer and less developed ones; frequently the same firm later branched out yet further afield, thus continuing the task of developing a monetary economic system among the African population. Rather than open a new shop of his own, a man might prefer to set up a son in another district; for if he opened a branch of the firm under his own sole control, the difficulty of finding a manager, whether a relative, a member of his own caste or sectarian community, or a stranger, made a risky enterprise even more hazardous. By making over the whole new enterprise to his son, when the young man had shown himself capable, he saved himself trouble and had the satisfaction of having done his duty as a parent. The rate of bankruptcy among small traders was always high, and a man who failed in one township tended, if he could find the means, to move out to a more remote settlement.[12] A successful trader, on the other hand, was more likely to move into a larger town with wider business prospects and better schools for his children.

Most shops were small general stores which sold the goods required by the rural African population.[13] In 1954 the average net income of such a trader was probably never much more than £400 a year. In the bigger towns general stores were partly replaced by specialised shops, but even so most retail trade was handled by general traders in bazaars. Bazaars made up of almost identical shops selling identical goods are typical of under-developed tropical countries.[14] The number of shops is always high in proportion to the number of customers because the shop-keeper is usually not simply a distributor of consumer goods, but is also a collector of produce which he despatches to wider markets. To ensure regular supplies the may be obliged to extend credit in the form of goods or money to the growers of the produce. Consequently, he himself is likely to need credit: usually he looks to wholesalers or large produce exporters for this.[15] Although, such a network of credit relations may have the backing of the official legal system in collecting debts, the shop-keeper, in the daily running of his business, relies in the last 'resort on his own detailed knowledge of and trust in his clients. This fact, as much as the limits of the credit he himself can obtain for running his business, reduces the numbers of customers to whom he can safely make loans. In this situation, knowledge and trust on all sides are essential, and such credit relations are often strengthened by being phrased in terms of kinship or pseudo-kinship.[16]

In Uganda, there was normally no question of kinship between Indian shop-keepers and African farmers, and a trader looking for support from a wholesaler frequently went first to kinsmen or members of his own caste or sectarian community. In a system of this kind, then, the traders, all selling identical goods, may not in fact be so much competing with one another in retail trade as in the buying of primary produce and re-selling it to wholesalers. In 1955 this was the situation in many parts of the rural districts of Uganda, but in the larger towns specialised shops were the rule.

In 1952, there was approximately one trader to every 270 persons in the Protectorate—a ratio typical of bazaar economies. In the past most rural shop-keepers had acted as retailers and as buyers of produce and suppliers of credit; but from the early days the administration had carefully regulated the collection of primary produce, especially cotton and coffee, and in the collection of these products had left little room for middlemen to organise the trade. Many of the government's official agents for collecting produce were small shopkeepers or men who subsequently set up as independent traders and relinquished their official agency, having used it to set themselves up in trade. The collection of certain grains and of hides and skins was not through government agents, and in these trades a government buying agency could not, therefore, be a first step in building up an independent business. To do so a man had to rely on his own resources or what credit he could obtain.

The acquisition of a collecting agency had always been one way in which a man might set himself up in independent business. With it behind him he needed little capital to begin keeping shop. For extra capital he could usually rely on the help of richer relatives or members of the same community, but even without the support of a collecting agency, a man, if he had the knowledge and the nominal backing of an established wholesaler, could order goods direct from England on three months' credit. He could expect delivery soon enough for him to sell sufficient goods to meet his commitments before they fell due. Most traders, of course, did not take the risk of ordering goods in this way without adequate support and always preferred to obtain them through a substantial wholesaler who could also be relied on to help in difficult times.

Although, most traders in Uganda by 1955 were not the principal suppliers of credit to Africans or the chief buyers of produce, the wealth of the African population, especially in the cotton and coffee growing areas, made retailing sufficiently profitable to maintain a large number of traders. If one of them could obtain a selling agency for goods in constant demand, goods such as sugar or bicycles for example, he was in a stronger position than his rivals. To obtain an agency of this kind he looked first to his kinship and community connections, as he did in many other aspects of economic and social life.[17] These connections did not govern Indian economics, but their importance was very great and was easily under-estimated, especially by non-Indians.

Cotton Industry

Nobody, not even the Indians themselves, saw their share in the cotton industry as an aspect of community membership; on the other hand, everybody was aware that the cotton merchants formed a rich small elite, and that as Patidar and Lohana merchants handled by a very large part of the crop, members of those communities were generally better placed if they wished to enter the industry.

When the cotton crop was ripe it was picked by the African, growers and taken to an accredited government agent at a specified near-by ginnery where it was weighed and paid for. These buyers were usually Indians, who might or might not be ordinary traders in the off-season and were not necessarily employed by the ginnery. The cotton allocated to the ginnery was processed and the seed (from which oil was expressed in other mills) was extracted from the fibre which was then baled for export. In 1952, approximately 90 per cent of the ginneries were owned by Indians, who had bought them between the First and Second World Wars when poor trading conditions drove most of the former European owners out of business. All baled cotton was purchased from the ginneries by the Lint Marketing Board, a statutory body which controlled the industry, and which auctioned the bales to authorised exporters. The greater part of the cotton crop of Uganda was sent to Bombay for weaving in the mills of Gujarat.

Export tax was paid out of the takings of the Lint Marketing Board which annually fixed all internal cotton prices, and the profits were placed in a fund for stabilising prices from year to year, primarily for the protection of the African growers. The amount of cotton a ginner might buy, and, therefore, of his profits, was also regulated by the Board. The owners of ginneries were in effect the agents of the Protectorate administration. This control of ginneries, as well as of the coffee hulleries, which extended to the number that might be built and operated, meant that the people who were able to gain an interest in them were in a highly privileged position. During the Second World War and after, the owner of a cotton ginnery was in effect guaranteed a substantial and regular income by the government.

This small group of Indian ginners in Uganda was almost unique in East Africa. Their wealth and a steady income were officially secured and they used the money from their investment-to establish themselves in other types of business and to extend their influence as patrons and suppliers of credit, both to men within their caste and sectarian communities, and also to other selected Indians. Even before the emergence of communities as entities separate from the general body of Indians, the secure wealth of the cotton ginners meant that the leaders of the older united associations usually came from within their ranks.

In 1953, there were 194 authorised ginneries in Uganda. Buganda and the Eastern Province between them produced 70 per cent of all baled cotton. In the five year period, 1948 to 1953, only some 12 per cent of the total came from non-Indian firms; 69 per cent came from Hindu ginneries, in particular from those owned by members of the Patidar and Lohana communities, who together owned 48 per cent of all the ginneries but produced 59 per cent of all baled cotton.[18] In Buganda the Patidars owned 14 per cent of the total number of ginneries in the country, whereas the Lohanas held only per cent. On the other hand, in the Eastern Province the Lohanas owned 11 per cent and the Patidars only 7 per cent.[19] It was this distribution which led people to say that Buganda was a Patidar fortress and Busoga a Lohana stronghold.

The distribution is explicable in terms of local history. The fact that more Patidars owned ginneries in Buganda probably meant no more than that there were more of them in that province at the time when it was feasible for a rich Indian to buy a ginnery. It does not mean that the caste of a merchant was necessarily important in acquiring an interest in or in running one. Occasionally, however, situations did arise in which communal affiliation was important.

In 1952, there were thirty-four oil mills in operation in the country which needed cotton seed as raw material. Of these, thirteen belonged to Lohana and nine to Patidar firms. As might be expected, most of the Lohana mills were in the Eastern Province and those of the Patidar in Buganda. The remainder belonged to Indians who were of different communities or who were in partnership with Patidars or Lohanas. An oil millers' association attempted to lay down policy for the industry as a whole, and in this voluntary association the Lohana community usually had the deciding vote. After a long period of controlling the allocation of cotton seed during the war, the Protectorate government decided in 1952 to allow a part of the year's crop to be publicly auctioned. The oil millers' association agreed that its members should not bid higher prices than those set by the government in the previous year. Until then the millers had been in the favourable position of obtaining seed without competition from other purchasers and most did not want a return to unrestricted bidding for it at auctions. The managing director of one of the Patidar firms—a party to the association's agreement -saw an opportunity of immediate profit. He persuaded nine other firms (all belonging to members of his own caste community) to bid beyond the agreed price. This they did and bought almost all the seed that was for sale.

The point of the incident is simple. Any Indian wanting employment, a loan, advice or help in a business, a political, or any other kind of deal, for preference went first to a small core of consanguineal and affinal relatives and then to members of his own community. This was equally true of the rich and the poor, and could have been illustrated by examples from the setting up of a shop to the acquisition and management of coffee and tea estates.

Industry

Industry in Uganda in 1955 was very little developed.[20] Africans, Europeans and Indians all owned and operated such factories as existed, but most were owned by Indians—77 per cent as against 23 per cent owned by Government, Africans and Europeans. The range of industry was narrow. Excluding the cotton ginneries, and there were, in 1954,598 registered factories: 228 of these were for the processing of coffee, grain and timber; another 142 were engaged in motor repairs, light engineering and joinery; and 131 were grain and seed mills. 51 per cent of all the factories were situated in Kampala and the surrounding district.[21]

The owning of a factory by an Indian usually arose out of his earlier trading interests. These were governed partly by the district in which he originally settled and the opportunities there for him to A fact as a middleman in handling local produce, and partly by his traditional knowledge and skills. The Lohanas, for example, settled early in Busoga and entrenched themselves both in the retail trade and in the cotton and coffee businesses. The Patidars established themselves in the same way in the adjacent lakeside province of Buganda, whereas further west the Ismailis and Lohanas controlled the collection of grains, and together handled most of the retail trader At a later date, the three communities owned most mills, coffee hulleries and ginneries in the country.

An immigrant's traditional occupation and skills might also influence his trading interests in Uganda. In India, if a ritual occupation was not open to a Brahmin, he preferred to earn a living in occupations connected with food or books or administration; and many in Uganda owned food or stationery shops. Only two, however, owned factories—a grain mill and a printing press. Most carpenters *(Suthar)* came to East Africa in order to trade; but of the twenty-six factories in Uganda owned by members of the sub-caste, twenty-four were joinery or furniture-making shops. By contrast, immigrants from the Punjab, most of whom were Sikhs and Sunni Muslims, did not in general come to East Africa for trade: they had neither the skills nor the connections with the established Gujarati traders to go easily into the retail business. They were mostly craftsmen of one kind or another. Many, indeed, had been recruited in India for government service in Africa, and subsequently set up on their own account in mechanical and not in retail trades Just on 29 per cent of the motor repair and light engineering shops in Uganda belonged to Sikhs and Sunni Muslims. A in industry, as much as in trade, the scene was dominated by Indians, and in particular by the Lohanas, the Patidars and the Ismailis. Because of the numerical superiority and wide distribution of these communities, the successful merchants who had been able to accumulate savings and invest in industry at the appropriate time mostly belonged to these communities. They owned 215 out of 598 factories (Patidars 80, Ismailis 71, Lohanas 64), where 'factories' do not include ginneries. The importance of this in giving opportunities to members of the communities was considerable.

Government Service

The number of Indians employed in the administration of the Protectorate was small (6.1 per cent of the gainfully employed Indian population), but their influence on their Indians and the country at large was most important. 1952 less than a dozen non-Europeans held positions in the senior division of the civil service. In the junior division, on the other hand, out of a total of 2,297, African employees numbered 1,856 and Indians 441. Of the Africans 1,551 earned only 200 a year or under, and none the maximum of £850 whereas only "Seventeen Indians earned an annual wage of £200 or less. The majority (3967 earned salaries between £200 and £550 a year. Only one had reached the maximum.[22]

Nevertheless, the position of these middle grade Indian civil servants frequently brought them subsidised housing and other rewards beyond their salaries; for they acted as clerks and sometimes as secretaries to official committees, councils and licensing boards, and they knew the plans and daily workings of the bureaucracy. In certain situations the information they commanded could be most important to a trading community. Moreover, it was to these men that senior civil servants usually turned in the first instance for comment and, advice-on measures which affected the Indian populations as whole. Their position invested them with unofficial influence and a power and prestige sometimes almost comparable with that of the ginners and other communal leaders.

The nature of this influence naturally varied with the men involved and the positions they held. To take one example only: when the rules of immigration into East Africa were tightened in the early 1950s, Indians in India often found it difficult to gain admission into the territory; but recruitment for a short period of service with the government (which was chronically short of administrative clerks) in practice allowed a man to settle in the country when his contract expired. The number of immigrants who could come to Uganda in this way was limited, but an established Indian civil servant could always give valuable private advice and perhaps bring influence to bear in obtaining an entry permit. Similarly, in the field of education, which deeply concerned the Indian population, the influence of a junior civil servant might amount to considerable power. An important position in the civil service was not necessarily measured by the salary attached to it.

Nearly two-thirds (322) of these Indian civil servants belonged to three communities—the Goans (235), the Brahmins (36), and the Sikhs (51), none of which was large or influential in the Indian community as a whole. The Patidar, the Lohana and the Shia Imami Ismaili communities, which predominated in all other spheres of Indian life, had relatively few members in government service (Patidar 28, Lohana 5, and Ismaili 7). Most regarded it as a poor substitute for, or at best a preliminary to a business career.

From the early days of the British administration of East Africa, when it was still under the general supervision of the government of India, Goan civil servants had been employed. Coming from Portuguese India, the majority were Roman Catholic Christians, and in Goa had been educated at 'English' schools for commercial and government service as clerks in India and abroad. Many spoke English as their first language and were so closely identified with the British administration that they had been classed as a separate 'race' in the population censuses of East Africa. They had also been provided with their own separate schools. The Goans were found almost throughout the civil service, unlike the Brahmins, who were mainly employed in the administrative and legal departments, and the Sikhs, who worked principally in technical departments.

As a rule, members of the Lohana and the Ismaili communities did not enter government service. They had been settled for a long time in East Africa and were established in trade. The early immigrants came from Kathiawad and Cutch, which were not under direct British rule, and most of them had not been to English schools. Unlike the Goans, they had neither the experience nor the skills needed in the civil service. They preferred if possible to enter commerce as soon as they could, and unlike the Sikh immigrants they had the skills and the connections to do so. The Sikhs, on the other hand, came as artisans and lacked the knowledge of commerce. Many, therefore, worked as civil servants for long periods before they accumulated sufficient experience and capital to go into business on their own account. The members of the Patidar community in government employment in the early 1950s were, for the most part, relatively recent arrivals and were mainly young men who intended to leave the service and enter trade.

After 1945, all administrative services in East Africa expanded and began a process of Africanisation. The number of qualified Africans was small and it was often difficult for the governments to man the civil services. During the same period the Aga Khan began to Westernise his followers and to urge them to participate all aspects of life in the countries in which they had settled. For their future safety, he argued, they must acquire the modern skills that would be needed in all independent African countries, and at the same time they would need to assimilate themselves with the Africans as far as -was feasible. Many Ismaili women were trained in English, shorthand, typing and secretarial knowledge, and were employed by the governments of East Africa in increasing numbers; but by 1955 it was becoming clear to most people that the privileged position of the Indians in the civil service would not last much longer and that with the establishment of Uganda as an independent state careers for Indians as officials might not continue. For the Goans, who had identified themselves with government service for more than sixty years, the change was likely to cause real hardship. Other Indian communities were likely to suffer less, though all would probably suffer from the loss of the former convenient lines of communication between them and the administration.

Africans and Indians

The concentration of Indians in towns and settlements and in trade and industry had important consequences in their relations with Africans. Most Indians were richer than most Africans; and because the Indians lived together in crowded settlements and were a specialised trading group they were highly conspicuous and potential source of envy and dislike to the Africans, who met them mainly as buyers of produce, shop-keepers and givers of credit. Not many Africans in Uganda or elsewhere in East Africa were successful traders; before the arrival of the British there had been no cash markets of the kind found in West Africa and in modern times most Africans still did not have the proper education or commercial skills needed in retail trade. But, after 1945 a steadily growing number began to take out licences and to compete in a small way with the established Indian -retailers. Every year many of them went bankrupt, and this fact, combined with dislike of foreigners, began to disturb the superficially good relations which had existed in Uganda between the Indians and the Africans.

Since 1924, it had been official policy to regard Uganda, in contrast with Kenya, as a primarily African country; but both a Africans and Europeans believed that the Indians had 'a strangle-hold on the economy'. The attitude of the early administrators who considered trade an intrinsically civilising and useful activity had vanished with that of an earlier generation of African rulers who had begged Indians to establish trading stations among their people. Both Europeans and Africans after the Second World War feared that the Indians might, however unlikely it seemed, find ways of safeguarding themselves by converting their economic strength into political power, thus, permanently excluding the Africans from commerce and industry. Administrative policy, therefore,, unlike that of earlier officials and African rulers who were concerned primarily with the development of trade, was to train African traders, and to support and advise them in every possible way until they had become an independent, self-reliant trading class. The process did not always improve relations among the different sections of the population.

The Africans first introduction to a monetary economy had been made by the Arabs but it had been the Indians who had' carried out the main task of its development. It was they who had undertaken the risks of pioneering and its real dangers to life and money. When much later the Africans entered the field and encountered some similar risks, those which inevitably accompany small-scale business in an under-developed economy, their frequent failures were all too readily attributed to the entrenched position of the Indians. It was invariably forgotten that the Indians had experienced comparable difficulties half a century earlier, and that their safeguards then had been the established trade on the coast and not official agencies and services. With a few exceptions it was also overlooked that the Indians, enclosed as they were within towns and trading settlements, by no means monopolised the whole market.

In 1952. the Department of Commerce in Uganda made a survey of retail trade, and found that 'the vast majority of traders... were Africans.'[23] During the war the Africans' interest in trading grew because keeping a shop meant that the owner obtained goods such as sugar, soap, cloth and bicycle spare parts, which were in short supply.[24] Even so there were less than a thousand African traders in 1945, though in the following years the numbers grew and showed no signs of diminishing.[25] There were several reasons for this growth. Men who had served in the armies abroad came home with gratuities which they invested in trade; their experience and education, too, was wider than most of those who had previously attempted to set up in business. Moreover a large number of people, including many Indians, saw that it was politic to encourage Africans to enter trade.[26] In Kampala an Indian merchant founded a school of commerce specifically for training Africans, and it worked closely with administrative officials in doing so.

For different reasons, then, the various sections of society in Uganda agreed that African participation in trade ought to be increased. How much this would threaten established Indian traders was uncertain. Some, especially those in areas of expanding trade, thought it would not affect them much.[27] Others, especially Indian merchants in less favoured areas, were less hopeful.[28] They had observed that African traders in certain districts of Kenya and Tanganyika had, with local political backing, wholly supplanted the immigrant traders. Moreover, by 1955 the technical skill of Indian shopkeepers was not much greater than that of many Africans, and the unremitting flow of help and advice did not go out equally to Africans and Indians. In the years after 1955 the 4 emergence of open hostility to Indian traders, accompanied sometimes by pillaging and destruction in the rural districts of Uganda gave reality to many Indian fears. Subsequent developments in all the independent countries of East Africa since then have done little to alter their fears of a bleak future as small traders.[29]

A certain number of the more successful Indian business men had invested some of their capital in industry, an area of the economy in which the Africans had hardly begun to enter. But, even here the policy of the administration, shown mainly in the activities of cooperative societies, was to reduce the Indian share.[30]

Some Indians, too, had placed their sons in professions such as the law, accounting, medicine, insurance and banking. By doing so they hoped to keep ahead of African advance, but it was a step open only to a limited number and was entirely dependent upon good Western education. For other Indians, too, a Western education was also essential if they were to survive, either as traders or employees.

Until the advent of representative government the Indians had been partly able to safeguard, or at any rate to keep watch on, their economic position by the special relationship which had grown up between their leaders and the administration. This relationship depended on the men chosen to sit on advisory bodies, and on the Goan and Indian civil servants who acted as intermediaries between the European administrative officers and the Indian public. Service on these bodies engendered sentiments of familiarity and respect and sustained a limited but important social life which embraced Europeans, Indians, and, before 1955, a few Africans.

With the growth of African nationalism and the Africanisation of the civil service this special relationship (characteristic of the later stages of colonial rule in many

British territories) was inevitably altered. By 1955 the Indian leaders began to realise that not only the political future of Indians in East Africa but the safety of their fortunes also hung on the kinds of relationship which they could cultivate with the coming African ruling class and its civil service. Everybody knew that it would be different from the old relationship with the Europeans; nobody could foresee its nature. Many thought that it might be more costly to the Indians, and though members of the poorer sections of the community did not doubt that the rich would survive, they were not at all sure that they themselves would.

NOTES AND REFERENCES

1. In 1955, there was little data available for an assessment of incomes in Uganda. In 1962 the Development Plan for Kenya, 1964-70 p 34 gave an analysis of Graduated person return, which 'throws light on me matter, 11 per cent of the Asian population had incomes under £120 per annum, whereas 91.4 per cent of the Africans were in this category. Of the Africans 0.5 per cent, and of the Asians 68.4 per cent, had annual incomes of £400 and more. Even in 1955, Uganda was probably a richer country than Kenya, and the African population, as a whole, was probably better off.
2. G. A. Currie, *Estimates of the Geographical Income for the years 1950-52,* East African Statistical Department, Nairobi, 1953. The figure for the Geographical Income includes, of course, an estimated value of the total income from subsistence fanning; H.S. Morris, *Immigrant Indian Communities in East Africa* unpublished Ph.D. thesis, London University, 1963, pp. 451-2.
3. Department of Commerce, *Annual Report*, Kampala, 1952, appendix 4
4. Colonial Report, *Uganda* 1952; H.S.Morris, *Immigrant Indian Communities in East Africa,* table 2, p. 453.
5. *A Report on the Census of the Non-Native Population of Uganda Protectorate* (1948), Nairobi, 1953, para. 181,
6. *Ibid* appendix 11 and para, 159.
7. *Ibid.,* paras. 179 and 180. The figure 56 per cent is probably too high, In small retail shops run by a family it is not easy to say who is or is not employed. In 1962 the figures for employees in

Uganda were put at 45 per cent of the economically active population, Dharam P. Ghai, An Economic Survey" *Portrait of a Minority,* D.P. Ghai, Oxford, 1965, p. 94.

8. *A Report on the Census ...* (1948), para. 182 and table 35.

9. Department of Commerce, *Annual Report* Kampala, 1952, appendix 4.

10. Laws of Uganda, 1951, vol. V, cap. 208, ss. 4 and 5.

11. Crown Lands Ordinance, 1903 and Uganda Order in Council, 1920. Cp. H. S. Morris, *Immigrant Indian Communities East Africa,* pp. 41-2.

12. W. Elkan, *Trade in Ankole,* East African Institute of Social Research (mimeograph), 1958. 'Some of the new shopkeepers have come in from other districts; for instance a new bicycle shop in Mbarara is a branch of an old-established firm in Masaka. But, the commonest pattern is for fathers to set up their growing sons in separate shops. I have often heard Indians say that it is better for a young man to have a business of his own than to help expand his father's business. They must have something of their own to develop their sense of responsibility, as one business man put it. The usual practice then is for the son to receive help with a new shop; part is given him outright and the rest he is expected to repay eventually. I enquired about ten newly opened shops and found that five of them were started for grown-up sons, two were "branches" of businesses outside Ankole and were, therefore, probably in the same category, one was a branch of a business at Ntungama, set up in Mbarara to enable the children to go to school, and the remaining two were men who had shifted—one into and the other out of Mbarara.'

13. Department of Commerce, *Memorandum No. A.T,C./54/3, Retail Trading,* Kampala, 1954. 'During the period of development up to twenty year? ago, few Africans showed interest or ability in trading. In order to establish trade which would provide incentives for the growing of crops immigration had to be encouraged of people who were prepared to set up shops all over the Protectorate. These pioneers in trade were mainly Asians who were able to withstand the difficulties of the climate and the hard conditions of living. Usually they established their shops in small settlements for mutual protection and assistance. From these settlements the Township and Trading centres of today have grown and Trading Ordinance has restricted Asian shop development to these centres. At this time there were so

few shops and demand was so limited that each shop stocked a wide range of goods and became what is called a bazaar. This type of shop persists all through the Protectorate'.

14. B.E. Ward, *Cash or Credit Crops?*, Economic Development and Cultural Change, vol. 8, No. 2, 1960, pp. 148-63; J.K. Tien, *The Chinese of Sarawak,* London, 1953, pp. 35-45.

15. J.K. Tien, *The Chinese of Sarawak,* chapter 8.

16. B. E. Ward, *Cash or Credit Crops,* pp. 148-63,

17. See H, S. Morris, *Immigrant Indian Communities in East Africa,* pp. 464-6, for an account of sugar agencies in Uganda.

18. Table 8. The Ownership of Ginneries in Uganda 1954.

    Table 9. The ownership of ginneries by district and community in Uganda (PATIDAR and Lohana).

20. By industry here is meant the manufacturing industries involving the production of goods or services in authorised factories. The Uganda Factories Ordinance 1952 denned a factory as any premises in which or within the close or curtilage or precincts of which persons are employed in manual labour in any process for or incidental to any of the following purposes, namely: 1. the making of any article or of part of any article; or 2. the altering, repairing, ornamenting, finishing, cleaning or washing, or the breaking up or demolition of any article; or 3. the adapting for sale of any article; being premises [where] the work is carried on by way of trade or for purposes of gain....' Business premises of this kind were counted as factories only if at least six people were employed.

21. Information relating to 1954 was supplied by the Department of Labour, Kampala, See also H.S. Morris, *Immigrant Indian Communities in East Africa,* table 7, p. 477.

22. Colonial List, 1952, Entebbe. See also H.S.Morris, *Immigrant Indian Communities in East Africa* table 8, p. 483,

23. Department of Commerce, *Annual Report,* Kampala, 1952, p. 5.

24. Department of Commerce, *Memorandum No. ATC/54/3. Retail Trading,* Kampala, 1954.

25. Department of Commerce, *Annual Report,* Kampala, 1952, p. 5. Although, African Traders are numerically preponderant, almost all of the wholesale trading is in the hands of Asians and Europeans, and Asian retailers carry far larger stocks and

achieve a much greater turnover than Africans. There remains, however, a clear indication that Africans are ready in considerable strength for an advance in trade.

26. In 1952, the Governor of Uganda in his address to the Legislative Council (Uganda Legislative Council Reports, November 1952) said; 'There is a wide recognition among the European and Asian commercial community of the importance of doing everything possible to assist Africans forward in commerce. A special officer had been appointed for this purpose in the Department of Commerce, and the advisory committees which assist the Department have given much thought to the subject'.

    W. Elkan *(Trade in Ankole)* wrote: 'Mbarara merchants are, of course, the least affected [by African traders] since in general they are their suppliers, not their competitors. In any case Indians are a good deal more realistic than is often thought and they know that their own security in this country will be greater if shop keeping is less exclusively an Indian domain. Many African shopkeepers have been helped to start up by Indians. An African restaurant in Mbarara, for instance, was started with money lent by an Indian merchant; his building cost about £4,000, Others receive generous credit from Indians.'

27. W. Elkan, *Trade in Ankole.* See above, p, 207, note 26. But, it is worth observing that when Elkan visited Ankole trade was booming.

28. In 1954, shopkeepers in small trading centres near Mount Elgin were pessimistic about their future. Even though the volume of trade might increase, they did not believe that they or their children would be allowed to share in it. Already the older men had not been able to set up their sons in rural shops and had been obliged to send them to the towns as employees.

29. The years since 1955, have done nothing to reduce a more general pessimism among Indians in East Africa, See D.P. Ghai, *Portrait of a Minority* p. 108.

30. In 1952, the Protectorate government enacted legislation for the purchase of ginneries for the benefit of African cooperatives at prices calculated on the sale of other ginneries on the open market during the three years before 1952. Under powers conferred by this legislation the Governor could acquire a ginnery because he was: of the opinion in respect of an undertaking that it is in the economic interests of the cotton industry as a whole that it should be acquired and its operation limited' (The Acquisition of Ginneries Ordinance, 1952, Clause 3, i).

He could also order its sale if he was: of the opinion in respect of an undertaking that it is in the public interest that provision should be made for its operation by an African co-operative enterprise' (The Acquisition of Ginneries Ordinance, 1952, Clause 3, ii).

By 1954, thirty unused ginneries had been closed and six others, fully operative, had been given to African Cooperative Societies, Indians feared that this legislation and procedure would provide a precedent for driving them out of industry of all kinds in Uganda in the future.

4

SOCIAL AND CULTURAL PROFILE OF THE INDIAN DIASPORA

Growth of the Indian Population in East Africa

Of all the ethnic groups resident in East Africa, the Asians have no doubt experienced largest population increase proportionately. 'Asians' is the East African synonym for all domiciled people of Indian or Pakistani origin. The term 'Indian' seems to be applied to guests from India, temporary visitors, Indian government agencies and the people in India-there are no non-Indian 'Asians' present as calculable minority groups in East Africa. The population increase in East Africa is higher than in the parallel linguistic and caste-groups in the Indian homeland.

This development, however, has come to a rather sudden halt and during the past decade, but especially since the East African nations achieved their independence. There has been a conscious and widespread attempt to curb the number of children, though there is no concerted effort yet of family planning. Economically more affluent and relatively more sophisticated families are certainly conscious of the necessity of family "planning. Upper echelon government servants, business executives, people of all linguistic and religious groups, not even with the exception of the Catholic Goans, are cognisant of the fact that scientific birth-control is as important to the settlers in East Africa as it is in India and Pakistan. The only objection to scientific birth-control is voiced by some of the older, tradition-bound Gujarati Hindus who claim that people have many children because they like them, because it adds to the love and affection in the family and 'that it has always been this way,' that God gives children. Some younger puritanical fundamentalists, such as the followers of the *Brha Bharatiya Sangh*, 'the greater India Union', organised on the model of the Hindu Fascist R.S.S. in India or the more radical among the Arya Samajists—a fundamentalistic reform movement founded roughly a century ago in the Panjab—claim that sexual continence *(brahmacharyam)* as taught by Mahatma Gandhi, Swami Dayananda Sarasvati (the founder of the Arya Samaj) and by other teachers of the Hindu religious lore, should be the sole answer to the problem of overpopulation. However, the ubiquitous feeling that the coming generation of Indian settlers does not have much of an economic and social future in East Africa is no doubt the most powerful single factor in the reduction of the birth-rate among the minority in the last few years.

Africanisation and its Economic and Social Implications for India

It is as yet hard to say whether the sub-communities as well as the vocations which have a lesser chance of survival through 'Africanisation' tend to be more actively conscious of the need of birth-control in their own kin-groups than the sections which write off the possibility of a return to India or Pakistan. The Panjabi communities, Hindu, Sikh, and Sunni and Ahmeddiya Muslims, are the most vulnerable and, hence, the most insecure, because the majority of them are government employees or attached to governmental and semi-governmental organisations which are likely to replace Asians by indigenous Africans within a short time. The fear possessing most Indians, that the taking East African citizenship, as recommended by the official voices of the countries involved, may not eventually help them to preserve their job and their livelihood, constitutes the most pervasive anxiety syndrome among all Asian groups, but, of course, particularly among 'servants'. Even stronger apprehensions are felt by the small *duka* (shop) owners all over East Africa, i.e., by the Gujaratis who have given the-image of the Indian as a petty, money-grabbing trader, to both Africans and Europeans in East Africa. These *dukas*, owned almost exclusively by Gujarati-speaking Asians, are being crowded out by the African co-operatives and by an increasing boycott from the side of the former African clientele. It is perhaps only the top industrialist and businessman, and the very few large-scale Indian farmers, who would bid for a future successful residence in East Africa.

Sectional and Communal Divisions in the Overseas Indian Minority

As seen from what little has been said so far, it is impossible to deal with the Indian minority in East Africa *en bloc;* there is virtually nothing of sociological significance about the minority which would hold for all its constituent groups. Ideally, each of these groups should be dealt with quite separately, for they form more autonomous sub-cultures than, say, the Jews and the Irish in Boston who have been written about in great profusion as distinct subcultures. Linguistic and communal divisions, trans-group relations, in-group coherence and the whole range of sociologically diversifying elements must be adduced if a study like this is at all to be seriously attempted.

Divisive tendencies in Indian society have been studied by many authors; in the East African region, David Pocock has written some excellent accounts;[1] Hsu's recent book[2] is no doubt the most incisive work written so far about the structure of division in Indian society. Sectional and communal divisions in Hindu society have been the focal theme of sociological and anthropological studies in the South Asian area for over two decades.[3] This has caused much chagrin in official quarters in India, as well as among modern Indians in India and the diaspora, who understandably frown at the study of divisions which they feel are harmful to Indian society; 'why do anthropologists insist on studying caste and division in India when there are so many more important and fascinating things happening there—this is a representative query posed by Indian administrators and intellectuals faced with sociological conversation. Yet, regardless of the understandable feeling that these divisions ought not to exist, no amount of soft-pedalling and ever-so-well meant whitewashing can disenthuse the anthropologist in India from analysing these divisions; the sociologist *qua* sociologist is not a social therapist unless called upon to be one: but by such attempted therapy he really opts out from the less inspiring, and more modest duty of the student of society to describe society as it is and not as it should be.

Caste corporate groups, and division between corporate units is not only crucial to the study and the understanding of Indian society—there is virtually no other tool available at present. Most modern Indians, however skilled in the professions, however erudite in sundry reading, do not realise the importance and the subtle dignity of purely descriptive studies; nor do they realise the important distinction between the 'is' and the 'ought'—in fact, there is an endemic confusion between the two, which may well result from the unilateral, other-worldly value system of the Indian tradition which makes the 'ought' and its protagonists the cynosure of the Indian mind.

When the modern Hindu in East Africa speaks about caste, he uses the English word 'caste' even when he uses his own language, i.e., Gujarati or Panjabi. This seems to be an unconscious defence and protest device against the possible charge of being old-fashioned and socially reactionary. When talking to caste-mates, or to other Indians when matters of personal or kinship importance are discussed, they will use the names of the caste in question—Lohana, Patel, Mochi, Khattri, Ramgarhia, etc., but they will use the correct Indian term *jati* (caste) descriptively only under strong, directed pressure in their discourse. Hardly any East African Hindu feels at ease, when referred to the fact that a caste *(jati)* is simply an endogamous group and that only the abolition of endogamy, or more positively, the large-scale introduction of caste exogamy would break the caste system, which they decry with much eloquence. Far apart perhaps from some of the very few learned Brahmins in East Africa, hardly anyone—not even the old, support the caste system dialectically. Yet, what they oppose, and what they suggest should be done away with, is again a figment of the 'ought'—so far as in East Africa, only few marriages have been inter-caste liaisons. The uninspiring, purely factual statement, held out by the social scientist to the East African Indian informant, that no amount of invective against the vacuous 'caste system' will help, as 'caste' is nothing but endogamy—at least in the East African setting—makes most Indians quite uncomfortable. If the point is pressed hard enough, young Indians—young not necessarily in age but in outlook, i.e., all people who would like to be identified with modern social aspirations—hasten to assure that even endogamy is breaking down, that inter-caste marriage is becoming frequent, and they would usually adduce a case from their own family or from some 'close friend' where exogamous marriages have occurred, or are about to occur.

The most eloquent critics of the institution are equally aware of the insignificant number of exogamous liaisons. There is an interesting shift in the semantics of caste-parlance; sentences like 'there are many unarranged, inter-caste marriages through love' or 'there have been at least two dozens of inter-caste marriages in my community' cannot be substantiated. When it is pointed out, for instance, that between such culturally close communities of the Lohanas and Patels there have been only ten marriages in East Africa over the past fifteen years, this is admitted but then the reaction is to the effect 'but this is changing fast... in another thirty years, everyone will marry whom he likes'. This diction is quite universal; it also goes to show how strongly the modern Indian in East Africa has been affected by the teachings of the cultural heroes of the age, Gandhi, Nehru, Bose, etc. Modern India's official culture is free of caste; that is to say, the parlance of its votaries is that of a caste-less society—the only hitch being that again, 'is' language is used where 'ought' language should be used.

Just how the caste system, i.e., the tradition of *jati-endogsimous* marriage is going to break down in East Africa in the near future at the present rate of inter-caste alliances, is hard to imagine, unless the political and social pressure on the minority accelerates this dormant potential of social change. It is stated, by one and all, that the 'caste system'—whatever that means to the East African Indians—has been harmful and that it must vanish. There is hardly any Indian of whatever degree of sophistication, who would argue, officially, in favour of the system. Suggestions that charity begins at home, and that the system should be broken from within the family structure, are taken in a prescriptive sense, and there is a strong tendency, on the rhetorical side, to assert that inter-caste marriages should eventually take place.

However, when it comes to the parental or grandparental, or the 'arranging' generation, few of them would initiate a match across the caste-lines, even if considerable financial benefits might result; but the older, 'arranging' generations would tend to give in to the occasional entreaties of young people who want to marry across caste-lines, if such advantages are evident. Hardly any of the 'arranging' generation would admit any grudge against their descendant's partner of another caste, once the marriage had come about.

The majority of East African Indians are Gujarati-speaking Hindus; they form roughly 70 per cent of the total Asian population. Among them, the Patels and Lohanas are numerically and, economically dominant—economically on a par, however, with the less numerous Shahs, most of whom are Jain by religion and the *banya,* i.e., people belonging to the merchant-caste by tradition. The rest of the Gujarati Hindus belong to the *'choti jat'* literally, 'small castes', inferior to the others in the indigenous Indian caste ranking, i.e., carpenters *(sutaria),* cobblers *(muchi, mochi),* barbers *(nao),* tailors *(darji),* all of which are summarily and incorrectly referred to as the *'fundr* class, *fundi* being the Swahili word for labourers in general, but carpenters or masons in particular.

Fundi covers both Gujarati and Panjabi groups; among the latter, it is almost exclusively the Ramgarhia Sikhs who are, thus, referred to, as quite a few of this highly enterprising community have gone into the professions and done very well indeed. Trade exclusiveness, one of the criteria of the old, indigenous Indian caste system, has hardly ever been adhered to in East Africa, except where expert skills have been traditional, and hard to come by outside the old caste-groups; thus, the Gujarati tailors are mostly *darji* by caste, the goldsmiths are almost 100 per cent *soni,* i.e., members of the Indian Gujarati goldsmith caste. Mobility is upward unilateral, though: no 'higher' caste people do the work the *fundis* do—i.e. no or very few banyas, for instance, would take to shoe-making or tailoring, though many of the professional people among the East African Indians of this decade belong to the castes identified with the *fundi* until very recently.

Panjabi Hindus are much less divisive among themselves, and though *Khattris* (quasi-warriors or ascriptive one-time rulers), *suds,* derived from Sanskrit *'sudra'* a person of the fourth and lowest classical caste *(varna)*—of the traditional scheme, and Brahmins did not and do not intermarry in India, there is, indeed, a noticeable increase in intermarriages among these East African Panjabi groups, and there is much less opprobium on the side of the elders against such liaisons than there is in the Gujarati groups.

The Sikhs, very close to the Hindus or, for all sociological purposes, identifiable with the Panjabi Hindus in matters of caste-ranking and structure, are about 10 per cent *Jat,* i.e., members of the Panjabi indigenous agricultural and petty-landowning caste, and 90 per cent Ramgarhias, which caste was ranked close to the bottom of the traditional ranking in the Panjab. Indeed, they form the bulk of the actual *fundi,* i.e., the acting masons, carpenters, etc. They are definitely the most successful and excellent artisans in East Africa, a fact admitted both by the indigenous Africans and the European settlers.

There is a small group of Panjabi Muslims of the *Sunni* tradition and of the recently founded Ahmeddiya or Mirza'i sect, diffusely present in the East African countries, most of them in government and other clerical services. There is free social intercourse between them and the other Panjabi speakers, as socialising is language-rather than caste-bound in East Africa.

Whether the Goans can be classified as Indian in East Africa is a ticklish question for anyone, except the anthropologist. For the latter, it is perfectly clear that the Goans are Indians, whether they want to be, thus, identified or not. They speak an Indian language (Konkani, very close to Marathi), and there is no other justifiable classification from any ethnical or cultural viewpoint. Most Goans in East Africa, however, are not too happy with this designation, and they would stress their 'Portuguese-style' Catholicism as a point of cultural difference. The few Goans in the professions', doctors and lawyers, are either radically Indian by a sheer effort of will, or they deny or ignore their Indian background and claim that they are Portuguese or Brazilian! But, even they have quite a hard time in convincing people that they do not understand Hindustani, the lingua franca of East African Indians. The phenomenon, incidentally, of 'not knowing', i.e., pretending not to understand a language identification with other speakers, is one of the more noxious experiences of the sociological profession.

Whether this is due to the prolonged non-acceptance of such a group by the host nation or by the mother-group, the case of the Goan psychiatrist who claims to be Brazilian is no less aggravating than that of the German-born Jew in Chicago who moved to Pittsburgh for a while in order to be able to tell people he was from Pittsburgh when they asked him where he came from. Many Goans under forty, however, do not speak Konkani even, having had a 'purely English' education.

Alienation of Overseas Indian Minority

The three Gujarati-speaking Muslim groups form a very important sector of the Indian minority. Among them, the Shi'a Khoja Ishmailis, the followers of H.H. the Aga Khan, are from any viewpoint the most conspicuously emancipated, and perhaps the most successful group among all the sections of the minority beginning with their apparel: their women wear western dress due to *a firman* (pontifical injunction) of the late Aga Khan. They are the most thoroughly modernised—at least on the outside—but certainly also the most alienated from among the Indian groups, tending to keep aloof from the others. Moreover, they have succeeded in creating a separate identity in the alter-image of all other people in East Africa.

The next largest Gujarati Muslim group are the Shia'a Khoja Ithna-Asharis, followers of the eleventh Imam. The *mullahs* of this community are frequently North Indians or Panjabis by birth, probably because there is more Arabic, and certainly more Urdu learning in those Indian and Pakistani regions.

The third and last Gujarati Muslim group are the Bohras or Boros. Whereas both the Ishmailis and the Ithna-Asharis are Lohana by descent, converted to Shi'ism at different points in the past, the Bohras are of Gujarati Brahmin background. The head of this sect, who bears the illustrious title *'Dai-ul-mutlaq'* ('emissary of communion', i.e., with the hidden Imam, the representative of the Prophet), sits in Bombay.

The denial of caste in the Islamic groups in India, Pakistan and Indian East Africa is a purely theoretical and pietistic claim. Endogamy within the various Islamic groups mentioned is as rigid as among the Hindus. There have been virtually no intermarriages between Ithna-Asharis, Ishmailis and Bohras, nor between any of the three Gujarati and the two Panjabi Muslim groups. I cannot be established that there is less latent opposition against possible marriages with non-Indians, whites that is, among the Ishmailis, than against liaisons with other-group Muslims. Such liaisons, which are not quite rare especially with Ishmailis who studied in Britain or elsewhere abroad and contracted their own match, are less frowned upon than marriages across religious, caste and linguistic lines inside the Indian minority. This may simply be due to the 'one-is-less-than-two-harms-done'—count: in an Indian-non-Indian liaison, only one Indian family is hurt in prestige and emotion, in the case of inter-community marriages within the Indian groups, two Indian families are.

Whereas the divisions between the five Muslim sections (three Gujarati and two Panjabi) are pretty clear, this cannot be said about all the Hindu Gujarati communities. There is a general identification of all Gujaratis except the Muslims as 'Hindus'; both Lohanas and Patels, when using the word 'Hindu', without previous contemplation, mean Gujarati-or-Cutchi-speaking Hindus only (Cutchi is a western dialect of Gujarati). The term 'Cutchi is used by most non-Gujaratis and for all Gujaratis in East Africa, and often by Africans for all Indians. Gujaratis do not semantically include Panjabis as 'Hindus' unless the fact that many Panjabis in East Africa are Hindu is directly pointed out to them; yet such cognitive knowledge does not in any way decrease the divisive tendency—one does not mix or marry with another group just because they are Hindu, but because they belong to the same linguistic and endogamous unit.

Just as in contemporary India, there is really no conflict between the *'chotijat'* 'small (low) castes' like the *sutarias* and *muchis*, and the dominant Lohana-Patel groups, because their respective ranking is so heterogenous that social, let alone matrimonial competition and eligibility does not really arise. On the other hand—again like in India—there is a strongly divisive, potentially hostile undercurrent between Patels and Lohanas, the 'culturally and caste-hierarchically closest communities. In the first place, the mutual alter-image between them is largely negative; Patel informants tend to call the Lohanas shrewd, the Lohana women flippant or unhappy, prone to despair and suicide; Lohana informants would say about the same with regard to the Patels. Yet, there is a strong readiness on principle to intermarry, and about a dozen Lohana-Patel intermarriages have taken place recently in East Africa. The fact that in these matches the men were Patel, the women Lohana, might be a case of hypergamy—the Hindu male can marry slightly below his caste-level without any orthodox opposition; and this is also a corroboration of the fact that in India, the Patels have a slightly higher caste-ranking than the Lohanas, where they live in the same or immediately adjacent areas.

The former Indian custom of non-commensality between the castes has vanished in East Africa. All castes interdine, and a significant proportion of non-commensality may be present only between the linguistically different groups. This, however, may also be due to the very different kind of food Gujaratis and Panjabis prepare—and there is little common taste in culinary matters. Very few Gujaratis are seen at the average Panjabi wedding and *vice versa.* Menfolk drink together, and there is real and total integration of every group in East Africa, indigenous, Asian, and European, on the sundowner (equivalent of the American cocktail) level. There is also an unwritten bond between meat-eaters and alcohol-drinkers, probably the strongest commensal bond across the caste- and language-lines in the minority. 'Advanced' often means just meat-eating and whisky-consuming.

Within the upper Gujarati communities, there is latent conflict but not so much among the Lohanas as among the Patels. At Nairobi and some other larger settlements, there is the 'Patel Brotherhood' and the 'Patel Club', the former being the ascriptively vegetarian and tee-totalling, the latter the 'indulging' section—always referring to the males, as very few women as yet 'indulge'. Tension between the Lohanas and the Patels seems to transcend earthly life—as in some places the Lohanas and the Patels have separate cremation grounds.

Among the Patels, there are two further endogamous units, the *Kharwas and* the *Lewas,* whose original locations are geographically distant in the Gujarat. This restriction to intra-caste endogamy is kept up by and large, conscious only to the older people who know about it, but who do not communicate it to the younger generation in the process of finding mates. Thus, though young couples in arranged marriages do not usually know about the intra-endogamous background of their match, the separation between the two groups persists in East Africa; a large proportion of the Patels in East Africa are *Lewa*.

Brahmins are few and far between in East Africa. Among the Gujaratis, there are about 300 families in all East Africa, mostly of the *Audich-section*; their socio-religious organisation is the Brahma Samaj in the main cities; among Panjabis, there are roughly one hundred Brahmin houses in all the territories. Brahmins find it easier to steer clear of communal divisions, for although no particular ritualistic status attaches to them, they are welcome as guests in all groups.

Communal divisions in this context are a purely anthropological matter; the casual observer, particularly when he listens to the conversation of the modernised Hindus who make strenuous efforts to give the impression that there is no such thing as communal division, is easily persuaded that they either no longer exist or that they do not pose a social problem any more; or that, where they exist, they are vestigial and about to vanish within the next few years. The rather embarrassing vociferousness and the vehement denial of division on *jati*-lines is quite clearly a device of overcompensation; unconscious to most of the younger people, it has possibly a cathartic effect on the speaker, against his better cognitive knowledge of the divisive situation.

Division on communal bases had a positive side also: it was the parochial groups alone that have so far created educational, medical and other crucial facilities, where an all-over appeal to the Asians, say, through the Indian Association, was never made or failed. This and similar non-parochial Asian societies are diffusely present; their function is somewhat theoretical—exhausting itself in the reception of international and Indian guests, and in giving status to their appointed leaders and in similar marginal offices. The organisations which build and sustain schools, hospitals, assembly halls, libraries, etc., are parochial without exception. On the practical side, the various communities, deeply suspicious of each other, readily admit each other' achievements, and compete in a wealthy way. There is hardly any Lohana, Patel or other Hindu, who would seriously impugn the excellence of the Khoja Ishmaili achievements by way of creating and sustaining social work, education, etc. on a large scale, and *vice versa*. Thus, all groups admit that the Aga Khan hospitals and schools are the best in the countries, closely followed by those of the Jain Shahs, and then perhaps by the Arya Samaj which is largely Panjabi.

Parochially founded and supported educational institutions today are nominally interracial in their teaching staff and in the recruitment of students. Even previous to governmental injunctions after *uhuru* outlawing discrimination on racial or communal grounds, there was always a tendency to include some students of different racial and religious origin, although the founding group would be dominant both on the staff and in the student body. The Aga Khan hospitals in Nairobi and Dar es Salaam have approximately an equal number of Ishmaili and other patients, though there is a preponderance of Ishmaili doctors and nurses on their staff. This, of course, is very largely due to the superior encouragement toward higher education and training in the Ishmaili community in general, as pioneers of western-oriented emancipation among the Asian minority.

All agree, in their small talk and in common parlance at least, that communal divisions must go and the younger and more radical people claim that they are gone, which of course is a sample of the aforesaid systematic confusion of 'is' and 'ought' endemic in Indian society. A rather interesting linguistic use is made, after *uhuru* of communal division on its most basic, i.e. endogamous level. The African and European allegation that 'Asians don't mix", meaning that they do not intermarry and that they to not *really* socialise with others, is often countered by stating that they *do* not intermarry at all, and socialise very little, with Indians of other castes and linguistic groups and of different religion—and that the relative seclusion of the Asian minority as a whole from non-Asians should be appreciated as an *a fortiori*.

When outsiders are present, the urgency of mutual assimilation is so strong that statements of the form 'the Patels (non-Patels speaking)... do (something negative or pejorative)' or 'the Khoja Ishmailis are.... (pejorative)' are becoming very rare indeed. Mutual generalising criticism is, thus, becoming a strictly intra-Indian affair.

The question is constantly being asked if and how Indians should integrate in the new African body politic; whatever may be the views about it, and they vary quite radically from person to person, the variance not being bound up with specific groups, there is always the stipulation that the Indians would first have to integrate themselves i.e. abandon caste and linguistic divisions, before the next step can be taken.

'Sundowner' level socialisation serves as a figurative paradigm for integration; just how seriously it is taken by non-Asians is not a speculation within the purview of this study. It is true, however, that inter-group and interracial reservations are completely relaxed where Asian men, and much fewer women, between themselves and with non-Asians, drink together. But, the very fact that drinking, on which there is still a strong stigma, is a positive leaven for integration, makes the word 'integration' suspect to the more conservative Indians.

Social intercourse in young peer groups, schools, scout organisations, sports clubs, etc., is complete and uninhibited. On the adult level, the B.S.S., the East African corollary of the Hindu Fascist R.S.S. *(Rashtriya Svayam Sevak Sangh,*

National Self Help Organisation) has Gujarati and Panjabi speakers of all castes in its fold, male only, as female companionship is thought dangerous and disruptive on the orthodox compeer level. Here the ease of social relations is forced, but there is total integration, except that Muslims would not join for obvious reasons.

It ought to be observed that, prediction is none of the anthropologist's job—all divisive tendencies may indeed break down in the not too distant future. Asians find it hard to appreciate the social scientist's refusal to prophesy, and his reluctance to state and to see unity which may well come about some day, but which just is not yet there.

Statements to the effect that religion ranks supreme in the Indian value systems are by now sheer platitudes; yet the statement that this feature extends to the Indian settlers in East Africa is important and has to be made quite categorically. Just as no secular value system has ever developed in India from indigenous roots. East African Indians have been arranging all their values on a non-secular scale, again with the ascetic as the cynosure in that scale. We must rule out the objections that come from all sides, that 'money' is the only value for the Asians in East Africa, as a facile and dilettante view of no use to the social scientist. For even the love of money ties in with the unilateral hierarchical, teleologically religious core-value of the Asians in this region.[4]

Like in India, the older Indian in East Africa tends to be taken in by the itinerant monk *sahdu, pandit,* story-teller, diviner and faith-healer who gets to East Africa from India as an invitee or on his own, even though most Hindus always assert that these people are rogues and no good, and that they should not be supported. The reception and the attitude toward 'saints' and other preachers of institutionalised 'big tradition' Hinduism is still more naive, and bespeaks a higher degree of floating credulousness than in the present day sister communities in India.

What kind of religion is it that the preachers from India disseminate and reiterate on their extended, usually quite lucrative East African trips? And what is the religion the Asians brought along with them? How has it been modified through the decades of Indian residence in East Africa? Here, the 'big tradition—little tradition' dichotomy will aid our analysis.[5] Officially, there is no 'little tradition' in East Africa. Hindu religious organisations have usurped the total capacity of official religious communication, and even the more esoteric among these societies (the Swaminarayan sect, the followers of Sai Baba, a.o.) identify themselves completely with the standards of the 'big tradition', i.e. the Vedas and Upanishads, the Bhagavadgita, and the didactic epic. The demographic cause for this is simply that there are hardly any rural settlers in the true sense; even the petty *duka* owner (shopkeeper) in the bush is not a villager among African villagers or herdsmen, but a permanent guest from the city, as it were, and too isolated culturally to establish a rapprochement with the African 'little traditions' that no doubt surround him.

A homogeneous cultural group has to settle in a locality for quite a while in order to develop original 'little tradition' tendencies of its own, and, for example, the rough and hardy Sikhs who trade hides with the people in Masailand and who live very much like their clients, hardly have the opportunity to develop 'little traditions' first because their womenfolk seldom live with them in the bush (and 'little traditions' do not develop where there are no women of the same culture group around), secondly, because the minimal Sikh prayers are so short and handy that the Sikh trader in Masailand will hardly feel the necessity for any superogatory religious activity.

First, then, the 'big tradition' proper among the East African Indians. The Muslims' religious life is easy to describe. Most of the East African Indian Muslims are Shia'a, professing an eclectic Islam with emphasis on a linear continuity in the transmission of the teachings through successors or successor-surrogates to the Prophet. Thus, the Panjabi Ahmeddiyas or Mirzai's ascribe a status identical with that of the Prophet to their founder in the nineteenth century. Similar in structure, but very different in temperament and style, the Ishmailis regard the living Aga Khan as the *hazir Imam* 'the present Imam—Leader of the Faith' ('present' in the sense of 'living', 'physically present'), and they claim linear descent from the Prophet's own line for him. To the Ithna-Asharis, though they do not believe in a contemporary accessible Imam, the continuity of the prophetic office is taken care of by anyone who is directly inspired by the voice of God, so that any votary who is pious and has some charismatic status is eligible.

The influence of the Hindu *avataravada* (divinity reincarnated in human teachers according to the spiritual needs of the time), to which Islam had been exposed for so many centuries and by which it had been thoroughly modified in South Asia, is strikingly evident in these forms of Islamic religion. The Bohras, Gujarati speakers of Brahmin descent, believe in a Hidden Imam, represented by the *Dai-ul-mutlaq* mentioned earlier in another context. There has hardly been any change in the practice of Islamic religion since the departure from India. There is a considerable amount of successful conversion among Africans, especially through the Ahmeddiyas, who are most energetic proselytizers and whose preachers 'go native' in a radical way; they master the African languages to a degree that enables them to preach in Swahili, Kikuyu, and other East African languages.

This does not hold for the Khoja Ishmailis, for their religious outlook has changed most radically since the time their ascendants came to East Africa. Whether the purely historical accident that the late Aga Khan, a modern intellectual, a humanist and a cosmopolitan issued *firmans* (canonical injunctions) which modernised the community by decree, or whether there is an inherent lenience in the Ishmaili version of Muslim teachings, or if they both combined to change the community, is hard to assess. Ishmaili Islam is the most highly personalised form; based on the ascriptive charisma of the Aga Khan's person, the highly reformist, sophisticated, and pragmatically extremely functional notions of the late Aga Khan have changed the face of this important, affluent and striking group. The late and the present young Aga Khan, a graduate from Harvard University, have been sending *their firmans* by letter or wire, and they are then read out from the pulpit, in the *Jamatkhana* (assembly halls—the Ishmaili name for their mosque and place of congregation) and these orders take effect immediately. Some of these *firmans* are of a strictly mundane nature, as for instance that the cost of a bride's gown should not exceed 30 shillings and that the number of wedding guests should be limited to a specific figure—the change-over to western dress has already been mentioned.

The Hindus and other non-Islamic groups among the Indians admit and admire the Aga Khan's leadership and regret that Hinduism has not brought forth a similar personality, or a similar pattern of incontrovertible, personal leadership.

With the exception of the Ishmailis, the official worship and ritual is identical among the other Islamic groups. They are supposed to say their formalistic prayers *(namaz)* five times a day, and it seems the Ahmeddiyas and Ithna-Asharis are modally the most regular. The Ishmailis have a special prayer book, culled from the Quran, but with certain modifications; they now pray again in Arabic, formerly in Gujarati. They stress meditation— the *Jamatkhanas* in the East African cities are indeed fairly full from 4.30 every morning, and a large majority attend the obligatory Friday prayers and conventions. The *Jamatkhanas,* some of them architecturally extremely modernistic, are not only places for prayer, but for a highly institutionalised type of community life; food is prepared in Ishmaili homes, brought to the *Jamatkhana,* and auctioned, so that people who do not cook (bachelors, or very poor people in all sorts of duress) can have a well cooked meal almost at any time—the proceeds of this food auction go to the poor-fund, and this feeds back into the various social and educational institutions of the Aga Khan.

The alter-image of the Ishmailis in the eyes of other Indian communities, however, is not too positive. In the first place, most Indians distinguish between 'Muslims' and 'Ishmailis', including the Ishmailis themselves. When asked, 'is Mr. X an Ishmaili?' most Indians will answer 'no, he is a Muslim': and if you ask an Ishmaili 'are you a Muslim?', he is likely to say, 'no, I am an Ishmaili'. In the eyes of the other Muslim groups, the Ishmaili ritual, prayer, and the general development of religion is heretical, too much removed from the orthodox conventions of worship. Though none of the Shi'a sects in East Africa would concur with the puristic postulates of the *ulema* (the official body of orthodox Islam), censure of the Ishmaili form of worship is about as strong as that of non-Muslim worship in general. There is a strong tendency among other Muslims and Hindus in East Africa to suspect Ishmailis in general of moral laxity, and in accordance with the official Indian culture 'immorality' etc. means any autonomous expression of the sexual. However, the only clue the non-Ishmailis can possibly have is that Ishmaili women wear frocks—baring one's legs as a female being is a *chose fatale* to the Indian mind even in 1965. Objectively, there is no modal difference in the 'moral habits' of the Ishmailis from any other Indian community, Muslim, Hindu, or other. Somehow, the image of an Indian woman not covering her ankles engenders suspicion. Interviewing Ishmailis of all economic groups, and of all relevant age-groups, it was found that their attitudes about morality, sex, and the invariable value concomitance of sex and morality is identical with that of all other groups, with not the slightest difference in the mode of appraisal 'and censure.

Influence of Hinduism on Islam in East Africa

Hindu influence, contextually and formally, is strong on all Indian Muslims. Hardly any Indian Islam is *ulema* Islam, and certainly no East African Indian Islam bears any trace of the '*ulema* strictures. But, although both Sh'ism and Sunism tended to incorporate many Hindu elements on South Asian soil, including the virtual acceptance of *avataras or* divine teachers in human form, incarnations or emanations of the godhead, it seems to this author that the East African Indian Muslims have absorbed more Hindu elements than they are conscious of. Hindu symbolism abounds in Ishmaili nomenclature—for example, a house in Dar es Salaam was named *Om Habibabad.* On inquiry, some Ishmailis around the house if they knew the meaning of OM (which is the basic Hindu-Brahmin vocal symbol, and as a written symbol comparable in importance to the cross of the Christians), they said it was some sort of a Persian or Arabic *"mantra'* (a *mantra* again is a secret, sacred Hindu or Buddhist formula). Of course, there is nothing whatever Muslim about OM, but the cathexis is all the stronger as its original content has been forgotten.

Hinduism in East Africa, like elsewhere, is in every aspect far more complex than Islam. Like in India, there is no such thing as a church or a pervasive ecclesiastic organisation among the Hindus. The only well-organised Hindu group, at least in matters of uniform ritual and credo, is the *Arya Samaj,* a highly fundamentalistic, simplistic, and theologically unsophisticated reform sect founded by Swami Daynanda Saras vati, a Gujarati monk, who taught mainly in the Panjab in the middle of the last century. It has caught the imagination of many East African Indians—among whom the large majority are Panjabi with a small Gujarati element —perhaps due to the feeling of a lack of unity among the Hindus of East Africa.

The founder of the *Arya Samaj* ('Society of Aryans') preached 'back to the Veda by which he meant a complete ritualistic identification and adherence to the oldest portion of the canonical scripture, the *samhita*—collections of hymns; he excluded the Upanishads and the other speculative tracts of the Vedic tradition, which set him into crass contrast with all other Hindu sects.

In Northern India, especially again in the Panjab, the unreformed, allegedly more conservative Hindus refer to themselves as *'Sanatani'* (eternal). The *Sanatan Dharma Sabha* ('Organisation of the Followers of the Eternal Religion') is contrasted with the *Arya Samaj.* Although, the *Sanatani* are opposed to the *Arya Samaj* by their allegedly more rigid traditionalism and orthodoxy, this distinction does not stand any critical scrutiny. The *Arya Samaj* is much more fundamentalistic, and doctrinarily much less tolerant than the *Sanatoria* organisation. The followers of the *sanatoria* tradition—and this means in East Africa, every Hindu who is not an *Arya Samajist*— use icons *(murti)* for their worship, and the main point of criticism the *Arya Samaj* teachers bring against the *sanatana* doctrines and practices centres on the latters' worship of idols.

But, neither the *Arya Samajists* nor the *Sanatanists* in East Africa are aware of the traditional implications of *murtipuja* (idol-worship), which has never been the worship of an inanimate object, but the aesthetical contemplation of an object in order to facilitate the contemplation of the divine in the devotee. Apart from some very few Brahmin priests *(purohit)* in East Africa which defend *murtipuja* on a scholastic level, the *Sanatanis* usually are diffident when faced by *Arya*

Samajist argument, and half-heartedly admit the shortcomings of *murtipuja*.

Among the followers of the *Arya Samaj*, which is organised on an all-East African level with its administrative centre in Nairobi, the official iconoclasm of this school does not affect most of its members to the extent that all of them forswear *murtipuja* completely; most women in *Arya Samaj* households carry on with worship of Hindu gods, and of Hindu icons in their homes; men, even when staunch Samajists, usually do not interfere. From about one hundred *Samaji* households which was surveyed, only six insisted on not having any residual *murtipuja* in their houses; they conduct the daily Vedic fire-ritual *(havan)* in the simplified and plain version prescribed by Swami Dayananda, and the women participate in it. In all the other cases, the women live their own parallel religious life; they worship through their *murtis* (icons) although perhaps not with the same eclat as the official *Sanatanis*. As a justification of the presence of icons in the house, the *Arya Samajist* may say that he too worships Rama, Krishna, etc. as teachers; but they deny the concept of *avataras*, i.e. of divine incarnation in the forms of these mythological figures.

Most *Samajists* chant the Vedic hymns without understanding their meaning, and the quality of the chant is poor; there is hardly any guidance as to correct incantation, etc.; also, the participation of women in the fire-ritual *(havan)* is totally unacceptable to the more learned, orthodox Hindus in India; Swami Dayananda's insistence on ritualistic equality of women stemmed from his desire to emancipate them socially. But, this regular ritual makes the *Arya Samajist* more conservative than the Sanatanis, who are 'the conservatives' by definition. The pouring *of ghee* (clarified butter) into the sacrificial fire during the *havan* is explained by followers who want to be 'modern and scientific' as having the purpose of purifying the air in the house! The *Sanatanis* do not have a unified, organised form of ritual, every active *Sanatani* very largely concocts his private ritual, largely on information obtained from some casual teachers or itinerant preachers from India, or by emulation and counsel from his elders or peers.

The *Arya Samaj* is a model for the 'big tradition'. But, as all the other Hindu groups have recently been exposed to highly sophisticated forms of Hindu thought, through literature and through the visiting swamis, the travelling salesmen of the Hindu Renaissance, the 'big tradition' pervades the whole community in an overt fashion, and we shall have to look elsewhere for manifestations of the 'little tradition'; to these we must now proceed.

There are situations where some 'little tradition' surreptitiously encroaches upon 'big tradition' in East Africa, in a manner which has no exact parallel in India, simply because there is hardly any physical contiguity between the two types of tradition in such a direct manner in India. The Indians of East Africa are urban people, whatever their ancestral background. In Indian cities, the 'little traditions', where they exist sporadically, are completely subservient to the 'big traditions' and the urban followers of 'big tradition' Hinduism look down upon 'little traditions' or deny their existence altogether. Not so in East Africa. We have heard no less than a dozen reports about occurrences in different locations in all the three countries; I observed three which I regard sufficiently typical. The one case was in Tabora, Tanganyika, where 'God has come into the house' *('ghar men Isvar aya')* of a man who claims to have daily visions of the god. Lord Krishna in his case, in person. A large number of people gather at his house which has now achieved the nimbus of a shrine and which is also marked by a flag like official temples. These visitors, by no means all women, come to witness the daily scene and very few people in the city, apart from *Arya Samajists,* would radically deny the 'truth' of these events. There is a tendency among 'modern' people to dismiss these things as *andhavisvas* (blind faith, superstition), but that is about the maximal criticism offered. Men, when together, tend to call it all fraud *(dhoka),* thus, giving a seal to their scepticism which is thought to be a sign of being modern. Every morning, then, the said person feeds milk to the 'photo' of Krishna, one of the usual rather ghastly polychromes that abound in non-institutionalised places of worship all over East Africa and India, by putting a *lotha* (conic brass vessel) of sweetened milk to the lips of the painting. We moved quite close up to the image, as the householder had invited me to visit his shrine set up in a niche in his home, lately enclosed by a wooden partition which he had erected after the deity had started giving his *'darshan'* (vision, sight). The milk, as expected, oozed down to the ground on the front side of the image, which natural fact was pointed out by some of the more sceptical folks in the neighbourhood. Most of the devotees at the place actually believe that the milk is physically taken and drunk by the god, thus accepting the offer every day, thereby, blessing the householder. People who deny it, pointing out the fact that the milk pours down the front as it would from any other vertical surface, are called *'nastik* (unbelievers) by the others, and this is a term of grave religious reproach.

Most of the 'little tradition' incidences, however, fall within the wide scope of 'possession' as used by the ethnographer and the culture-and-personality oriented psychologist. The orthodox term (Gujarati and Hindustani in East Africa) is *mata* (or *devata) lag gayi* literally 'the Mother (or any other deity) has affixed herself (i.e. on the person affected)'. In most cases, the Universal Mother *(Jagadamba),* or some other mother-deity, is the focus of mythological introjection; *Jagadamba* is the most frequent Gujarati appellation for the 'big tradition' mother goddess otherwise called Durga, Kali, Shakti, etc., in other parts of India. But, though the goddess is of 'big tradition' provenance, her uses here are 'little tradition' uses; and of course, it is never quite certain whether a deity with a Sanskritic, i.e., 'big tradition' name, is not a Sanskritisation of some local village deity, absorbed into the official pantheon. The frequent identification of *'Mata'* (mother) with Shitia, the goddess of smallpox, would be a pointer in that direction.

In most cases in East Africa, this sort of possession is accompanied by the ascribed capacity of divination, soothsaying and healing. I studied a man in his early fifties in Old Kampala (Uganda), who has since hoisted a tall pole with a red flag—red being the emblematic colour of the mother goddess—and a *trishul,* the trident symbolising both the 'Mother' and her divine spouse, Shiva. Regularly every Sunday at 9 p.m., he invokes the blessings of the "Mother', begins to tremble and shake vehemently within a few minutes after his invocations, which are in Gujarati. After that, he calms down completely and for the rest of the performance he acts and talks perfectly normally as it would seem. He distributes holy ash and *prasad* (sweets offered to the deity) to the rapt audience, which numbers between 10 and 50 every week. He then answers queries about the future and solves problems of anyone who asks him any specific personal questions.

A British-educated, delightfully charming and attractive Lohana girl of about 20 told me 'I believe him completely, because he is really in close contact with the Universal Mother whom I also worship'—interestingly, the young lady's father is a staunch and active *Arya Samajist*—but his wife and daughters are not disenthused by this austere fact: the bell tolls at almost every hour of the day in the little house temple which the women in the family run in dire opposition to the *Arya Samajist* injunctions against idols. However, when I asked the young lady whether the divinations of the man possessed had always come true, she first answered in the affirmative; after some reflection she added 'but once, when I wanted something very very badly, he promised me I would get it. But, then it did not come through! When later on I asked him to justify this false outcome, the holy man said that what God gives you, my little daughter, is always the best for you'.

The most interesting case was that of a Lohana woman of about 40 at Mwanza, Tanganyika, whose house has been visited in a somewhat bizarre fashion by the Universal Mother. It is a very ordinary house. A while ago children heard strange songs and footsteps one night and when they opened-the door to the little shrine in the morning, there were cinnabar powder footprints of a small female foot, though without the big toe, on the floor in front of the idol; by its side, there was a crude *trishul* (trident sacred to Shiva and the Universal Mother), also of *kunkum* (cinnabar powder). This, so the woman and her devotees reported, was repeated several times, and subsequently, the footprint and the *trishul "were* covered by the woman with a piece of glass, in order to preserve the holy token. Sizable numbers of women and some men have been visiting the place every day since, and the matter got into the *East African Standard* and the *Nation,* the two most widely read English language dailies in East Africa—as did some similar events at sporadic intervals.

A Gujarati lady doctor, an M.B.B.S. from Bombay, herself suggested to me to witness the scene because she had felt perturbed by the scepticism which I had pronounced in a talk to the local Hindu community, criticising the whole syndrome from a pastoral view point. The lady doctor, whose age is about 35, is herself a staunch believer in the powers of the woman and she introduced the latter to me in person. I am personally almost certain the woman is a latent catatonic-schizophrenic with a strong paranoid tendency. She functions normally enough in her home, looking after nine children of her own, and her husband. She talks gently, though nervously and apologetically when objective questions are put to her. She is not illiterate. Every morning she takes her bath, then proceeds to her shrine. She invokes the goddess with a short, obviously self-composed Gujarati prayer, which she says with hands upraised, and which hardly lasts five minutes. In course of this, and for about ten minutes after she has concluded her prayer, she trembles vehemently, her eyes are closed and she perspires profusely; yet, it did not strike me as an unpleasant sight. Now when she emerges, her hands are frequently full *of* *kunkum* (cinnabar powder), and this is the most awe-inspiring feat in the eyes of the pious public. It is hinted that the *kunkum* is somehow mysteriously put into her hands by the goddess herself.

Some of the ladies expressed the view that at several occasions, the whole little shrine was full of *kunkum,* walls, floor, ceiling, and everything, after she had completed her prayers. I inspected her hands, and there were indeed slight cinnabar powder traces between her palms. It seems that the moment she enters her shrine, she touches the little altar, or the space between the image of the deity and a little wooden partition around it. The image is one of the common gaudy oleographs, probably torn from a calendar, and it is not even framed in glass. Below the actual 'photo' of the goddess, who sits astride the tiger, the *vahana* (carrier animal of the goddess Durga or Shakti) there is a thick layer of *kunkum,* broad at the base, and tapering off at the spot of the paper where the goddess' feet are painted. This *kunkum* was supposed to originate *in loco,* and when it wears away as it does, the goddess replenishes it at night. Little bits of *kunkum* thus probably come into contact with the protrusions of the woman's palms as she touches the area; she then rubs her palms vigorously, which movement is interpreted as a gesture of prayer by the devotees; but this process obviously spreads the powder all over her palms. If this is the actual procedure, it is probably quite unconscious, because the woman evidently forgets, or does not absorb these preparations as her own—which is quite typical for several types of schizophrenia. The people who are really upset about these recurrent and prestige-giving events are the *Arya Samajists,* who refer to all of them, and especially to the reaction of the audience, as *andha-visvas,* which is a literal translation-neologism from English meaning 'blind faith', but which Asian English speakers re-interpret as 'superstition'. They also imply that these matters involve deliberate fraudulence; in the case of the Mwanza woman, however, I am perfectly certain that there is no such thing as deliberate make-believe; it is one of the pathological manifestations of 'little tradition' Hinduism for which the majority of all Hindus has always found some place.

A young man in Nairobi, about 32, Panjabi *khattri,* clerk in a bank, who speaks perfectly good English, is married, and has two children, has been having *'darshan'* (vision, consummative 'sight' of the chosen deity) and other 'spiritual experiences' of Shiva and Shakti, the consort of Shiva, a synonym of *Jagadamba,* the Universal Mother, ever since he was a boy of three, so he told me. A *trishul* (trident symbol of Shiva and Shakti), has been appearing in blood on his forehead, on his arms and chest, and so did the mystic syllable OM in Nagari script. About ten years ago, so he told me, he found a *guru* in Nairobi, strangely enough an old Sikh of the Ramgarhia caste, who taught him 'how to meditate and see God correctly'. Helped by his *guru,* and aided by his own previous experiences, he had been in states of 'profound meditation', in which he sees brilliant lights, and the full vision of the god and the goddess, sometimes together, sometimes separately. Once, a few years ago, he further told me—as he had told his friends and relatives—he was in deep *samādhi* (consummative trance, the final postulate of the Hindu's contemplative exercise) for three days on end. Though he sat in his room at home all the time, a person who was his exact double did all his work in the office, signed papers for him with precisely his handwriting, and when he returned to the office on the fourth day, nobody had noticed his absence. He also met a man of the *darji* (Gujarati tailor) caste from Arusha, Tanganyika, who was an expert in *'maili vidyd'* ('dirty' techniques, viz. sorcery)—as was, incidentally, the brother of his own *guru,* who changed into a big bird and began sucking his (the speaker's) blood.

This is a pathological, but not infrequent example of little-big tradition transaction: the experiences themselves are very much of the 'little tradition', but the jargon is entirely that of the Hindu Renaissance 'big tradition' of modern India, the style, without modification, that of Vivekananda, Shivananda, and copious other edificatory literature of the contemporary Hindu revival.

These are not just isolated cases; on a cautious estimate, there must be around two to three hundred instances, currently, of the pathological-cum-little tradition framework in East Africa. Adducing some examples in detail as we did was not to accumulate empirical data for corroboration; what is important for our study is not so much the number of occurrences, as the size of the audience to these phenomena: this is a problem well-known to the student of culture and personality, viz. the definition of the mentally 'normal' and 'abnormal' in terms of acceptance, neglect, or rejection by the environmental society. We are not so much concerned,, therefore,, with showing a great number of pathological cases, accepted with positive evaluation in a specific religious tradition in a transplanted milieu, but with the exemplification of an interesting syndrome important for cultural analysis: the terms 'normal' and 'abnormal' in a clinical sense are completely vacuous, if they are not used within a specific audience *vis-a-vis* the agents or performers for this audience. Most of the cases that can be adduced to exemplify a 'little tradition' overlap with Hindu 'big tradition' in East Africa, which goes to show that the most bizarre behaviour pattern can and does gain prestige if there is a sanctioning audience. But, again, the psychological accoutrements of this situation are of no real concern to us in this study; what is important is to realise that the Hindu settlers in East Africa have achieved a complete fusion of 'big' and 'little' tradition elements, albeit at the cost of both theological and psychological congruity.

Unlike in South Africa[6], the gods and goddesses by which the Hindu subjects in East Africa are affected or possessed, are exclusively 'big tradition' deities. The Gujaratis and Panjabis who migrated to East Africa did not have any godlings comparable to, say, the Seven Sisters of the Dravidian rural pantheon. They came with a predominantly urban background, and with urban, i.e., mercantile purposes. Whatever 'little tradition' had encroached upon the settlers' parents or grandparents from the rural areas of the Gujarat or the Panjab had been crowded out by 'big tradition' parlance and its postulates, so that it requires a considerable amount of probing to find 'little tradition' residues except on the pathological fringe. Most of the 'big tradition—little tradition' overlap goes on inside the Hindu households in East Africa, special fasts *(brat),* the daily *puja* (formal worship at the house shrine), are carried out largely by the women. These are oriented towards the Sanskritic gods, i.e. the deities of the Hindu 'big tradition', in Gujarati and in Panjabi, with a sprinkling of Sanskrit invocations among the former, and of course the Sanskrit stereotype formulae of the *Arya Samajis.*

There is a very large Gujarati sect which might be said to represent an Essenic form of crystallised 'big tradition' Hinduism. It is the Swaminarayan cult created about a hundred years ago by a highly ascetical Brahmin and his followers in the Gujarat. Their disciplinary and doctrinary canon is the *patrika* (literally, 'letter'), a set of rigid rules of ritualistic and personal behaviour. This sect has large and well-kept temples in almost all East African cities, and in some places (as in Tororo, Uganda) their shrine is larger and more elaborate than the other, more general Hindu temples. The Swaminarayanis are also more exclusive than other Hindu groups; although they do not object to other people entering and worshipping at their temples, their services are more uniform, more formalised, and more intensive than most of the other Hindu forms of worship. They are also highly selective about visiting preachers; they invite only preachers from the mother-body in the Gujarat, specialists in the teachings of the sect. Their present swami, who is 'the same as Narayana (God, Vishnu)' visited the region; when he spoke, a screen had to be put up to conceal the female audience from his vision; the homes in which he stayed had to be evacuated by all women of the household between menarche and menopause. Their doctrines, however, do not seem to be different in essence from those of the orthodox Hindus around them; they worship Vishnu and his various human incarnations (Rama, Krishna), as well as Shiva, the Devi, and the other main deities of the Hindu pantheon, images of whom are installed in the Swaminarayan temples side by side with 'photos' of the three monastic founder-Brahmins. These original teachers, however, are seen as supreme in the hierarchy of all spiritual preceptors of mankind. This again is no different from the attitude of all other Hindu sectarian foundations, whose inceptors have all acquired divine status, and are in principle directly identified with the supreme deity. On the dogmatic side, the Swaminarayan theology is an almost unmodified take-over from the modified-dualistic teachings of Ramanuja (eleventh century A.D.).

The Sikhs, with their simpler and highly formalised Gurumukhi corpus of prayers form their canon, the *Guru Granth Sahib,* must be classed in the 'big tradition' whatever the origins of Sikhism were three hundred years ago. They have their regular *kirtas* (litanies) on Sundays, with a steady and large number of devotees, both male and female. There is no doubt that the attendance is more proportionate, between men and women, among the Sikhs than among any Hindu group. Sikh women do not seem, on an average, to be as eager for domestic worship; the Panjabi Hindu women are less eager than the Gujarati and Cutchi women—the average time given daily to formal worship would be something between 1-2 hours among Gujarati women, and from between ten minutes to half an hour among Panjabi Hindu and Sikh women.

East African Hindus follow a great variety of sects of very different degrees of religious sophistication. Most of these sects hail from the middle of the sixteenth century A.D. and later, and there is hardly any adherence to the classical schools.

The doctrines directly inculcated in religious education—through processes of deutero-learning rather than through formal religious instruction which is almost non-existent in East Africa—were propounded by village saints, preachers, and reformers of the Indian middle ages; a majority of the East African Hindus, and almost all women follow the simple, rustic, ethical-cum-ascetical doctrines of those teachers. The sophisticated, however, have been more recently influenced by the teachings of the Hindu Renaissance, i.e., the reform movements of the last eighty years that spread all over India. Even from among these, some are decidedly on the pathological fringe, as the followers of Sat-Sai Baba, a saint of Muslim background but ascriptively a Hindu mystic, of the late eighteenth century. His present successor, who lives near Bangalore in South India, is reported to 'know everything that is said, done, and thought anywhere in the world', and to be able to cure all diseases which medical people have given up as beyond remedy. This cult is magicocentric, its votaries tend to go into mild stages of trance, which is remarkable as so far all the literature on Sai Baba has been published in English only; during their regular meetings, one person reads the deeds of Sai Baba in English and then translates it into Gujarati, sentence by sentence.

At Nakuru in Kenya, there is a Lohana shopkeeper, referred to as Hirji Baba Maharaj. He is approaching 70, a quaint looking man with a greenish turban of his own design. He has been travelling from place to place all over East Africa, and in about forty years he has won a following of several thousand Hindus, mostly Lohanas, Patels, and 'small *jati*' Gujaratis and Cutchis. He chants and interprets the Hindi Ramayana composed by Tulsidas, a village-Brahmin of North India, who flourished in the sixteenth century. Hirji Baba seems to be the only Hindu teacher who has made some converts among Africans—there are about a dozen Jaluo and Kikuyu followers, who have learnt Gujarati and Hindi, participate in the *bhajan* (litany), follow other Hindu ritual, and have assumed Hindu names. A few years ago, a whole boat was chartered by his devotees, whom he led to several shrines in India, and back. To any non-Gujarati Hindu, the concomitant ritual seems pretty 'old-fashioned'—but when a modern East African Panjabi uses this term in the context, it has the same feeling-tone as the modern American use of 'sick'. Itinerant monks invited to Hirji Baba's meetings—as well as to other religious functions among the Gujaratis—are placed on an altar, worshipped through *araii* (oil-lights waved around them in a circular motion as around temple icons). Their feet are washed with milk and sweet water, the water distributed as *caranamrt* (a libation poured over the deity's or the holy man's feet, literally. Toot-nectar') and drunk for spiritual merit and benefit. Such occasions are not rare and far between, they occur right around the main streets of Nairobi, Dar es Salaam and Kampala.

While the hitherto mentioned groups form the majority of the East African Hindu body politic, there is an increasingly large number of people, distributed with varying density over all the constituent linguistic and caste groups, who follow one or more of the teachings of what could be termed as the Hindu Renaissance, the modern, English language-using simplification and popularisation of the scriptures by an eclectic, quasi-Sanskrit oriented, rhetorical 'big-tradition' echelon of preachers beginning with Swami Vivekananda at the turn of the century, and continuing today with an ever increasing host of monastic and lay teachers and organisations that have their headquarters in many parts of India, and—as with the Ramakrishna Mission, the Divine Life Society, or the self-Realisation League, in western countries as well. Strangely enough, East Africa is the only place with a sizable Hindu population, where the Ramakrishna Movement has not established itself (it is quite well established and influential in neighbouring South Africa); one of the reasons may be the total absence of Gujarati- and Panjabi-speaking monks in that organisation, as all the Ramakrishna-Vivekananda monks are Bengali or Dravidian speakers. The honours are shared between the school of the late Swami Shivananda Sarasvati of Hrishikesh on the side of naive religious appeal and, for the religiously more astute, by the Sri Aurobindo *ashram* at Pondicherry, which has become a world-wide movement. It is largely the Patel community that got enthused by it, and one of its leaders, now retired from active life, has moved permanently to the *ashrarn* in South India.

Shivananda Movement

Swami Shivananda, of South Indian Brahmin descent, had been a medical practitioner in Malaya, saw the light and became a *sannyasi;* and set himself up at the foot of the Himalayan range in Hrishikesh on the upper Ganges, a centre of monastic activity in North-Western India. Within ten years he established a 'Forest University', wrote literally scores of books on religious topics, health, morals, and became by far the most successful popularizer of simplified, theistic, eclectic Hinduism which uses English as its tool of communication. He appealed to an audience that knew some English and no Sanskrit, or a vernacular only—all of his books and most of the periodical writings of his institution appear in the major Indian languages. They included Indian Government employees, officers in the armed forces, lawyers, school-teachers, in short all the people with whom E. Shils[7] deals in his excellent study. Shivananda was prolific, pompous and puritanical, the ideal combination of the official culture of modern India, 'healthy' in the sense of stout and 'light-coloured', he fitted into the image of the Hindu hierophant. His followers do not object to the sanctimoniousness that is so disturbingly obvious to any critical reader, simply because there is no word, and hence no concept of this sort in modern Hinduism. He created the Divine Life Society, with followers in California and in Nairobi, in Bonn and in Dar es Salaam.

Almost all educated Hindus in East Africa have some acquaintance, and most of them the profoundest admiration for the Shivananda movement. His teachings are perhaps most typical, comprehensive, and the most representative of the simplified 'big tradition' Hinduism that officially prevails in East Africa; a Hinduism which emphasizes bourgeois virtues, yogic and 'spiritual' exercises, a naive *mens sana in corpore sano* acceptance of all religions and all teachers of religion without explicit value comparison, and an eclectic reading of the most frequently translated texts of the Hindu tradition, especially the Bhagavadgita, though hardly any of the canonical Upanishads. Literally thousands of East African Hindus have made Swami Shivananda their *guru in distans,* although he never set foot outside India since he took up the monastic life. The fact that Hindus refer to him as the 'Himalayan Sage' or the 'living incarnation of the Divine' goes to show what ascriptive charismatic status can do. Hrishikesh is certainly no more in the Himalayas than Arusha on Mt. Kilimanjaro.

By far, the most sophisticated version of modern Hinduism available in East Africa is the Shri Aurobindo cult. Aurobindo and his spiritual consort *'la Mere'* a French Jewish woman who joined him many years ago, established fame through his English writings, and through the exquisitely organised *ashram* which combines healthy living with 'spiritual' life, meditation, yoga exercises, plain food, a euphoric atmosphere and a cosmopolitan flavour. Aurobindo himself, though Bengali by birth, never learnt his mother-tongue in a literate sense, and published all his writings in English, much more sophisticated but no less sanctimonious than the writings of Shivananda and the other swamis of the Hindu Renaissance.

The Theosophical Society has made some headway in East Africa and there are Lodges in all the larger cities. Many theosophists are simultaneously admirers or followers of Aurobindo, as of Swami Shivananda. The 'esoteric' writings of Mme. Blavatsky are read and admired. Only English speakers are among the active theosophists, as few of the theosophical writings have been translated into Gujarati. On the ritualistic side, however, the theosophists continue their domestic worship according to their respective Hindu background. Whereas the Aurobindo cult has attained ritualistic status-pictures of Aurobindo and *'la Mere'* abound in Patel houses, and candles are lit in front of them in the style of regular Hindu worship—there are no pictures of Annie Besant, Blavatsky, or other founders of the Theosophical Society.

Jainism

The Jains are among the most wealthy and influential of the Gujarati- and Cutchi-speaking groups. The section which is particularly strong in East Africa, is the Visa Oshwal community, which has the most autonomous and efficient educational institutions, next in size and calibre only to the Ishmaili institutions of the Aga Khan. Although, Jainism originally forbade agriculture as a profession that entails the taking of (microbic) life, the Visa Oshwals of Jamnagar, Porbandar and adjacent areas were originally farmers, though they came as tradesmen to East Africa. Jainism is an atheistic religion, it denies the authority of the Hindu scriptures, but its ritual and its attitude towards life is very similar indeed, especially to modern puritanical Hinduism. Most East African Jains are not too cognisant of the radical differences between Hindu and Jaina doctrine, and though their temples are separate, most Jains—especially women—invoke Hindu gods and goddesses along with the Tirthankaras, the semi-mythical founders of Jainism.

This about summarises Hindu practice in East Africa. Prof Hsu's otherworldly unilateral orientation[8] finds full corroboration in the East African Indian outlook. Otherworldliness breaks through at every moment, and the pleasures of life are viewed with religious suspicion even by the many who indulge freely in them, creating highly dysphoric feelings of remorse and guilt. Hindus and Sikhs in East Africa who have made over a certain number of millions tend to stop eating meat and drinking alcohol even when they had been partaking of both in their less wealthy days.

After this rundown on the workings of applied religion and ritual in Indian East Africa, it now remains to describe the Hindu teachings as assumed by the communities. This is much easier and requires less bulk: Hinduism as prescriptive ideology is rather simple in the diaspora, and with the exception of literary involvements (Aurobindo, Theosophists, etc.) the idea part of East African Hinduism can be stated with ease. Unlike the lay Christian or the lay Muslim's ready answer to questions of the form 'what is a Christian' or 'what is a Muslim', the East African Hindu finds the corresponding definitional question somewhat embarrassing, for although he can give a discourse on what he thinks is *right* to do and to think, he cannot give a definition of Hinduism or of 'being a Hindu', because the theological apparatus essential for such a definition is lacking in East African parlance. The Eastern Mediterranean teachings are simple and on the lay level, of a piece. The Hindu teachings are not, unless those of a single school like the *Arya Samaj,* universalised, which is an unpalatable idea to all but the *Arya Samajis*. The average East African Hindu, particularly the younger ones, when asked this question would say 'My parents were Hindus, they told me I am a Hindu, but I really don't know what it means'. This, however, does not countervail a pervasive set of religious ideas held by the subjects.

On the contrary, their articles of faith are readily enumerated: the East African Hindus believe—as did their forebears in India—in an all-pervasive divinity, usually appealed to as Vishnu, especially in his *avataras* (incarnations) as Rama and Krishna, or as Shiva, with or without his spouse (Devi, Jagadamba, Shakti, etc.) or the hyposta-sized World Mother alone, without Shiva. Divinity is also manifest in minor representations of a heroic, demoniacal, or human form like Hanuman, the monkey-warrior who assisted Rama in his recovery of Sita, the tatter's spouse, herself an incarnation of the world goddess Lakshmi, Vishnu's eternal cosmic partner. Hanuman is both the epitome of chaste, unwed, loyal piety and religious devotion *(bhakti)*. Along with it, all Hindus with the exception of the *Arya Samajis* who are vehemently anti-anthropomorphic and iconoclastic—believe that divinity is both 'formless' *(mrakar)* and endowed with anthropomorphic or theriomorphic 'form' *(sạkar)* according to the spiritual needs and competence of the devotees, but that the approach through 'form', i.e. through one of the divine incarnations is easier and closer to the heart of most 'common people'.

The main text referred to and quoted from is the *Bhagavadgita,* the most important, though non-canonical text of the Hindu Renaissance. Its extreme eclecticism appeals to the modern Hindu, its implied herolatry adds to the appeal. It contains religious and quasi-ethical injunctions and provides a definite code of living for the Hindu non-specialist. The fact that this text is non-canonical, and hence not a compulsory creed for a Hindu, is hardly known to anyone in East Africa. The emphasis, especially amongst the Gujaratis and Cutchis, is on pronounced, intensive devotional practice *(bhakti, bhajan* and *kirtan*—religious litany and congregational worship in the home and in temples and at casual places of assembly, in fellow-devotees' homes). Most East African Hindus are aware that there are many other ways of propitiation of the divine apart from *bhakti* but then, following the general tenor of the middle-class Hindu Renaissance, *bhakti* is regarded as the best and the least extravagant, and does not presuppose the knowledge of Sanskrit and philosophy which is nonexistent in East Africa.

Practice of Religion in the Overseas Indians

The relation between religion and life is just as intensive and paramount among East African Indians as Hsu has seen it in India. The quasi-pragmatical aspect of it, the direct impact of the numinous on life in society is again expressed in that unique eclecticism which makes both the logician and the humanist nervous, the theologian apprehensive, and the anthropologist delighted. All East African Hindus assume that goods are dispensed on the basis of *karma,* i.e. that life's sorrows and joys (but especially its sorrows) are due to *purvasamskaras*—i.e., to the aggregate effects of the individual's deeds and attitudes in past lives and in the present life, and that their present attitudes and activities will determine the course of things to come. At the same time, most East African Hindus *also* state that whatever happens to them is due to one's *taqdir* (fate), 'Nothing can happen unless it is written on a person's forehead'; 'Nothing happens which God has not fixed and decreed'. These are sayings of wealthy, relatively well-read and 'modern' Hindus in East Africa, quoted from conversations held in 1964. The obvious contradiction does not occur to them unless it is pointed out by some itinerant scholar'.(either one believes that happiness and sorrow are due to one's own past actions and omissions, or contrariwise, that they are somehow predestined by an external force, divine or demoniacal. Historically, the latter notion is a direct bequest of Islam in India.; The use of the Arabic, hence Islamic term *taqdir* in Hindu parlance does not strike the Hindu as a contradiction in terms, unless some outsider presses him into a logical-theological decision, which he is most reluctant to do.

Like all naively religious in the world, the East African Hindu assumes that all religions teach basically the same things—namely, rules for a moral life. The notion that morality might have to be separated from religion and that ethical themes are thematically distinct from religious teachings is totally foreign, horrifying and distasteful to him. The same holds for East African Indian Muslims, Jains, Sikhs and Catholic Goans. Most men, particularly the 'modern', claim eloquently that they 'don't care for religion', and that it is only their womenfolks and the very old who do; but this is sheer make-believe. The entire value system of the East African Indians is strictly religious, and there is no trace of a genuinely secular evaluation of moral situations. The conception of a rationally or intellect based morality or an ethical value orientation devoid of religious reference is as yet completely unthinkable to our subjects.

Very similar in proportion to the sister-groups in India, religion is one of the few permanent sources of relaxation and entertainment—and for the women, perhaps the only respectable one. There are Hindi 'cinemas' galore, there is drinking and card-playing at home and with friends and in the club, but from among 800 informants constituting a cross-section of the Hindu and Muslim Indian population of East Africa, only four men and two women who were not fascinated by religious problems. These four were occidentally trained university lecturers and academic assistants at the various branches of the University of East Africa.

It is futile to talk about social customs in India without constant religious reference. There is no divergence from this nexus on the East African scene. There are no secular social institutions of an indigenous kind in India—sports-clubs, bridge-clubs, etc. and any voluntary associations of the type Hsu[9] denotes as 'clubs' are western imports; and without any modification, this holds for East African Indians. Men do join clubs, there is the 'Patel Club' in the bigger cities, setting itself apart from the conservative 'Patel Brotherhood'—the former consciously emulating western club style. There is Rotary, Lions International, Round Tablers in all larger cities and the membership is on an average one fourth to one half Indian. There is the Masonic Lodge, which has a high percentage of Indian members. But, none of these are indigenous, and one might even construe the desire to join a Lodge as a transmogrified form of ritual-seeking, not just of good fellowship or mutual aid, as with occidental joiners. Social life remains ritualistically directed life, regardless of whether ritual is openly performed by the women, or inveighed against by the 'modern' males who need a cathartic agent to compensate for the oppressive overt ritualism at home, when constantly exposed to occidental models of club-making or secular socialising.

Customs around the life-cycle are *ipso facto* religious in any Indian setting. Women do go to the hospital now for delivery, but most women over 40 had their first babies delivered by Indian midwives at their parental home. Most of the early childhood ritual is omitted, and remembered only by the older generation. The investiture of the boys with the holy thread *(jeneu)*, indispensible in upper-caste India, is usually no longer performed as an isolable ceremony, but coincides with the young man's wedding—when the investiture is done a few days previous to his wedding. No one except the professional temple-priests *(purohit)* wears the thread after his wedding whereas the high-caste sister communities in India still observe the custom today. Even the East African Brahmin males—who form a tiny proportion of the total Hindu population—hardly wear the sacred thread. No one takes to the traditional fourth or monastic stage of life, but there is a strong admiration of men who have taken it in India, and who are invited as preachers.

Marriage rituals are quite unchanged from the Indian base: the Gujarati and the Panjabi groups conduct their weddings more or less as they do in India, with the basic rite—the circumambulation of the sacred fire, the seven steps, the ascending of the stone by the bride for 'firmness of the house' being identical for all Hindus. The groom's party *(barat)* arrives by car, and fortunately the young man is not made to approach the bride's house on horseback as he is required to do in India. Each community has its own *purohits* or priests, usually employed by the temple authorities of the various communities. Marriage is still an expensive business, the dowry system is strong and oppressive, resented by most, continued by almost all, and rejected, in a somewhat Utopian fashion, by younger parents. An overwhelming majority of all marriages, Hindu, Sikh and Muslim, are still arranged by the parents, but the children have a veto to a far more real degree than in the Indian sister communities.

Death ritual is unchanged, too, though simplified, and the feeling of ritualistic pollution is all but non-existent. Hindus cremate their dead, in electric crematoria in the largest cities where open cremation is frequently disallowed by municipal regulation. The Hindu cremation grounds are usually close to the cemeteries of other communities. There are minimal obsequial observances, for which the temple priests may be called in. Only men over a certain age attend the cremation; young people and all women stay home and conduct *bhajan* (litany). The immediate kin of the deceased do not cook for a day, sometimes for as many as three days, and close friends do the cooking in their own homes bringing the cooked food to the mourners.

The interpersonal relations between men and women are as tense and obtuse as they are in India, and it is here that stagnation is almost complete. There is virtually no premarital romantic contact except among the very young who have gone to college or who have been employed in occidental-style firms; foreign-returned young people make it a point to be different, and there is some amount of dating, with the parents' consent; the Ishmailis seem to be the least inhibited relatively speaking in their dating patterns, and the coffee houses and restaurants in the larger cities are full of young Ishmailis, especially on Saturday mornings, eyeing each other with interest and wanting it to be known that they do so. Inter-caste marriages, are exceedingly rare, in spite of most peoples' claims to the contrary. There is a slightly higher proportion of cross-caste dating among the young emancipated.

In marriage, and among the male and female adult in any social situation, the mutual ignoring pattern is unchanged. There is complete avoidance—at least overtly—and there is no display of concern or tenderness of any sort between husbands and wives, which would be regarded not only as bad etiquette, but as bordering on the immoral. Here again, the Ishmailis are exceptional to a degree, one does see interested smiles and warmth between males and females in that community, but this is one reason why other communities—Hindu and even Muslim—tend to regard the Ishmailis as a whole as morally corrupt or at least suspect. Husbands simply do not and may not show any tender feelings to their wives *coram publico,* they have to use curt, terse language with them in front of others, particularly the elders in the house, and any ever so faint show of mutual affection is frowned at by the old, and pointed out as morally reprehensible. Daughters-in-law with a modern outlook who insist on having their husbands' attention in the joint house, are the epitome of wickedness in their in-laws' eyes.

An unmarried girl who acts in a matter-of-fact manner in the modern sense, as in taking employment in such technocentric organisations as television, radio, the Press, or sales promoting business, or even the mere fact that she went to school in Britain makes young men suspicious very much like their parents, about her eligibility as a wife. Even the most 'advanced' young men tend to bracket such girls as 'club-types', and once this nomenclature is applied to any girl, her marriage chances are profoundly jeopardized. This is a pattern of stagnation—for the Indian sister communities have by and large abandoned such preconceived notions, and it appears that young men in East Africa frequently perpetuate an evaluation pattern set by their grandparents in India. The identification of 'purity' with virginity is axiomatic, and naively uncritical even among completely westernised people. The young men's naivete about women and their notions of romantic love are in part created, and wholly reinforced by the Hindi movies which form the focus of East African Indian secular entertainment across all the groups constituting the Asian minority; Hindi movies are, incidentally, preferred by a sizable lower-middle and labour class majority of Africans, to British and American productions, and there are many Africans who hum and sing Hindi film tunes. The Hindi screen is full of totally unrealistic paste-and-cardboard romances, with male-female relationships as they never existed" in India or indeed elsewhere, and emotional conflicts are resolved by a song or a dance or both. These film songs seem to inspire and inform most of the erotic conceptions of the Indian population, young *and* old—the former overtly and proudly in their parlance, the latter surreptitiously. As most young people can drive and can use their parents' cars, there is a fair chance to take out a girl once in a while and 'drive her around', and this process occurs usually, but by no means only, within the driver's caste. Prospective mates are allowed to enjoy such drives, or go to the movies. Indulgence of a mild sort amounts, on a cautious guess, to about 10 per cent, and though (American and British) movie-inspired kissing is good style, there is little necking and hardly any petting at such occasions; premarital full sexual intercourse among young adults of the same social and economic grouping is virtually non-existent, and its suggestion elicits shocked horror.

Young men who studied abroad usually have had their sexual initiation overseas, but they do not apply it until they get married; courting an Asian girl without a view to a marriage but with a view to sexual consummation is rare, and if the chance arises, this western-informed, premarital consummation is not often carried through. Parents who have sent their children abroad for 'schooling' live under a constant fear that their offspring might not return or bring a European mate; frequently, mothers and fathers expect pledges of complete avoidance from their children before they send them abroad. A girl who is suspected of having lost her virginity, either abroad or at home, is not likely to find a marriage partner at all, regardless of her religious and caste background. The same, of course, does not apply to men. Unlike in puritanical circles in the western world, where a young man may indulge and be connived at with a knowing pat on his shoulders and a smirk, the young Asian who is known to have 'enjoyed' is censured with genuine rebuke, though he may be faintly and clandestinely admired by his own male peers. The elders then refer to him as having developed 'bad habits', which means that he has made or makes extramarital or premarital love and drinks—and nothing else; the notion that sex and drink go together as universally concomitant vices is so deep-rooted that the suggestion that some persons may enjoy the one to the exclusion of the other is met with complete unbelief. There are 'love-marriages', i.e. marriages not arranged by the parents, which constitute a negligible proportion of marriages in the higher income brackets and are virtually unknown in the lower income brackets. The male partner, especially among the 'modernised' and affluent, makes bold of the fact that he broke the old outmoded fashion to which the majority adheres.

Postmarital courtship follows an unvarying pattern—immediately after the wedding, the bride moves into her husband's home; marriage is consummated within the first week, but apart from the young men who have had some experience abroad, it usually takes from 6-7 months for the first pregnancy to occur. Honeymoon trips after the wedding are as yet quite unusual, and two Panjabi couples who did venture on an East African *safari* tour were talked about with some scorn as having been on 'Hari OM' or 'Hanuman',[10] and though young folks to be married would like to plan a honeymoon, the suggestion is usually received with some embarrassment. For about one year after her wedding, the young woman is supposed to—and usually does—wear expensive, colourful *saris* as part of the extended ritual. The Ishmailis form an exception once again, for due to a *firman* of the late Aga Khan no wedding dress must cost over 30 E.A. shillings, regardless of the financial status of the bride's family.

In the previous decades, the East African Indian birthrate tended to be slightly higher than that of the sister communities in India. The present generation, however, is very definitely conscious of the population problem, and the very acute problems of family growth in the present critical, transitional situation. There is a fairly pervasive intention among younger couples to limit the number of children to three or four, and most modern means of contraception are known and employed. Vasectomy has become known during the past few years, and about half a dozen men in some of the bigger cities had undergone the operation, or had seen to it that their wives underwent the parallel operation to prevent further conception.

One of the most positive features of East African Indian social life is the manner of child rearing. With a great majority of the total Asian population still living in a joint family setting, the rest being recent split-offs from larger units, the number of infants, toddlers and children, siblings and cousins, in a house of four rooms averages from three to six. They are brought up with great affection, and the boys with overly great indulgence. The patience of the adults and adolescents in the house—grandparents, parents, older siblings and cousins—with the screaming youngsters, particularly the boys, is absolutely amazing for anyone not reared in the Indian tradition.

The only negative feature, fairly pervasive in all the constituent communities, is of no real pedagogical concern to the growing children, but it is a psychologically disorienting agent within the adult family: in continuation of the Indian tradition by which the grandparents assume considerably more right than the parents to handle and play with the young children, grandparents in East Africa tend to compete with the parents for the affection of the small children as well as for that of the pre-adolescents. The situation is particularly toxic when there is tension between the mother-in-law and her daughter-in-law; whenever the child acts up, the former tends to put the blame on the younger woman who, due to her lower position in the domestic hierarchy, cannot usually defend herself, especially as her husband tends to side quite openly with his mother against his wife. The methods of parental *vs.* grandparental competition for the children's affection are often quite insidious and they pervade almost all facets of daily relations within the house.

There is a definite preference for sons. Panjabi and Hindustani speakers, just like in India and Pakistan, called their little *daughters 'beta'* which means 'son'. This teknonymy is a North Indian one —when pointed out to an average audience in North India, the preference is usually admitted; in East Africa, it does not imply any emotional discrimination in the sense that girls are not wanted —here for once, the East African Indians clearly show some ideological advance— it is simply the linguistic left-over of an institutionalised Freudian slip and would probably be dropped if an effort were made. Fathers and grandfathers are extremely tender to their little sons and to their daughters, little and grown-up, mothers and grandmothers to both at all ages, and all males in the house to the female children. There is virtually no beating, although the threat of beating is often made as a corrective or deterrent.

The paternal attitude to sons, particularly the eldest son, changes when the boy reaches adolescence; the relation becomes formal, often stiff, and the two feel socially uncomfortable with each other. The same holds for the oldest brother and his younger sibling brothers—there is hardly any personal intimacy between them, but there are indications that there is a lot of floating hostility between the eldest brother—who is likely to be the head of the house when his father retires or dies—and his 'real', i.e., sibling brothers.

The Gujarati parent seems less indulgent than the Panjabi, particularly in matters of religious indoctrination, which is quite radical in Gujarati Hindu households. There may be a higher degree of secular disciplining among Panjabis, but religious and ideological training which the average Gujarati householder devolves on his children is virtually absent with the Panjabi Hindus and Sikhs. Gujarati parents expect their children—from toddlers to adolescents and young adults—to attend the evening prayers in the house, and by the time the child reaches school age small-congregational family prayer has become quite natural. Such procedure is rare with Panjabis.

The pattern is slightly different with the various Muslim groups. Ithna-Asharis and Bohras apply some pressure on their young to perform their prayers at least informally. The situation is different with the Ishmailis. Almost all of them, young and old, regard the *Jamatkhana* as their spiritual and social home and place of congregation, and the Friday visit is compulsory. The sermons are combined with social meeting, fund-raising, auctioning of food cooked by individual women in their homes and carried to the *Jamatkhana,* where bachelors or people who just did not cook can buy good home-cooked food, the proceeds of the auction going to the poor-fund. With the Ishmailis, the bringing up of the young in the faith is a very gentle, unobtrusive, almost a playful procedure, but it is absolute.

It is a mute question whether ritualistic purity in the manner observed and stressed by anthropologists reporting on India proper does at all apply to East African Hindus. Precautions, actions, and attitudes concerning ritualistic purity are at best vestigial. Menstruating women do not participate in any religious activity, and the Gujaratis usually stay out of the kitchen. Women usually —though not as invariably as in India—take their bath before performing their formal worship in the house-shrine. There is none of the 'natural horror' of entering the shrine or performing one's worship without a bath as is the case in the sister communities in India.

The joint or extended family system is still the rule among the Asian settlers. In theory, 'modern people', that is people who have passed their Senior Cambridge Examination—often regarded about all a good settler ought to want and aspire for himself and his children—tend to break away into nuclear groups, though the intention is hardly ever formulated. There were too many people in my father's house—so we moved into one of our own', or some such statement is most usually made as an explanation. Very often, younger brothers rejoin their father's or elder brother's joint household, and even where a genuinely nuclear family has been formed, there is constant upward visiting, i.e., the younger brother and his wife visiting the senior joint house. Younger, unmarried but adult brothers tend to join such new, spacier setups, though such cases have become countable only in very recent years. There is no doubt a great desire, among the younger generation, to nuclearise the family system.

In the majority of joint set-ups, the average number of couples under one roof is 2-3 among the Panjabis, and 2-4 among Gujaratis, irrespective of their religion; again, the Ishmailis are moving away into a more radically nuclear ecological form, as the late Aga Khan's scheme of providing a house for each family, on a co-operative tenant-into-owner basis is taking effect increasingly; this of course might, in theory at least, work for a reinstatement of a joint household system, except that these tenements are really too small to harbour larger family units. As in the classical Indian system, a 'joint household' simply means a senior man and his wife, their sons with their wives, their unmarried sons, and the unmarried daughters, who move away into their own virilocal setting when they marry.

Separate cooking among the various couples is rare in East Africa. One woman, usually the wife of the eldest son, supervises the cooking which is frequently done by African servants.

It is impossible to make a general assessment of interpersonal relations with respect to the degree of amity and discord, except in such socially structured relations as mother-in-law to daughter-in-law, oldest brother to younger brothers, etc. The father-oldest son relation seems to me more strained, though less overt among the Gujarati than among the Panjabi groups, whereas the latter are more overt but possibly not so intensively negative. Younger sons, and especially the latecomer male in the family, tend to get away more easily; as they are not expected to take over the father's responsibility, there is no high degree of potential competition, and their age often makes them equal with the oldest grandchildren, which adds tenderness and indulgence to the parental treatment of the very youngest direct offspring.

As to the oldest son's relations to his *father,* I would concur with G.M. Carstairs statement about the father-son relationship among Rajputs in Rajasthan, that 'the son does not have a psychologically independent sex life as long as his father lives'—even though the son may have several children. The feeling-tone of this statement applies to East African Hindus, with the exception of families where the fathers have already had occidental education or experience. The elder sons' relations with their wives in the house during his father's lifetime form a parallel extension: the sons do not have a psychologically independent sexual existence, oldest sons tend to be quiet, almost catatonic in the presence of their wives *en face* their fathers, they will not joke, will not dare to show any interest or affection for their wives; neither will they address their wives except to pass on domestic orders of the 'go and fetch.....' type.

In company of guests, oldest sons will answer 'yes' or 'no' if any questions are directly put to them, and they will not usually inaugurate a conversation themselves, in the paternal presence. Sons openly side with their mothers against their wives, and even some 'modernised' young men make bold of this fact. 'Women should have a secondary place in society', is not just a facile statement of the Rotary Club in-between lunch-

and-speech conversation type, but a very germane reflection of the consanguinity syndrome in Hindu society.

Interpersonal relations with outsiders are a much more positive and pleasant matter. What strikes any student of East African Indian society, be he a casual visitor or a skilled observer, is the literally boundless hospitality of one and all toward the guest and the stranger. This goes for all communities with the possible exception of the Goans who due to their emulative 'European' style of living seem to feel that it is not good manners to feed one and everybody who comes by. They try to view guests on western models of modified hospitality: guests come invited only—in crass contradistinction to the Hindu view: the Sanskrit word for 'guest' is *atithi,* literally, 'one who comes without an appointment'. With all other communities, Hindu, Jain, Sikh or Muslim, refusal to treat a guest—any guest, not only a member of the community of the prospective host—to food and drink, and if required, to stay, is unthinkable. I conducted highly structured tests to check this radical hospitality and found it proved in all cases.

From an aesthetical viewpoint, living conditions are in no way better than with the equivalent economic groups in India. There is no improvement in artistic choice and taste. Most houses, cutting across all the Indian communities, decorate their interior with the Ravi Vanna type oleographs and polychrome representations of gods, goddesses, Gandhi, Nehru, Vallabhai Patel, Sabhas Chandra Bose, kings and queens of the Hindu pantheon, film actresses from the Indian screen, sectarian and national Hindu leaders from the past 400 years, and an occasional photograph of Queen Elizabeth and Prince Philip, or even Elvis Presley stuck into the frames of the aforesaid products. The walls are replete with cheap. chintz, and the oleographs themselves are perfectly ghastly, super-realistic, gaudily-coloured and embarrassingly banal. The choice has little to do with the economic level, for these artifacts are found among millionaire industrialists and the poorest *fundis* alike. Paper flowers abound on the tables and windowsills, even when the garden around the house produces fine specimens *en masse:* these seem to be reserved for the house-shrines only, though even their paper flowers tend to outnumber the natural plants. From among four of the leading Asian industralists in East Africa, only two families have genuine, elegant and refined Indian and European art in their residential premises.

The rooms of the affluent are overloaded with items of the same spurious kind, and the secret of empty spaces as a token of genteel living is not known, and the suggestion frowned upon.

In all Indian houses in East Africa, almost all living and bedrooms have photographs of the inmates of the house hung up or propped against chimney pieces and horizontal surfaces; the wedding photos of the oldest and the other senior couple is an invariable addition to the domestic gallery.

The standards in the other arts are equally poor. The Indian programme of the Voice of Kenya blares Hindi film music through many hours of the day, with classical and other good Indian music occupying a very small part of the total musical broadcasts. Phonographs are owned by almost everyone, with large collections of shellac records with almost 100 per cent 'filmi' music and there is a certain amount of scorn directed at the very few who would listen to or introduce good Indian music into their homes. As opposed to the All India Radio programmes which have been creating a well-nigh universal taste for good music in India in spite of initial protests, there is no movement to improve the standards of musical taste in Indian East Africa. There are one or two hapless teachers of Indian classical music and classical dance (*Bharata Natyam, Manipuri,* and the 'oriental' eclectic type) in the three largest cities, but their clientele is negligible in number and influence. There is still a feeling among most parents that it is not quite proper for a girl to learn dancing, and that it is a 'waste' for a boy to learn music. As a particularly noxious side-effect of this puritanism which is rampant among the East African Indian elders we notice the phenomenon that once music and dance do come upon the scene—either vicariously through records and radio and film, or through occasional attempts by the daughters of the house, no distinction of any sort is made, and with a shrug, there is 'dance' in the house, with no differential judgment between

Bharata Natyam and the Twist, and none between the sentimentalised film music and a classical *khayal*. Most of the young people who have gone through Senior Cambridge and who have 'mixed', know the Twist and other recent imports, and they love it; as in India in this decade, in saree or *sawar-kamiz* or slacks, the Twist has come to stay; *Bharata Natyam* has hardly arrived. Virtually none of the dance-and-music loving Indians of East Africa—would be able to distinguish a sequence of *Bharata Natyam, kathak,* and *Manipuri,* from 'filmi dance. These unpleasant features have to be pointed out in view of the fact that the sister communities in India, on the same and on lower economic levels, have taken quite extensively to the study and the practice of the genuine Indian fine arts.

Most Hindus in East Africa, challenged about the inferiority of religious paintings and oleographs in their temples and their homes, react with a shrug and with statements to the effect that 'pictures of God inspire us to be religious'—references to the need of aesthetical quality within the religious iconographic framework are not understood.

The East African Indian cuisine is no different in essence, from that of the sister communities in India and Pakistan. The Gujarati Hindu groups eat highly spiced, watery and largely vegetarian food with lots of chutneys, turmeric and sugar, cooked exclusively in oil. Khoja Ishmaili food and other Muslim groups eat spicy food with plenty of fish and meat, with the exception of pork—though a small percentage of the younger, especially the more 'advanced' Ishmailis do occasionally partake of it—whereas other Muslim groups are strict about this classical avoidance. The Panjabis eat simple, not too spicy, relatively wholesome dishes, cooked in *ghee* at all times; their staple is *roti* (hot flat wheat-cakes of whole wheat, '*chappatis'* in the old British Indian terminology), the staple of the Gujaratis is rice and *rotii,* a smaller, and oil-baked version of the Panjabi *roti.* Almost all Panjabis, Hindu, Muslim and Sikh eat meat (with the exception of beef), though strict *Arya Samajis* and most women over 50 do not. The most highly modernised visit European-style restaurants in the cities; those who do usually do not ask questions about the zoological provenance of the meat: quite a few Hindus who frequent restaurants believe, or profess to believe, that 'steak' is made of mutton, and 'hamburgers' of ham.

There is a strong stigma on the consumption of any alcoholic drink, among all communities except the Goans. A high proportion of Asian men drink whisky, *the par excellence* drink and the epitome of drink in general, but only a small number of the women under 40 join their husbands after some initial reluctance in the first years of marriage. Fathers encouraging their daughters to share a drink are totally unthinkable.

The meat situation is more complex—among all Hindus, there is a stigma on meat eating, even though most of the meat eaters make no secret of it. Most of the Gujarati Hindus and Jains are strict vegetarians except that many of the young among them have modified their habit into the 'eggarian' variety-for on a strict count, meat, fish and egg are all 'meat' in the Hindu tradition.

Most men smoke cigarettes, very few smoke cigars and pipes. Hardly any woman smokes, and even among the youngest, Britain-returned and most 'advanced', only a few would smoke, with the ' exception of Goan women who often do. Sikh men do not smoke, as Sikhism forbids it quite rigorously. But, Sikhs who shave off to 'modernise' usually take to smoking like other Hindu males.

Everybody drives cars, young and old, male and female. Only twenty years ago, very few women drove and the ones who did had to brave universal censure—but since World War II, large numbers of Indian women in East Africa have taken to driving and do it as naturally as women in the western world. In fact even the untrained observer who compares city life in India and in East Africa will notice this as a striking—though sociologically hardly a very significant—feature; very few women in urban India drive cars; many Indian women in East Africa do. This is not only due to the economic difference—among economically equal urban groups in India, there is still a latent opposition to women who 'get around too much', and the car is the epitome of urban 'getting around'.

The contrast between the older and the younger generation is enormous and must be an indispensable final topic of this study. It is rather difficult to assess differences in the degree of contrast between the various constituent groups. Stagnation is stronger among the Gujaratis than among the Panjabis, but least strong with the Khoja Ishmailis—it is perhaps not too incautious a statement to say that the cultural and ideological discrepancy between young and old is stronger in the more emancipated groups, and the least marked among more stagnant groups as the Jain Shahs and some Cutchi Hindus. The older generation complains about the lax morality of the young and even doctors and other professional men over forty attempt to keep a strict watch over the 'morals' of their sons and, *a fortiori,* their daughters. Just as in India today, 'morals' has a purely sexual connotation, with a much weaker anti-spirituous and anti-gambling-and-dissipation undertone.

A man or a woman of 'good morals', who does not have 'bad habits', is one who does not indulge in any non-marital nor too much in marital sexual activity (the woman who involves her husband too much, or is suspected of doing so, sexually—is immoral by extension and assumption). Drinking *vs.* teetotalling forms the second and much less critical criterion of 'morality' in the Indian value hierachy, unsuccessful gambling the third and weakest. A 'good' girl or boy would be one that stays at home, eats food with his parents, does not go' to cinema' too often or with people not known to the parents, and does not ponder any sort of interpersonal relation with a non-kin person of the other sex. An 'immoral' youngster, in the eyes of the older generations, would be one who stays out of the house and does not tell the parents where he has been, indulges or is thought to indulge in romantic activities or tastes, and takes drinks outside the house.

It is important to bear in mind that there is no difference in the intrinsic value-judgments of young and old. When the young rebel, they do so by doing, or pretending to do or fancy the 'immoral things'; they do not criticise fundamentals, i.e. the implicit value judgments, for they feel about as guilty as their parents about these censured indulgences.

The cultural and psycho-socially significant distinctions between old and young are smaller and more trivial than the unskilled observer would think. Young and old women drive cars; young men drink hard liquor, so do old men; young and old men, and many women, have taken to meat eating; young men and women, returned from abroad, or exposed to patterns of western living, meet at parties, go to the movies, dress in what the last generation would have called immodest garments, might do the Twist or engage in occasional necking; young men might boast of not going, or having never been to a temple—but so do old men. The older women's complaint that the young have abandoned religion is purely rhetorical, as their own husbands except for a small percentage, never practised religion in any ritualistic fashion.

Yet, this is not the point; the entire value-system is unilaterally directed to and informed by the religious lore. A Panjabi Hindu doctor in Kenya, trained in Britain, who has 'never been to a temple' once expressed the view that they know nothing about religion, I am a worldly man, I am not interested in religion, in he relation between the *Atman* and the *Brahman,* in rebirth and the question whether our actions depend on past impressions or whether God dispenses them, in the possibility of the cessation of birth and rebirth through yogic contemplation, in *Karma,* the *avataras*—elaborating his denial in precise theological language; by the time he was through he had listed about all the main teachings of the Hindu theology. The irony of this example might be brought out for the western reader by an analogy of the very unlikely English physician telling an investigating anthropologist 'I am not at all interested in the Christian religion—they call me a Christian, but I know nothing about periochoresis, traducianism, the relation of the Son and the Paraclite, the eucharist'. The Indian doctor's statement is typical, the putative British colleague's very improbable.

There is no doubt that the younger generation diverges radically from the older. Although, as was shown in some detail, young men, and women have not entered inter-caste marriage liaisons in statistically significant proportions, they all favour it in principle, where the older are either overtly or covertly negative and antagonistic. One gets the impression that those among the older who verbally encourage inter-caste marriage would rather see others than their own kin enter such liaisons. Women over forty hardly ever support the idea and the frequent statements of the form 'whatever makes my son or daughter happy, he or she should do' is modified, under guided query, to indicate that cross-caste liaisons would not make the parents happy, though they would resign themselves to the situation should it arise.

It is overwhelmingly evident that western impact on the technological side is much stronger here than in India and Pakistan. On the ideological and on the cultural side, however, there can be no such unequivocal statement. The impact of western models on the various Asian communities is highly diversified in every except in the somewhat naive sense that 'all Asians' have better education, better houses and better chances. If we arrange the degree of acculturation to western models—apart from technological models where there is no distinction between the constituent communities—in a descending order of assimilation, the Khoja Ishmailis would rank on top, closely followed by Panjabi Hindus and Muslims, Sikhs, Gujarati Hindus (Lohanas, Patels, 'small' castes), Bohra Muslims, Ithna-Ashari Muslims, Visa Oshwal Jains and Shahs. This scale is purely exploratory and somewhat impressionistic, and one would not insist on a fixed hierarchy of assimilation and acculturation to western influence.

In fact, that the corpus of western influence is itself very limited in scope. No scholars, humanists and high-class British writers were among the East African white expatriates, and no top-level intellectual societies on the London, Oxbridge, and discursive Anglo Saxon salon-level were created that could have had an enculturating influence on the Asians. The British who came to East Africa were government servants, soldiers, farmers or businessmen—and apart from some occasional visiting anthropologists, archaeologists, and other scientists who came 'to the field', and who taught and teach in uneven density at the various institutions of what is now the University of East Africa—the British settler's pastimes were hunting and *safari*, golf and tennis, sports and sundowners rather than discursive thought, intellectual conversation, Bach and such other activities that might disseminate sophistication.

The Indians in East Africa have not had the benefit of direct contact with the British and European intellectual world, and those who went and go abroad for studies, do so with narrowly set targets: the medical or dental profession, law, perhaps engineering; none of these professions or the preceding training are culture-giving *per se:* it is quite possible, and rather easy, to take a medical degree in London without ever having heard anything about modern British literature and philosophy, and the fine arts, etc.; of some fifty England-returned professionals, all of whom having spent a minimum of three years in Britain, two had gone to the Albert Hall, and one to Co vent Garden, though all had 'seen' the British Museum, whatever that means. It would for these reasons be unfair to the Asian and the western elements that coalesced in East Africa to stipulate a humanistic or aesthetically discursive climate where there never was any institution of precedence.

The values held by the average British and European expatriate population are intellectually naive; they range from traditional Christian to pragmatic-secular values and the slightly more sophisticated and better-read attitudes of the British judges and higher magistrates whose contact with the Indians was not dense and sufficient for the devolvement of any intellectual interest to the minority at large. Young men read little except technical books for their professional advancement, some novels, some Shakespeare, etc. for their Senior Cambridge—but not after—and almost no modern literature; this is not true about the peer generation of the sister groups in India, where T.S. Eliot, D. H. Lawrence, and even Kafka are being read along with the time-honoured Tennyson and Dickens. Visiting roughly one hundred houses of upper government servants and businessmen of all Indian communities, we have seen but three book collections exceeding one hundred items of a discursive or belletristic type. Pious literature in English and Gujarati abounds, but that was bought by the more directly religious minded last generation. Paperbacks are read, American and British mysteries, the sexy penny-novel, amateur motoring and engineering. Readers Digest are littered around the bed and living rooms of many English-reading houses. The Dale Carnegie kind of 'how to be successful' literature is bought and read, and some sex-technique and happy-marriage literature is found in some of the most unexpected pious homes.

The impact of formal education on the early school and the high school level acquired in British modelled private schools and, to a lesser degree, at the non-parochial public schools often creates a suspense or a breakdown of communication between the adolescents and the elders at home who have not been exposed to this pedagogical model. There is a marked difference in this respect between the above type of schools and the Asian parochial schools (Ishmaili, Arya Samaj, Sanatan Dharm, Jain, etc.) where religious values are directly instilled as a more or less official part of the curriculum. These children seem to remain ideologically closer to their elders. Interviewing several boys and girls studying at the most fashionable and expensive schools which had not admitted Asians before *uhuru*, the following points seemed to emerge—the interviews were conducted separately and the subjects did not know each other: there is very little or no rapport with those members of their immediate and distant kin who had been brought up under the orthodox or conservative tradition transferred from India; there is close identification with the Asian, European, and less so with African peers who go to the same schools and who are taught in scholastic standards of the British model schools, with western cultural values guiding their staff and the text used. Kinship ties are accepted as inevitable, but with considerable grudge, and interfamilial personal relations continue only with those who have themselves adopted western educational values.

It is only the last generation that has undergone purely western-style formal education; the elders who are still in charge of the majority of Asian households have had hardly any formal education, and if they did, it was of the Indian parochial type, thoroughly suffused with Hindu or Muslim religious values which were thought to be universally valid and beneficial for the growing-up generations at the time of settlement.

By and large, the older generation still identifies occidental impact with loose, latently immoral and ethically degenerate and undesirable living. The most direct proof is the almost completely negative moral judgments the non-Ishmaili Indians have formed about the Ishmailis, the latter being the epitome of western culture in an Asian milieu, in the image of the Hindus and conservative Indian Muslims. The idea that the western model conduces to promiscuity, drink, laxity in general, and atheism is fairly pervasive with the older generation, and not infrequent with people between 35 and 45. The younger generation—between 20 and 40 exposed to western education since their childhood is trying hard to assimilate whatever it can cognitively perceive as not injurious to their self-image: modern cars, British and American movies, occasional occidental diet and restaurants, with family, friends, or surreptitious visits to coffee houses, etc. with a peer of the same or the opposite sex, with the acceptance in principle of individual, not caste-directed courtship.

Kitchen utensils, cutlery, crockery, etc., are entirely occidental, the large size metal *thali* which serves as the food-plate in India in the sister communities of the East African groups today, has been all but abandoned; most people still can use their hands for eating, but they do it with some embarrassment and prefer the use of knife and fork. For large-scale ritualistic occasions, the *thali* and the fingers are occasionally used, particularly among the more orthodox Gujarati. Houses are built very much as among the sister communities in India, on the basis of income, though not diffusely in the various communities; Gujarati Hindus tend to save money and invest, and their wealth can hardly ever be predicted from the looks of their houses, furniture, etc. Panjabis tend to spend much of what they earn on pleasant dwellings, with relatively little worry about long-range investments and savings.

Most Asians are quite gadget minded, TV, radio, transistorised and other, photography and cinematography are popular and frequent pastimes. The posed group is still the only known and accepted technique, the family album a compulsory chore for the guest.

In conclusion, it must be said that western impact provides the form rather than the content of modern living among the Asian minority. This should be understood in a structural sense; it is not that, say, Indian food is eaten from European crockery, or that a battery-operated halo resolves around the icon in some Hindu temples—all this is true and amusing, perhaps amazing but not really important. But, there is hardly any direct enjoyment of value-free food, drink and sex or the other goods of an emancipated, open society, as appurtenances to the sort of detached eudaimonism which many Indians in East Africa could afford. There is no self-criticism in any fundamental cultural sense, no self-persiflage, hence little sense of humour: loud laughs and practical jokes, emotional ebullience under drink, and occasional vernacular gibes where the *cochonerie* is taken for a punchline—these are the notions of a sense of humour, very much like in India, though an analytical, self-persiflaging generation of writers and thinkers is emerging there. The stylistic and ethical ennui of verbal pompousness, religious and rhetoric sanctimoniousness, and kin-bound complacence is not known, its suggestion not understood except by a few college teachers and their very narrow circle of peers.

The hallmark of modern culture in its ideological sense—humanism, self-reliant, kinship-free planning, autonomous value judgments, etc. inclusive—is secularism; this has not transpired to the Asians of East Africa. Nationalism of the Indian or the now-let's-be-African type permeates the words and the thoughts of their finest leaders, non-secular, basically religious morality the rest. Modern technology is foisted on all this, but then there is no contradiction between any technology and any personal ideology. For all this, no one can blame the Asians; there simply was a lack of precedence for acculturation. The West to which the Indians of East Africa have been and are exposed, is not the West of Mozart, Picasso and Bertrand Russell, but the West of the tea and sisal estate manager or expert, and the government officer whose intellectual and golf handicaps are very disparate indeed.

NOTES AND REFERENCES

1. David Pocock, 'Difference' in East Africa: a study of Caste and Religion in Modern Indian Society', *Southwestern Journal of Anthropology* XIII/4, 289-300; 'Inclusion and Exclusion: A Process in the Caste System in the Gujarat'; *S.W.J.A.* XIII, 19-31.

2. *Clan, Caste and Club,* van Nostrand, New York and London, 1963.

3. M. N. Srinivas, McKim Marriott, S. Č. Dube, M. Opier, Milton Singer a.o.

4. The East African Jains belong to the Visa Oshwal and Navnit Vanik castes. The former were farmers and landholders originally, the latter traders.

5. This terminology has been used for about two decades by Indian and British-American anthropologists like Redfield, Srinivas, Milton Singer, McKim Marriott and others. Roughly, the 'big traditions' are the religious-literary parts of any of the world's great religions. The 'little traditions' are the non-codified, pre-systematic or non-systematic modes of worship and ritual, witchcraft and sorcery, faith-healing, under the auspices of particularised ritualistic deities and demons, usually of rustic provenance. Whereas the functionaries of the 'little tradition', often belong to the pathological fringe, the priests of the 'big tradition' are literati, who handle the official version of the scriptures and the ritual. The two traditions, however, overlap at every step in India.

6. Vd. Hilda Kuper, *Indian People in Natal,* University Press, Natal 1960; there are extensive descriptions of possession, divination and kindred occurrences in that area, though Mrs. Kuper does not use the 'big-tradition-little tradition' tool as a heuristic device.

7. Edward Shils, *The Intellectual Between Tradition and Modernity: The Indian Situation.* Mouton & Co., The Hague, 1961. The book, like most critical studies of modern Indian culture, has been vehemently criticised in India.

8. Francis L. K. Hsu, *Clan, Caste and Club,* van Nostrand, London, 1963. This is by far the most perceptive study of caste and religion in Hindu India, and supersedes most previous research to date.

9. A phonetic play on the English word, 'Hari OM' is the Sanskrit formula at the beginning of the big tradition prayers and of

many invocations. 'Hanuman' is the name of the devout monkey-warrior of the Ramayana, known to every Indian as a most venerable hero of semi-divine status. The fact that these highly elated terms are used goes to show, by a process of psycho-linguistic overcompensation and vindictiveness, how unpleasant the idea of a newly wed couple enjoying itself away from the man's prescribed parental home is to the conservative.

10. G.M.C. Carstairs, *The Twice Born*, Hogarth Press, London, 1958.

5

AN EVALUATION OF THE ECONOMIC CONTRIBUTION OF THE INDIAN DIASPORA

An attempt has been made in this study to describe the main patterns of economic activity of the Asians settled in the three East African countries. This attempt seems worth making not only because of the intrinsic importance of the subject itself but also for the light it may throw on other facets of the life of Asians in East Africa. However, any such attempt is severely restricted by the lack of adequate data on the role of Asians in the East African economies. What follows,, therefore,, is no more than a rough sketch of the dominant patterns of economic activity of East African Asians, built up from bits and pieces of available data and supplemented by qualitative observations.

Size, Structure and Growth of Asian Population

The first step in this economic survey must be an assessment of the size, structure and growth of Asian population in East Africa. The census reports show that the Asian population in the three countries increased from 183,800 in 1948 to an estimated 352,300 in 1963, an increase of over 90 per cent in 15 years. This increase is, of course, the result of both a natural increase in population and a considerable net immigration into East Africa. Unfortunately, we do not have adequate information to separate out the effects of these two sources of population growth. Some very rough estimates made by the writer indicate that as much as 60 per cent of the population increase may have been due to immigration alone. It is, however, noteworthy that there has been a steady decline in net immigration into East Africa since the mid-fifties when it was running at an annual average of 10,000 persons. In contrast to this, the 1962 figures show that new permanent immigration of Asians into East Africa was almost exactly offset by permanent emigration from these countries; while the figures for the first quarter of 1964 in Kenya show that the permanent Asian emigration was almost double the Asian immigration.

Pattern of Asian Migration

It is not intended here to offer an explanation of this pattern of migration nor to speculate on the future trends in migration. The subsequent sections will deal with the employment opportunities for Asians in East Africa and will thus offer a partial explanation of the above trends in migration. Suffice it to say here that the slowing down in the rate of growth of the East African economies in recent years and the increasing difficulties in the way of Asian immigration have combined to bring net immigration to a trickle. It seems that for some time to come the main source of the expansion of the Asian population will be internal. Estimates of the natural growth rate of the Asian population vary between 2.5 and 3 per cent per annum. There are, however, strong indications of a gradual decline in the rate of population growth, caused mainly by a decline in birthrates. It would be a safe assumption to make that the natural rate of growth of the Asian population is unlikely to exceed 2.5 per cent per annum in future.

Structure of the Asian Population

Even more important from an economic point of view is the structure of the current Asian population. Despite a substantial inflow of Asian immigrants in the past, the general shape of the age-distribution of this population has tended increasingly to approximate rapidly expanding and locally born population with high fertility and declining mortality rates. The result is that the population 'pyramid' has a broad base and a very slender apex. Typically, about 42 per cent of the entire population consists of persons in the 0-14 years age-groups, with over 54 per cent in the 15-59 years age-group and slightly over 3 per cent in the 60 and over age-group.

This is in marked contrast to the age-structure to be found in countries experiencing a slower rate of population increase, which have a higher proportion in the working-age groups. The effect of this pattern of population 'pyramid' of Asians in East Africa is to impose a heavy burden on the 'productive' section of the population for the sustenance of a relatively larger proportion of 'dependents'.

Geographical Distribution of Asians

We are further interested in the geographical distribution of the Asian population in East Africa. Of the total Asian population of 352,300 in 1963 in the three mainland territories, more than 50 per cent or 180,000 reside in Kenya; which the Asian population of Uganda and Tanganyika is estimated 82,100 and 90,200 respectively.[1] Of this population, about 60 to 65 per cent were born in East Africa, the rest immigrated from India and Pakistan. It may be of interest to notice that the Asian population represents 1.3 per cent of the total population of East Africa.

An important characteristic of this population is its high degree of urbanisation. In 1957, no less than 75 per cent of the total Asian population in Tanganyika lived in 14 townships and 60 per cent in the five largest towns. Similarly, in 1959, 75 per cent of the Asian population in Uganda was reported to be living in urban areas. This proportion is likely to be even higher now because of a marked drift of the Asian population towards larger towns and cities all over East Africa in recent years. The 1962 census in Kenya reveals the extent of this drift: no fewer than 85 per cent of the Asian population in Kenya was reported to be living in the five largest towns. There are more Asians living in Nairobi alone than in the whole of Uganda or Tanganyika.

The urbanised pattern of Asian settlement in East Africa is in marked contrast to the pattern established in other countries, where Indians have settled in considerable numbers such as British Guiana, West Indies, Fiji Islands and to a lesser extent, South Africa. It ought to be observed that the urban pattern of Asian settlement in East Africa was partly due to the several economic restrictions placed on the members of the Asian community. Meanwhile, it is important to note the far-reaching political, economic and social consequences of the concentration of Asian population in urban areas. It is this factor which has been responsible for the 'Indian look' of almost all the major towns and cities in East Africa. Furthermore, it has facilitated the organisation of the Asian community into a number of tight, closely-knit communal groups and, hence, increased its isolation from other races. Economically, it has reduced the dependence of the community on other races. The fact that many businessmen, lawyers, doctors, accountants and other professional men derive a large proportion of their earnings from the Asian clientele, further reinforces their natural propensity to look to the Asian community for all their needs and aspirations.

Economically Active Population

A description and evaluation of the Asian role in the East African economies can only be made in qualitative terms at the present stage. However, in order to put our subsequent discussion in proper perspective, it is necessary to give a few statistics about the number and industrial distribution of the economically active section of the Asian population. The census reports indicate that the economically active[2] population constituted about 25-27 per cent of the entire Asian population in the three East African countries. This is a much lower proportion than among the European community; the main reasons for this are, of course, the higher proportion of European women in employment, as well as a lower proportion of children and retired persons in the European population of East Africa. Another remarkable feature of the Asian community, again in sharp contrast to the European, is the relatively small proportion of the economically active population working as employees. However, the territorial patterns in this respect are sufficiently divergent for us to consider each country separately.

In 1962, Kenya had the largest class of wage and salary earners, who at 36,100 constituted a little less than 70 per cent of the economically active population of the Asian community. At the other extreme is Uganda, where the corresponding figure for employees is only 9,900 persons, about 45 per cent of the economically active population. Tanganyika is somewhere in the middle with 12,100 employees, about 50 per cent of the economically active population. The rest of the economically active population is made up of employers, own-account workers and unemployed. The higher proportion of employees in Kenya is in part due to the advanced state of the economy, but mainly due to the substantially larger number of persons employed by the public sector.

In Kenya, public sector provided employment to 33 per cent of the total Asian employees in 1962; the corresponding figures for Tanganyika and Uganda are 25 per cent and 18 per cent. The importance of the public sector in Kenya is mainly, though not wholly, due to the location of the headquarters of all the EACSO services in Nairobi; very nearly 40 per cent of the employees in the Kenya public sector work for the Railways and Harbours, Posts and Telecommunications and the Common Services Organisation.

We have far more detailed information on the industrial distribution and income levels of Asian employees than of the self-employed and employers. However, before we come to a detailed analysis of employees, it is necessary to say something about the broad industrial classification of the entire Asian population of working age. A study of the various census reports shows that there is considerable similarity between the pattern of industrial distribution of the Asian economically active population in Uganda and Tanganyika. Broadly speaking, between 45 to 50 per cent of the total Asian working population in both these countries derive their livelihood from commerce, defined to include wholesale and retail trade, banking and insurance. Manufacturing and public services each account for a further 10 per cent of the working population. In Tanganyika, transport and communications, and in Uganda agriculture, including cotton ginning and coffee curing, are the next important category, accounting for about

9 per cent of the working population in each country. The rest of the population derive their livelihood from the provision of various services, from construction, etc. The pattern in Kenya differs somewhat, mainly because a much higher proportion of the working population are dependent on employment for their earnings. Consequently, we find that commerce is relatively less important as a source of livelihood, while public services, transport and communications, manufacturing and miscellaneous services are more important.

The great importance of commerce as a source of income for Asians in East Africa is clearly brought out by the above figures. However, some readers will be surprised to find that the contribution of commerce is not greater still, for Asians in East Africa are often described as a 'race of shopkeepers.' Next in importance are public services, manufacturing, transport and communications, and miscellaneous services. Agriculture is perhaps the only major industry in East Africa where Asian participation has been relatively unimportant.

Gender Perspective of Asian Labour Market

We can now turn to a detailed analysis of the Asian employees in East Africa. The official statistics show that there was a steady increase in the number of Asian employees throughout the post-war period until 1960, but that the numbers employed have been falling in the last four years. This fall in employment has been general and not confined to Asians alone, and is a reflection of a considerable slowing down in the expansion of the East African economies in recent years. The impact of Africanisation of public services and the economy did not make itself felt until 1963; its effect on the employment opportunities for Asians will be discussed in a subsequent section.

Here we may notice another important development in the Asian labour market in the post-war period: a steady relative increase in the importance of female employees. In Kenya, the number of Asian female employees has gone up from just over 600 in 1948 to 3,750 in 1962, while the number of total Asian employees has risen by a little over 60 per cent during the same period. We find a similar, though not such dramatic, trend in other parts of East Africa. In 1962, females constituted about 10 per cent of the total Asian labour force in East Africa. As might be expected, most of them are employed as either secretaries or clerks, mostly in commerce, or as teachers and nurses.

Sectoral Classification of Asian Employees

A breakdown of employees by industrial sector shows that about 30 per cent were employed by the commercial sector in Uganda and Tanganyika, and about 34 per cent in Kenya. Manufacturing was the next most important source of employment in Uganda and Tanganyika, while in Kenya transport and communications was an equally important source. The transport sector accounted for 15 per cent of Asian employees in Tanganyika, while agriculture, including cotton ginning and coffee curing, provided 12 per cent of the employment in Uganda. Public and other services were also fairly important sources of employment in all the three countries. We, therefore, find that one out of every three wage and salary earners is employed by the commercial sector, while the other employees are fairly evenly distributed among manufacturing, transport and communications, and services.

Occupational Distribution of Asian Employees

It is, however, more revealing to analyse the occupational distribution of employees in the three territories. Although, this information is available only for Asian male employees in Uganda, it is fairly representative of East Africa as a whole. The 1962 figures for Uganda show that out of about 9,000 male Asian employees, over 30 per cent did clerical or secretarial jobs, 16 per cent were "employed in an administrative, executive or managerial capacity, while 11 per cent had professional and technological qualifications. Skilled 'manual' workers such as sales staff, carpenters, bricklayers, mechanics, etc. accounted for a further 30 per cent of total employees. These figures do not take account of the occupations of the self-employed and employers among the Asian community. There is little doubt, however, that the great majority of the persons in these two categories would be classified as administrative, executive or managerial personnel;

a further substantial minority would consist of technologists and other professional persons. On the basis of observation and whatever little statistical evidence is available on the subject, we may hazard a guess that about 35 per cent of all the Asian workers perform executive, administrative or managerial functions, perhaps another 25 per cent are engaged in what we have described as 'skilled manual' jobs; a further 20 per cent do secretarial and clerical jobs, and about 15 per cent can be described as engaged in professional and technical occupations. It will, therefore, be seen that the majority of Asian workers furnish 'middle-level manpower' to the East African economies, while their contribution to the 'high-level manpower' is also substantial and growing rapidly. One remarkable feature of the Asian manpower in East Africa is the relative paucity of 'unskilled' persons among its ranks. The implications of the occupational distribution of the Asian labour force for future employment opportunities are far-reaching and will be discussed in detail in a subsequent section.

Asians Standard of Living and Income Distribution

Before we come to a general assessment of the contribution of Asians to the economic development of East Africa, it is necessary to say something about their standard of living and distribution of income. Once again, we have more information on the average earnings of wage and salary workers than of the self-employed and the employers. In the case of Kenya, an analysis of the Graduated Personal Tax returns reveals the following pattern of income distribution by race:

Percentage of taxpayers in each income group by race: 1962

Income Group	*Africans*	*Arabs and Somalis*	*Asians*	*Europeans*
Under £120	91.4	86.0	11.0	1.5
£120—159	4.7	7.2	4.3	3.2
£160—199	1.7	1.9	3.3	0.6
£200—399	1.7	2.0	13.0	2.5
£400 and over	0.5	2.9	68.4	92.2
Total	100	100	100	100

Source: Development Plan, 1964-70. Kenya, p. 34.

The main weakness of the above table from our point of view is that the last income group ends at incomes of £400 and above; we do not,, therefore,, have any information on the income distribution of persons earning more than £400 a year. Nevertheless, the table reveals some interesting patterns; it shows that roughly one out of every three Asian workers earns less than £400 p.a. Perhaps even more revealing is the fact that no less than 11 per cent of the Asian tax-payers, or about 5,385 persons, had an income below £120 p.a. in 1962. It is forgotten too often that a substantial minority of the Asian population in East Africa has income levels barely sufficient to provide for the basic needs of the family. The table also brings out the great disparities in the income levels of different races.

There are reasons to believe that the average income of Asians in Uganda and Tanganyika is higher than in Kenya. The average earnings of Asian employees both in Uganda and Tanganyika are higher than in Kenya; furthermore, as compared with the other two countries, a higher proportion of the Asian workers in Kenya are employees. Since the average income of employers and self-employed tends to be higher than that of the employees, we may conclude with reasonable certainty that the per capita income of Asians in Kenya is lower than that of their brethren in the rest of East Africa.

The above sketchy picture of the distribution of income among the Asians of East Africa needs to be supplemented by some qualitative observations. There is a very small layer of the Asian population in East Africa which can justifiably be described as 'affluent' even by the standards of the richest nations of the world. This group consists of a handful of industrialists, plantation-owners— sisal in Tanganyika, and sugar in Kenya and Uganda, coffee curers and cotton ginners in Uganda, owners of large department stores and import houses, and a few professionals such as highly successful barristers, doctors, architects and engineers. Their great affluence is underlined by their chauffeur-driven limousines, beautiful and spacious houses, lavish entertainment and frequent trips abroad to Europe, India and Pakistan.

The great majority of Asians in East Africa, however, fall in what might be described as 'middle income group' with incomes ranging from £300 to £900 p.a. This group consists of most wage and salary earners, a sizable number of professionals and a great majority of retail traders dotted all over East Africa. The standard of living in this group varies considerably; at one extreme are those in the upper reaches of this income bracket, who lead a reasonably comfortable life and may enjoy the luxury of a motor car and other consumer durables. But, perhaps a majority of persons in this group make do with a minimum of such comforts and may have to confine their recreation to listening to radios and transistors, or to an occasional visit to cinemas. For the most part, persons in this group would live in two to three roomed flats, in contrast to the spacious and well-laid-out houses of their more affluent brethren.

Lastly, there is a sizable and growing group of persons who may without exaggeration be described as indigent. This group usually consists of persons with large families, living in overcrowded slums, barely succeeding in making their two ends meet with an average family income of well below £200 p.a. Most of the members of this group constitute the core of the semi-skilled or unskilled section-of the Asian labour force; some eke out a living from a small retail business located on the outskirts of urban areas or in the emote outlying districts. It is this section of the Asian working population which is often ignored in the popular as well as the more serious accounts of the Asians in East Africa.

The above account of the income distribution among Asians may be made more concrete by reference to the average earnings of Asian employees in the three East African countries. It was shown above that employees constitute a little more than half of the total Asian working population. An account of changes in their earnings would, therefore, provide an important evidence of changes in the economic well-being of the Asian community as a whole. Kenya has the best statistics on employment and earnings, which go back to 1948. These figures show that between 1948 and 1960, the index of average earnings rose from 100 to 189 for Asians, from 100 to 199 for Europeans, and from 100 to 268 for Africans. Thus, the average earnings at current prices had slightly less than doubled for Asians between 1948 and 1960.

In order to determine the increase in real earnings during this period, we adjust the 1960 figures by the Nairobi Cost of Living Index. This adjustment shows that the real average earnings for Asians have only increased by 20 per cent between 1948 and 1960.

Disparity in Wage and Salary among the Africans, Asians and Europeans

The statistical evidence from Uganda also supports the hypothesis that the rise in average Asian earnings has been slower than that for either Europeans or Africans. Between 1958 and 1962, earnings per head for Asians increased by a mere 9.2 per cent, while the corresponding increases for Europeans and Africans were 22.9 per cent and 53.3 per cent respectively. The main reason for this disparity in wage and salary increases between the three communities is perhaps to be sought in the fact that whereas the wage level for Asians is determined essentially by economic factors, that for Europeans and Africans is influenced considerably by non-economic factors.

The rise in Asian wages has been kept in check throughout East Africa by a general decline in employment in recent years as well as by increasing competition from the rising class of educated Africans. African wages, on the other hand, despite a contraction of demand, have shown a rapid upward trend mainly because of the successive minimum wage laws and the progressive Africanisation of the better paid jobs. European salaries are determined more by the salary structure in U.K. than by the local economic conditions; hence, an adequate explanation for changes in European earnings, which would be beyond the scope of this study, has to be sought in relation to similar changes in the U.K.

However, these differences in the increase in earnings between the three races are quite insignificant in comparison with the great racial disparities in the level of average earnings. In Tanganyika, the average cash earnings for Asian males amounted to £564 p.a. in 1962; the corresponding figures for European and African males were £1,560 and £75 respectively. A study of earnings in Kenya and Uganda tell a similar story. Our main interest, however, is in Asian earnings. For purposes of comparison, it may be noted that the average cash earnings of Asian males in Kenya amounted to £551 in 1962 and in Uganda to £592.

A study of the Asian wage structure in the three East African countries brings out two interesting points. First, the average earnings of Asian women are in general far below the men, especially in the private sector: in Uganda, average earnings of Asian males in the private sector at £561 p.a. compare with average earnings for females of £398. Secondly, the average earnings in the public sector are well above those of the private sector in all the three countries; to take our example from Tanganyika, the average earnings of Asian males in the public sector amounted to £776 p.a. in 1962, while the figure for the private sector was £497. The main reason for this disparity is undoubtedly the possession of higher skills by employees in the public sector, thus, enabling them to command higher salaries.

We shall round off our discussion of the income distribution of Asians in East Africa by emphasizing the limitations of using average income figures as an index of economic welfare. Once again, the Kenya data is the most comprehensive in this respect and will be used to illustrate our point. An average earning of £551 p.a. for Asian males obscures the fact that a very substantial proportion of the male employees had much lower incomes; in Kenya on less than 33 per cent had earnings below £360 p.a. Finally, it may be of interest to note that in the private sector (outside agriculture) only 8 per cent of the Asian males earned £900 or more per annum, compared with 84 per cent of European men; in the public sector the corresponding figures were 10 per cent for Asians and 92 per cent for Europeans.

We shall now attempt a general assessment of the contribution of Asians to the economic development of East Africa. The distinctive Asian contribution to the development of East Africa can best be understood and appreciated within the framework of a series of restrictions placed on the economic activities of Asians in the colonial period. These restrictions had the effect of confining Asian economic activities to certain limited industries and geographical areas; they go a long way in explaining the current pattern of geographical and occupational distribution of Asians in East Africa. We shall mention here only the most important of these restrictions.

In Kenya and Uganda, Asians were precluded from owning and cultivating land, thus, denying them any openings in the agricultural sector. This restriction was reinforced by a series of ordinances in the three countries preventing Asian traders from conducting business outside specified cities and townships. These two measures effectively prevented Asians from establishing a foothold in the rural economies of East Africa; however, they did not altogether stop certain economic transactions between Asian traders and African rural dwellers. Lastly, there was considerable discrimination against Asians in public employment throughout the colonial period. The formal aspect of this discrimination stopped in 1955 with the abandonment of a racial salary structure in the public services of the East African countries. But, a series of administrative rules combined with accumulated prejudice to keep the Asians from the top executive and administrative posts in the civil service. It is,, therefore,, not surprising that the best energies and ability of the Asian population have tended to be concentrated on the fields which are open to them—rule, industry, the professions and skilled employment.

Historically, the most important contribution of Asians to the East African economies has been the extension of the monetary economy into the subsistence areas—a prerequisite for any economic development. A whole array of early explorers, administrators, and missionaries testify to the indispensability of Asian traders and artisans in the opening up and development of the interior. Their function was essentially the introduction of attractive imported consumer goods to large sections of the rural population throughout East Africa, thereby, stimulating their desire for money incomes; until recent times Asian traders also acted as the main outlets for produce from the indigenous rural economies. Asian dominance in the distributive sector of the economy laid them open to charges of exploitation, which will be discussed later. Here it is important to emphasize that Asians continue to perform the old but vital function of introducing and extending the money economy in such areas.

Since the Asian *dukawalla* or shopkeeper is still a characteristic feature of townships and small urban centres throughout East Africa, it is necessary to say something about him. To a typical *dukawalla* living in a remote township, life offers few excitements, and hard work little compensation. The working day is long, usually starting at 7 a.m. and continuing late into the evening. The shopkeeper, who generally lives in a small brick house adjoining the shop, will typically be helped in his chores by his relatives; but he may barely manage to save enough for his children's education or for his daughter's dowry.[3] Life in the township offers few amenities; there is very little by way of organised recreation and entertainment. The tedium of enforced leisure may partly and occasionally be relieved by social calls on the few Indian families in the neighbourhood. But, in general, there is little colour or variety in a dreary routine.

However, contrary to some popular myths held abroad, not all Asians in East Africa are *dukawallas* living in remote parts of the country. Today, their main economic contribution is the supply of high- and middle-level manpower and of capital. This combination of capital and technical know-how in one section of the population is a great potential asset to the economy. Unfortunately, we do not have adequate data to assess quantitatively this crucial contribution to the total stock of capital and skilled manpower.

According to Guy Hunter's estimates, in mid-1961 there were 67,500 skilled persons in East Africa, divided into two categories: the first consisted of just over 18,000 professional men of graduate or equivalent level, senior administrators, and senior managers in commerce and industry; and the second covered about 49,500 in the next layer of skilled manpower, including technicians and sub-professional grades (for example, the second echelon in agricultural extension work), executive grades in the civil service, middle management in industry and commerce, and teachers with secondary education but without a university degree. Hunter's estimates show that Asians provided a little less than 40 per cent of the people in category I and about 50 per cent of those in category II, in the whole of East Africa.[4]

We have no information on the occupational distribution by race of high-and middle-level manpower in East Africa. But, a few sample surveys and general observation suggest that in category I the Asian contribution is especially large in medicine, law, engineering, pharmacy, accountancy and business management generally. In category II, Asians provide most of the skilled, manual personnel such as mechanics, electricians, tailors, carpenters, salesmen and supervisors. A large proportion of persons in category I consist of European expatriates, whose numbers may be expected to decline rather sharply in future. Thus, the limited flow of African trained manpower will be needed not only to provide for the needs of the expanding economy but also to make good the expected loss of European expatriate manpower. It is, therefore, clear that a simultaneous withdrawal of Asian skilled manpower from the country could deal a crippling blow to the economy and act as a serious constraint on the development potential of East Africa.

Asians have made an equally important contribution in the form of savings and capital for the expansion of the economy. It is true that when the Asians originally immigrated to East Africa they brought relatively little capital with them; but it is also true that the savings made by them could have been used to increase their consumption rather than accumulate capital. A high proportion of this capital was originally generated in commerce, but it has in vested in of the economy, especially in the manufacturing and construction industries. Again, it is not possible to quantify share of Asians in the national stock of capital, but a rough idea of their contribution to economic growth may be obtained by mentioning the main economic activities in which they have been pioneer entrepreneurs.

In Uganda, cotton ginning and coffee curing were long a complete Asian monopoly, though in the last decade or so African co-operatives have greatly increased their share. At the moment all the sugar produced in Uganda is grown on the plantations of two Asians, who are also the leading industrialists in East Africa; the growing steel complex in Jinja owed its inception to one of them. Likewise, the timber and saw-mill industries were originally developed in Uganda on the initiative of Asian businessmen. In Tanzania, many of the largest sisal and other plantations are owned by Asians; while in Kenya, they have contributed greatly to industrial expansion in the post-war period. It is, in fact, difficult to think of any significant sector in the East African economies where Asian capital, entrepreneurial ability and skills have not made an appreciable contribution.

The economic success of the Asian community in East Africa has been due to the possession of certain qualities essential for economic development. The early Asian settlers were imbued with 'quasi-Protestant ethics; they were remarkable for their strong commercial sense, capacity to work long hours, low propensity to consume, and passion for accumulation of capital. With the increase in riches, the new generation have relaxed their single-minded pursuit of wealth. Nevertheless, a substantial number of younger Asian businessmen possess in abundance many of the qualities that enabled their forefathers to amass large fortunes. The qualities noted above, while vitally important for economic development, are essentially 'unheroic' and are not likely to endear their possessors to other communities. Asians have had more than their share of criticism from Europeans in the past and increasingly from Africans.

For long, Asians had a virtual monopoly of wholesale and retail trade and the marketing of minor cash crops, especially in Uganda and Tanganyika. Their dominance in the distributive sector of the economy exposed them to widespread criticism for alleged dishonest practices and to charges of exploitation. It is difficult to define the latter term precisely; in most cases it is undoubtedly used as a term of abuse without referring to any specific practices. To the extent that it is not used simply as a term of abuse, it may be expected to refer to a variety of sharp practices from which Asian businessmen, like the businessmen of other races, cannot claim entire freedom. These may include the problem of short weight, misleading information, overcharging, or any number of other ways by which customers feel themselves cheated. But, in a majority of cases, criticism is levelled against the widespread practice of bargaining in Asian shops.

Any system of bargaining must inevitably lead to the charging of different prices to different customers, and thereby to complaints of exploitation and racial discrimination. It is perhaps also true that many Asian traders have shown themselves more interested in quick profits rather than in steady, long-term gains, and have not hesitated to exploit temporary scarcities to make windfall gains. All these malpractices have served only to promote ill-will and distrust between the customer and the trader. It has been noticed that none of these practices are peculiar to Asian traders in East Africa; indeed, they are the stock in trade of businessmen all over the world, especially in underdeveloped countries. But, in East Africa, because of the dominance of Asians in wholesale and retail trade, criticism of such practices is often couched in racial terms.

At another level, Asians are sometimes accused of holding back the progress and participation of Africans in the economy of the country. It is undoubtedly true that the presence of a large, economically sophisticated community had the effect of retarding African participation in the commercial sectors of the economy. But, to argue from this that the absence of the Asian community would have resulted in generally higher levels of income for Africans is to commit an error in elementary economics. In the preceding section, it was shown that the Asians have made a vital contribution economic development; it is difficult to believe that East Africa would have developed to anything like its present level without the full and active economic participation of Asians.

The above criticism can be reinterpreted to imply that Asian business firms have not consciously aided Africanisation. There is undoubtedly much truth in this charge. Asians have for the most part been solely concerned with their own economic salvation; in the past they have pared relatively little energy for the economic advancement of Africans. The skills and training which Africans have acquired from Asian business firms have been the by-product of their employment with the latter rather than the result; of conscious attempt to promote the economic position of Africans. Having said this, it is difficult to see how it could have been otherwise. Most of the Asian firms are small, essentially family concerns; in many cases the employment of Africans in 'responsible' positions would have meant a loss of jobs for some members of the family—something very few Asians are prepared to accept. However, the old attitudes and habits are gradually breaking down in the face of pressure from Africans leaders, and—only occasionally—in the pursuit of enlightened self-interest. Some Asians have started business in partnership with Africans; many of the larger commercial and industrial firms have initiated policies of Africanisation. Towards the end of 1964, the (Asian) Dar es Salaam Merchants Chamber announced a comprehensive scheme to accelerate the participation of Africans in the commercial and industrial sectors of the economy through loans, partnerships, and training in commercial techniques.[5] Despite these recent moves, one cannot help feeling that the Asian response to the need to increase the share of Africans in wholesale and retail trade has not been sufficiently swift or thoroughgoing.

In recent years, the Asian community has been widely criticised for exporting capital. The imminence of independence in East African countries, accompanied as it was by widespread fears of a breakdown of law and order in Kenya and Uganda, led to a crisis of confidence among the immigrant communities, resulting in a tall in domestic investment and a large outflow of capital abroad. With the attainment of independence and the return of confidence, there 'has been a slight reversal of the above trends, but there are still many individual Europeans and Asians who continue to transfer a abroad part their current income. The response of the immigrant communities to conditions of uncertainty and fear of exchange control has been similar to that of the affluent classes all over the world. The only solution to this problem—the imposition of control on transactions in foreign "exchange—has been successively rejected by independent African governments as well as by the colonial governments. It is difficult to see how, short of foreign exchange control, the capital outflow can be stopped altogether.

There is little doubt that the coming of independence will increasingly mean large shifts of income and assets from non-Africans to Africans. This has already been foreshadowed in the policy declarations of the ruling parties in the three countries. The recently published Development Plans of Kenya and Tanganyika attempt to translate these policies into concrete projects. Before we consider them in detail, it is necessary to point out that the achievement of high rates of economic growth in East Africa could greatly ease the economic problems of the Asian community, while a stagnant economy could have serious effects on their economic prospects. Their actions and attitudes could determinant of the rate of growth. Asian business men and industrialists are of total investment; if they do not pursue expansionist policies, the efforts The East African governments to accelerate the rate of economic growth will be largely frustrated, thereby, seriously exacerbating the economic problems of the Asian community.

Africanisation and its Economic Implications

A very high proportion of the Asian labour force in East Africa, amounting to between 60 to 70 per cent, derive their livelihood from commerce or from employment in the public sector. Here the economic prospects for Asians appear rather gloomy. An accelerated programme of Africanisation in the civil services has already gone some way in redressing the past racial imbalances; it is likely to be pursued vigorously for some years to come. But, Africanisation by definition leaves little scope for either the recruitment or the promotion of Asians. Different categories of Asian employees will be affected differently; the most numerous category, consisting of clerks, typists, and others holding junior executive posts, will be hit hardest by programmes of Africanisation. Those in the teaching profession, particularly in the secondary schools, should have relatively little difficulty in finding jobs over the next few years. With regard to other graduates and persons with professional qualifications such as accountants, doctors, lawyers, architects, engineers, dentists, and so on, the prospects or employment in the public services will depend entirely on governmental attitudes.

There is little doubt that for many years to come there is likely-to be an acute shortage of skilled and educated manpower in both the public and the private sectors. But, this does not mean that the Asians with the necessary qualification will automatically assured of employment. The East African governments have up till now shown no great enthusiasm for employing Asians, even where Africans with the requisite qualifications are not forthcoming. This has undoubtedly resulted in an outflow of educated Asian manpower to countries like Canada, the U.K., India and Pakistan. An intensification of this trend could be a severe setback to efforts, solve the manpower crisis.

For many years to come there will be ample economic opportunities in private practice for professional persons; this is especially true of professions for which Africans have hitherto shown little inclination, such as engineering, accountancy, architecture or pharmacy. But, persons with such qualifications will always command an international market, and the lack of openings in East Africa need not spell economic disaster for them. In any case, they will always constitute a tiny minority of the total Asian working population.

In the private sector, many of the leading expatriate firms are pursuing a policy of Africanisation at all levels, and are, therefore, reluctant to take on new Asian employees. It is unlikely that the Asian predominance in wholesale and retail trade will last for long. One of the aims of the Development Plans drawn up in the three East African countries is to increase rapidly and substantially the share of Africans in commerce. This is perhaps stated most clearly in Tanganyika's five-year plan, which specifies that the co-operative movement should expand to secure 10 per cent of the total turnover of wholesale trade by 1970; the target for retail trade is 10 per cent by 1970, and in the long run some 30 per cent to 40 per cent of the total volume.[6]

The Tanzania Government has worked out a comprehensive scheme to implement these targets; and it also plans to place the marketing of all crops in the hands of co-operative societies or of African farmers. This would deprive Asian *dukawallas* of a valuable source of income. Similarly, the

Kenya Development Plan puts forward various proposals to enhance the share of Africans in commerce and industry; the most important of these is the decision to establish a chain of People's Shops managed by the National Trading Company, which will be formed under the aegis of Kenya Industrial Development Corporation. In Uganda, too, plans are afoot to help African traders through loans, subsidised rents, training programmes, and so on. All these measures, if successful, would imply an absolute reduction in the turnover of wholesale and retail trade handled by Asian businessmen. Thus, the commercial sector is unlikely to absorb the increase in Asian labour force.

The pressure of African competition is already beginning to make itself felt among small retail stores, especially in villages and other small centres, and has resulted in a drift of Asian traders to the towns and cities.[7] The indications are that this pressure will be future intensified, and in a few years time the erstwhile ubiquitous *dukawalla* may cease to be a part of the landscape in small urban centres. It is only the large import, wholesale and retail businesses owned by Asians which with continue to have a future in East Africa.

This leaves us with the industrial and agricultural sectors as possible openings for the increasing Asian labour force. Undoubtedly, a rapid growth of the manufacturing and construction industries could ease their unemployment problem. But, here again, the resultant demand for unskilled and semi-skilled jobs would be largely satisfied by the existing African labour supply; while only a few Asians may expect to be employed in managerial and executive posts. Is there any considerable scope in agriculture? Although, Asians were prevented by legislation from acquiring and cultivating land in the past, the old reasons for this discrimination no longer apply Agriculture might, therefore, be thought of as a possible solution to the 'Asian problem'; however, for a variety of reasons, this seems most unlikely even if, such policies were adopted. The question of land arouses the deepest emotions among Africans and any suggestion of alienating land for Asian settlement would Lam into bitter opposition. Quite apart from that, Kenya has no substantial unutilised land capable of cultivation. Even if the other two governments were to encourage Asian settlement, it is doubtful whether many capable and enterprising Asians would take kindly to agricultural life. Nor is it reasonable to assume that the governments be prepared to inject large sums of capital and technical know-how to make these schemes viable. It does not, therefore, seem that agriculture is likely to employ any substantial number of Asians.

The above analysis does not hold out hopes of a bright economic future for Asians in East Africa, to that extent it confirms the current widespread pessimism among the Asian community. Economic difficulties will perhaps manifest themselves in growing unemployment, pressures on average earnings, increasing economic competition from Africans, and generally in a gradual erosion of the many privileges which Asians have enjoyed in the past. But,, all this will have the effect of closing the economic gap between and Africans and may contribute to racial harmony in East Africa. Furthermore, for some years to come there may be a substantial net emigration of Asians from East Africa to India, Pakistan and the U.K. The emigrants will consist for the most part of retired civil servants and businessmen, of unemployed and of those with little prospects for employment, and finally of those with high educational qualifications in search of better economic opportunities, just as their fathers were a generation ago. Some of the Asian economic problems will, therefore, be exported in this way. For those who choose to stay on, their most enduring guarantee must lie in their complete acceptance as East Africans. To this process of acceptance, they can make a powerful contribution by a genuine commitment to the ideals and aspirations of an independent East Africa.

The governments and people of East Africa must, in turn, be vigilant against incipient racialism. It will be a bitter tragedy for East Africa and, indeed, for the whole continent if racialist tendencies which are unfortunately in evidence in certain quarters gather momentum, and racialists gain the upper hand. There are very few countries in the world where racial minorities do not suffer discrimination in one form or another. One, therefore, ought not to judge East African countries by very harsh standards. But, if racialism prevails in East Africa, will our leaders be able to hold up their heads at international conferences and condemn, in good conscience, the injustices and humiliations heaped on Africans in South Africa and Negroes in the United States? Let us, therefore, continue to hope that East Africans will be spared the anguish of seeing the ideals of equality and brotherhood they fought for and cherish, lie shattered at their feet.

NOTES AND REFERENCES

1. The quantitative data used in this chapter is derived from the following publications:

   Annual Statistical Abstracts for Kenya, Uganda and Tanganyika.
   1948 population census in Kenya, Uganda and Tanganyika
   1952 and 1957 census for non-Africans in Tanganyika.
   1959 population census in Uganda.
   1962 population census in Kenya.
   Annual reported employment and earnings in Kenya: 1948-62.
   Annual employment and earnings in Tanganyika: 1961-62.
   Annual enumeration of employees in Uganda: 1958-62.
   Economic and Statistical Review; March 1964.
   Kenya Statistical Digest, June 1964.

2. The term economically active population' refers to all persons working as employers, own-account workers, unpaid family workers and employees, as well as those currently unemployed but in search of jobs. It excludes housewives, students, children, retired persons, etc.

3. R. H. Desai, The Family and Business Enterprise Among the Asians in East Africa', paper presented to the Conference of the East African Institute of Social Research, Makerere University College, 1964.

4. Guy Hunter: *Education for a Developing Region: a Study in East Africa,* Alien and Unwin, 1963.

5. *The Nationalist (Dar es Salaam),* 17 August 1964.

6. Tanganyika's Five-Year Plan for Economic and Social Development, Vol. 1 Preliminary Edition, April 1964, p. 47.

7. 'The big increase in the number of African shops... has taken place in the last ten to fifteen years'. In 1961, there were 36,157 African retailers licensed. 'Very few of these African shops are

in towns or trading centres; almost all are situated in the interior'. In 1961 there were 10,090 non-African retail businesses, and 3,921 wholesalers, of whom the great majority were Asians, with a small number of Europeans: 'though the Asian traders are less numerous than the African, they handle, even at the retail level, much the greater part of the business'. *A Survey of Wholesale and Retail Trade in Tanganyika* (Economist Intelligence Unit, London, 1962), pp. 19 and 36-7.

6

POLITICAL PARTICIPATION OF THE INDIAN DIASPORA

Asians Compulsions for Joining Politics

It can be categorically stated that the great majority of the Asians in East Africa never actively participated in politics, if by participation in politics we mean in the Aristotelian sense, the exercise of rational thinking in a public discussion over controversial political problems. Rather they, both as a community and as individuals, reacted to politics and to political events with the crudest animal instincts of survival and security. This can be witnessed by the alternate waves of optimism and pessimism that betook them in recent years whenever a political speech by an African leader seemed to threaten their security or to preserve it. For a large part, they were content with the existing pace; their brand of political participation was intermittent and sporadic depending on occasions when their peaceful existence appeared to be challenged.

Serious politics has been a business of no more than a few individuals. What motivated these few to participate actively in politics is anybody's guess. There is evidence to show that there existed, at least in the British days, some correlation between being a member of the Legislative Council, and improving one's business prospects or professional clientele. This is not surprising: one's prestige and status improved with being a member of the Legislative Council, whether one was handpicked by the British as in the early days, or, as later, elected by one's community. The reason for joining politics, in most cases, was primarily personal. The function of presenting 'the Asian point of view' (if there was one) was secondary and incidental. With the Africans the reason for joining politics, though partly personal, was also strongly influenced by the need to force the pace of political evolution these territories. With the Asians, again with the exception of a few, the need to take a stand on measures of political evolution came as a necessity, sometimes unpleasant, after joining the Legislative Council rather than as a contributing reason for it.

Why is it that a great part of the Asian population in East Africa never consistently active role in politics? Illiteracy, which in large part explains the non-participation in politics by the African majorities, hardly explains the Asian position. We must, therefore, look for some other explanation.

The orthodox explanation, with perhaps a degree of truth in it, is that the Asians came to East Africa principally to trade and not to rule. This explanation has a virtuous undertone; they, in other words, came to East Africa not with the imperialist motives that had driven the Europeans to scramble for Africa, but with purely economic motives. Applying the push and pull theory, it was for most of them the push imparted by the relative economic poverty in their countries of orgin, and the pull of brighter economic prospects in East Africa, that were instrumental in persuading them to part painfully with relatives and friends and undertake a long sea voyage to an unknown continent. There were some who came, or more correctly were brought as indentured coolies to build the railways, yet here again the economic aspect of the push and pull theory was the operative factor. As far as the Europeans are concerned, the paramount factor was political not economic. The Marxian thesis of colonies for the economic gain of the colonial powers is not strictly applicable in Africa.

Is it then that the lack of Asian participation in East African politics can be accountable by the fact that the Asians who came to East Africa were mostly traders and businessmen? If it is, it then becomes difficult to explain why their brothers in British Guiana, in Fiji, in Malaysia and in South Africa were not equally restrained in their political activities. After all, their immigration into these countries was as much motivated by economic, rather than political, considerations as the Asian immigration into East Africa. If anything, the proportion of "coolie-immigrants' to pure 'trader-immigrants' was considerably larger in these territories than in East Africa, and politically, therefore, they should have been less sophisticated than the Asians in East Africa. We must, therefore, look for some other explanation.

A second explanation, as naive as the above one, is that the Asian in diaspora is a meek gentleman not concerned about politicking in a foreign land. The evidence in Fiji, in British Guiana and in other places contradicts this theory as well.

A third explanation is that the Asians could not take part in politics because the East African territories were administered on a colonial (or protectorate or trust territory) basis by an imperial power, the British, who tolerated politics on their own terms only. Admittedly, an imperial regime imposes restrictions on the political activities In its colonies (the British sense of democracy and freedom of speech hardly even crossed the Channel), and for a community, which was itself an immigrant trading community and at that a distinct race, the practical effects of a colonial rule over their political activities must have been both physically as well as psychologically inhibitive.

Although, there is something in this explanation, it does not fully explain the morality of the Asian position. Laws against political demonstrations are no reason why demonstrations should not nevertheless take place, if one truly believed in the cause of justice. Colonial laws hindered but could not altogether prevent political activities in India, or among the Asians in East Africa. The political quietude of the Asians in East Africa must, therefore, have some other reasons.

The first of these reasons is that the Asians were a relatively privileged class in East Africa. They were, of course, denied certain privileges, for example, ownership of land in the Kenya Highlands and attainment of positions of top grade in the civil service, yet they had virtually a free hand in the main occupation that interested the bulk of them—trade and commerce. There was, therefore, no good reason for them to spurn the British rule.

The second reason was that even if the Asians were to act, the revolutionaries in the political struggle....for independence, the prize was certainly not political power. They could never hope to seize power from the hands of the British, the way the Indians in Fiji and in British Guiana could. This was fully understood by every Asian in East Africa.

It was the tacit acknowledgement on the part of the Asians in East Africa of this limitation on their political aspirations that exerted a sobering influence in too open a manifestation of political radicalism—again barring a few farsighted individuals. The reluctance to participate actively in politics cannot, therefore, be explained exclusively in terms of the commercial interests of the Asians in East Africa, of in terms the nature of the colonial rule. Two other factors were at least as significant: the fact that they had nothing in particular to shout against, since the prevailing peace and order under the British was good enough for their purposes; and the fact of the silent acceptance of the reality of power in East Africa.

Why was the attainment of political power in the territories of East Africa an ideal not within the grasp of the Asians? An understanding of the reasons for this, and the effects it had on the political behaviour of the Asians, is important in any assessment of their role in East African politics.

The first important reason is, of course, the plain arithmetic of numbers. Constituting, as they did, never more than 1½ to 2 per cent of the population, the Asians could never hope to hold water in any bid for power the way their Asian counterparts in British Guiana and in Fiji could, where their numbers constituted about 50 per cent of the total populations.

But, in politics numbers in themselves do not constitute the full answer to the problem of power, as evidenced by the history of the British and other colonial powers rule over populations vastly superior in number to their own, and as evidenced by the ability of dictators to rule over their countries with nothing more than police methods.

Thus, where the authority to rule is not based on superior numbers, it is based on superior power. The sanctions behind the British rule in Kenya, Uganda and Tanganyika resided not in Nairobi, Kampala or Dar es Salaam but in London. Ultimately, it was the authority (and what goes with authority: control of the law, the police and the army) which emanated from London that could sustain the continued rule by the white minorities in these territories over their subject races vastly superior in numbers to their own. The point of this observation is borne out by subsequent history, particularly of Kenya, of the gradual withdrawal of the sanctions apparatus by London and the consequent almost overnight crumbling of the power of the white minorities.

Sanctions were, therefore, an important ingredient of the European power in Africa, and an element completely lacking on the Asian side. It may be a controversial point for historians, but it is not too difficult to believe that had the Asians in East Africa a sanction machinery to back any bid for power, they might have staked their claims as well as the Europeans.

The only type of sanctions that the Asians could apply in support of their political claims were moral and economic sanctions. But, these too were very limited in their actual application. Their economic sanctions resided in the fact that they held in their hands at fairly substantial proportion of trade and commerce of these countries. They could, in times of crisis, use these as weapons in the political struggle. They could, for example, either threaten to close down their shops or, at worst, pack up their things, including capital investments, and leave East Africa.

Although, a usable form of sanctions, in the absence of a legal and political apparatus in the background, economic sanctions have severe imitations and can be used only sparingly. Therefore, although the Asians were sometimes successful in extracting minor concessions from the British rulers, this was more because of an acknowledgement, on the part of the governments, of the Asian economic power, rather than a consequence of direct application, or threat of application, of these sanctions by the Asians. In any case, the Asians had too many stakes and vested interests of their own in the continuing prosperity of these countries, to want to create instability through the use of their economic power.

The economic weapon, therefore, was never sufficiently powerful for the Asians to" stake out large political claims, and this, in an important way, limited the political ambitions of the community.

The other sort of sanctions that the Asians could apply were moral sanctions, again neither very reliable nor too readily applicable. Moral sanctions have meaning only when applied against those who, at least tacitly, accept the validity of the prevailing moral standards. The plea that the reservation of the Kenya Highlands only for the Europeans was a piece of discriminatory legislation which smacked of inequity, was a plea that might have cut some ice with the ordinary Englishmen in the English countryside. On the Europeans in Kenya and for their political mentors in London, with their standards of political morality doctrinally rooted in colonialism, such arguments, of course, would have no effect.

The demands of the Asians in East Africa sometimes were buttressed by the moral support of their erstwhile mother-country, India. But, the Indian Government seldom obliged the Asians in East Africa with more than moral support in their fight against the inequities of the Highlands policy or the restricted immigration laws Generally, the Indian Government, and the Indian people, in their attitude towards their brothers in East Africa showed a complete lack of patience which they often expressed by chiding them, as parents would their naughty children, to behave decently in a foreign land..

This contrasts well with the attitude of most countries towards their nationals abroad: for example, the attitude of the Turkish Government towards the Turks in Cyprus. It was perhaps as well that the Indian Government was reticent in supporting the political demands of the Asians in East Africa, for it brought a sense of realism among the Asians about the limitations of their political manoeuvrability.

The Asians in British Guiana and in Fiji had the backing of numbers to make it worth their while bidding for power on democratic—one man one vote—basis. The Europeans in East Africa could not sustain their power on democratic principles, but had the support of a sanctions machinery resident in London to make possible their continued rule over Africa for more than half a century. The Asians in East Africa had neither the numbers that their brothers in British Guiana and Fiji had, nor the sanctions that their European counterparts in East Africa.[1]

A bid for power was, therefore,, from the very beginning, a hopeless venture from these two points of view. But, there was a third factor also which restrained the Asians from participating in the power-politics of the territories. And this was a realisation that even if they were to agitate actively for African independence, the result would be only a change of masters—African masters instead of the British—and not any greater share in the politics of the country. This might or might not have been borne out by subsequent history, but it was almost universally accepted that the change of masters would not necessarily involve the upgrading of the political status of the Asians.

Whether or not the Asians in East Africa were conscious of the effects of these factors on their political behaviour, it cannot be denied that at the level of meta-politics these were the factors that considerably debilitated the strength of Asian politics. At the level of the Asian masses generally, the popular view as, and still is that the Asians were primarily traders, not politicians. At the subconscious level they could sense that there were important forces operating which made it highly unlikely that they were going to be anything more than traders. How these, in fact, affected the conduct of Asian political participation, where there was any, in other words, how these affected their political organisation and their attitude towards elections, is the problem that we shall now turn to.

Nature of the Operation of Asian Politics

The realisation that the attainment of political power was beyond the pale of the Asians either under the British or the African rule, and the resigned acceptance of the fact that politically they were the most vulnerable community in East Africa, partly because they had so much vested interests at stake and partly because they lacked any effective and reliable sanctions at their command, these had always exercised a mellowing, almost paralysing, influence not only on the content of Asian politics but also on their political conduct.

First, then, the manner in which the Asians conducted their small politics. Throughout the British period, the focus of Asian politics had been the individual, brought to limelight either through his own efforts or placed in a position of status by the colonial governments.

There were never existent compelling reasons for the creation of political parties. On the contrary, all the circumstances militated against their creation. There was the official ban on the formation of political parties, much more severely imposed by the British in Kenya during the years of the Mau Mau Emergency than in other parts of East Africa. But, even if there were no legal restrictions, there might still have been no Asian political parties. The legal restrictions worried the Africans much more than the Asians. The latter had no strong incentive to form parties, as we know parties in their traditional meaning.

The few times when the Asians did form parties, like the Uganda Action Group (more of a ginger group than a party), and the Kenya Freedom Party, these were formed *ad hoc,* and basically to challenge the existing Asian leadership on "some politically controversial issues. As soon as these issues were resolved, these parties dissolved.

The more normal vehicles of political expression were not parties as we generally know them, but what may variously be called front organisations, associations or congresses. In Kenya, there was the Indian National Congress (partaking of the same name as the venerable congress in the mother country); in Uganda, there was the Central Council of Indian Association; and in Tanganyika, there was the Asian Association.

The function of these organisations was to act as a two-way channel of communication between the Asians and the governments. The British Government had recognised these organisations since they served a useful function of picking up the Asian leaders for service either in the Legislative

Councils or in various government boards and committees. Although, consisting of only a small number of paid-up members, these front organisations purported to represent the entire Asian community, and had their public meetings open to all the members of the community. The result, of course, was that these organisations were always starved of finances. A permanent paid secretary was a luxury that they could indulge in only from time to time depending on the state of their finances. These, quite naturally, had not very wholesome effects on the efficiency of these organisations and there for eon the political health of the community.

There was often a lack of communication between the organisations and the public which they purported to represent, with the result that Asians was hardly their strong merit. This, in turn, merely accentuated the individualistic nature of Asian politics, and explains why there was no serious and consistent practice of discussing political problems at a rational and public level, except when these organisations sporadically arranged public meetings to discuss problems that had arisen *ad hoc*. It is difficult to say, however, how the character of Asian organisations and the nature of their politics could have been otherwise, since, except for a few ambitious individuals, politics was not a paying proposition for the community as a whole, for reasons that we have already seen above.

Bad Press

Another effect of weak political organisation of the Asians that may be mentioned in passing is the consistently bad press they had both during the British period and after. The Asians were often painted in most unkind terms, for example, as exploiters and collaborators of the British, and although there is some degree of truth in this as there always is in all forms of political mud-slinging, the Asian organisations hardly ever made serious attempts to rebut these allegations, except again, intermittently and on an individual basis.

Absence of Institutional Mechanism on Political Issues

The weakness of the Asian organisations was not only at the level of each territory, but also at the interterritorial level.

There was almost daily contact between individual Asian businessmen in the three countries, and to some extent, there must also have been an exchange of views over the common problems of the Asians in East Africa, but such contacts as existed were never institutionalised with the result that not only was there no interterritorial support for each others' political demands, but there was also complete lack of a system of mutual advice on each others' problems.

Such lessons as were learnt by the Asians in one country from the experiences of their brothers in another country were purely incidental, *ad hoc,* and uninstitutionalised. Thus, the Kenya Freedom Party which was created in February 1960, although not consciously modelled on the Uganda Action Group set up at the beginning of 1959, yet had common features with it both in respect of the circumstances in which they were created and in the policies that they adopted.

It was difficult not to learn from the experiences of the brothers over the boundaries, but the lessons were learnt casually rather than through a concerted effort. In general, however, Kenya set the pace in determining the general mood of the Asians in the territories, partly because there was always so much more happening in Kenya than in Tanganyika or Uganda, and partly because Nairobi was so much more Asian than either Kampala or Dar es Salaam. After 1958, however, the roles were reversed because of the faster political development in Tanganyika and Uganda. Kenya lagged behind, giving an opportunity to the Asians in Kenya to learn from the experiences of their brothers in Tanganyika and Uganda.

Since there existed no traditional type of political parties among the Asians, except for short periods in Kenya and Uganda, and since Asian organisations in the political sphere were very weak, the task of getting elected as members of the Legislative Council or the Executive Council in the British days was very much dependent on the efforts of the individuals who aspired for such public office. This, of course, meant that only the more rich among the Asians could afford to join politics and contest elections, or those who had either good communal support or rich friends to finance electioneering campaigns.

Obligation of Asian Voters on Religious and Linguistic Basis

Communal voting was at once the inevitable outcome of individualistic politics and the scourge of Asian politics in East Africa. That the candidates should emphasize communal, religious and language differences among their Asian voters so as to muster support for themselves, is, however, not a new phenomenon, and had a parallel, with their African counterparts who incited tribalism to win votes. The only difference was that from the national point of view, Asian politics were insignificant anyway, so that communalism among them made little or no difference to the national politics, as did tribalism.

Communal Card

But, as far as the Asians were concerned the effects of communalism were not always healthy. The British Government quite effectively used Communal differences, whenever they felt that the Asians acting as a group would prove a nuisance, if not a positive obstruction to legislation. This, therefore, sapped whatever little political strength that the Asians had.

Demand for Self-Determination

Worse still, the communal voting and communal seats in the Legislative Council were fissiparous in their effects on the already weak Asian organisations. Thus, when British India was partitioned into India and Pakistan in 1947, the Muslim Asians in East Africa demanded the partitioning of Asian organisations. They, thus, created their own organisations, like the Central Council of Moslem Association in Uganda and demanded separate seats in the Legislative Council.

There was nothing very surprising about this development, since in any elections carried on communal basis, it was only a realistic assumption that the Muslim Asians would inevitably be outvoted by their Hindu rivals. The communal phenomenon had its more serious, and tragic (for the Asians) implications in the at least 'theoretical possibility that all the 'minorities' among the Asians should strike out for a claim of 'self-determination' and demand to be separately represented in the Legislative Councils. As far as the Sikhs of Kenya are concerned the issue had in fact gone at one time beyond mere theoretical possibility. The actual creation of a separate seat for the Sikhs happily did not materialize.

Policy of Divide and Rule

Communal representation plagued Kenya Asian politics more than it did Tanganyika and Uganda. Kenya had always been a hotbed of rival racial, tribal and communal factions, and the British Government cannot be credited with making even a minimum of effort to discourage these fissiparous tendencies. Theirs was a realistic policy of playing one faction against another—this is true even if it has now become a cliche.

The British colonial policy of divide and rule was an extension of and perhaps only another name for her traditional policy of balance of power in Europe. Just as it served the British interests best when there existed a balance or an equilibrium of power among the different nations in Europe, so a balance of power between the different races, tribes and communities in the colonies served her interest best.

In Europe, Britain traditionally supported the weaker nation against the stronger (Belgium in preference to Germany, for instance); similarly, in the colonies, British policy was to support the weaker faction against the stronger: the small tribes in the small tribe-big tribe conflict, the Muslims in the Hindu-Muslim conflict, and so on right down the line.

In Uganda and Tanganyika, where communal divisions were not so pronounced or so much played up by the colonial government, as in Kenya the Asians resisted being represented in the Legislative Council on strictly communal basis. This did not, however, prevent voting on communal line during the time of elections. Among other effects of communal voting there are two that are worth mentioning. First, with the exception of a few, the people who were supposed to be representing the Asian opinion in the governing councils of the three territories were elected not necessarily for their policies, but more often for their communal popularity. The second effect, and a corollary of the first, was that although there were always elements within the Asian communities who were much more radical in their political thinking than the rest of their people, they could not gain a voice in the governing bodies for lack of communal support, either because they belonged to small communal groups, or because their support was scattered over different communal groups without having a full support of one large community to enable them to win elections. It was against this background that the Asians faced the challenge of African nationalism.

African Nationalism and the Asian Response

Nationalism for the Asians was not a new experience. Many of them had known it in the 1920s and 1930s and even as recently as in the 1940s. It was until recently customary for the Asians in East Africa to celebrate the anniversary of the independence of India and Pakistan. Although, they were so far from their countries of origin, the independence of India and Pakistan was an emotional reality for them, in the celebration of which they could not but help participate. While this was an understandable human reaction to the success of a freedom movement in which they were emotionally involved, it was a reaction which stopped at the coasts of India. The emotion of freedom and the sentiment of anti-colonialism were not, except in the case of a few individuals, operative in the context of East Africa. Why?

In retrospect, it would seem that if the Asians in East Africa had shown the same amount of exuberance for freedom, and if they had completely identified with the African aspirations, and still more if they had taken the initiative to start the struggle against colonialism even when the Africans were not ready themselves, then the Asians might have reserved for themselves a position of respect and leadership among the Africans today.

Now, why did not the Asians transplant in the East African soil their spirit of anti-colonialism which they had experienced much before the Africans? Various explanations can be given for this, ranging from the most sinister plots to the most palpable excuses. The truth may lie somewhere in between.

One explanation, with some degree of truth, may be that the Asian immigrant in East Africa was a different kind of person from his brother back in India. Incidentally a similar observation is made of the Englishman too: the Englishman in a colonial situation was a different kind of creature—almost Fascist—from the Englishman back at home—liberal, humanitarian. The Asians in East Africa were a trading community who came here primarily to improve their economic fortunes. They could, therefore, be pictured in the most sinister terms: a hypocritical people who opposed the British regime in India but favoured it in East Africa so they might continue to enjoy economic prosperity.

Put in this way, it seems an ugly truth, if rather simplified. There was, however, an obvious dichotomy between what the bulk of the Asians felt in their hearts about African nationalism, and the public stand that their leaders had taken, both in their actions and in their pronouncements. In their public pronouncements, the Asian leaders in all the three territories had, except in a few isolated cases, from the very beginning taken a positive stand in favour of constitutional development towards self-government based on adult universal suffrage and a common roll. In other words, the Asian leader had envisaged independence under African majorities as the ultimate goal to aspire towards in the three territories—even in Kenya.

Thus, as far back as 15 February, 1946, the president of the Kenya Indian Association in outlining the 'aims of Indians in Kenya' had strongly opposed any attempt by the British Government prematurely to give self-government to Kenya under the existing European majority in the Legislative Council, in the same way as today the African states are opposed to a premature independence to Southern Rhodesia under white supremacy. The president had then warned that if the Labour were to succumb to the threat of non-constitutional assumption of power by the Kenya Europeans, then the Indians would have no alternative but to bring all non-European races on to a common platform and advise some common action.

In the same vein, the Asian leaders, in their public pronouncements, favoured the representation of the Africans by the Africans themselves in the Legislative Councils at a time when they were represented by unofficial Europeans; they almost invariably supported the African demand for increased representation in the Legislative Councils; and they fought for the principle of equality for the races including, for instance, the opening of the White Highlands for the Asians and the Africans as the as for a Europeans, and the ending of racial segregation in public places.

There can be no doubt that even when privately the Asians had reservations about the ability of the Africans to rule themselves, they were sincere about their public stand, and were influenced partly by ideological considerations of equity and justice, partly by a realistic consideration that power must eventually pass into the hands of the Africans, and partly because their own countries of origin, particularly India had taken an open stand against the continuance of colonialism as an important objective of their foreign policies, and were exerting their diplomatic influence to this end through organisations like the United Nations and the Commonwealth.

But, there is also no doubt that, excepting again a few individuals, the bulk of the Asians were ambivalent in their attitude towards the rising force of African nationalism. In public, it was necessary for the leaders to accept the inevitable and call it virtue; in private, one could indulge in the sin of thinking at variance with African nationalism. What follows is a possible explanation for this attitude, not a justification for it.

Fear is a natural reaction of human beings against the unknown. This is doubly so for a man with vested interests which might be threatened by the unknown events. In retrospect, the Asians would perhaps seem to have been unduly pessimistic, but fear was nonetheless a dominant characteristic of the Asians during the 1950s.

Why did they then continue to invest money in business in the 1950s? The answer must be that the Asians expected the British rule to continue for several more decades. In this they were in good company; the United Nations Mission which visited Tanganyika in the fifties reckoned that it would be a couple of decades before the country was ready for independence. However, once their expectations were proved false, the Asians were quick to send their capita abroad.

Now, why were the Asians dominated by a sense of fear, rather than optimism as they should have been at the prospect of independence? Again there could be various explanations, ranging from the one that the Asians were merely birds of passage who were beginning to see the end of their season in East Africa and must face the unpleasant task of returning to their homelands or finding new grounds, to the explanation that the Asians did not understand the nature of African nationalism because of a failure of emotional communication between the Asian and the African leaders. There is some element of truth in all this, but one cannot get away from two basic sociological facts that were at the root of such fears: one was that the Asians were a separate economic class with vested interests; and the second that they constituted a minority immigrant community which could easily be identified as belonging to a different race altogether. It was as if two revolutions—economic and racial—were springing a surprise at the Asians who happened to be at the other end of the stick. And there hardly existed any mitigating factors: visibly there existed almost no strong African group whose interest could be identified with the Asians. Furthermore, events moved so fast that the Asians—conservative in their ways in any event—could not adjust themselves quickly so as to identify themselves with African nationalism absolutely.

African nationalism was, therefore, black African nationalism, even though there were individual Asians who were genuinely in basic sympathy with the African aspirations. Self-determination was known and seen in racial terms by the Africans and not in purely national terms.

African nationalists had shouted for self-governments, not necessarily good governments—self-rule was decidedly purported to be better than foreign rule. The majority of the Asians had accepted the idea of self-government for the Africans, but they were also concerned that there should be good government, good in their ability to maintain law and order while they continued with their business. The British Government at least provided them [with that. Chances were that the African governments might not, since theirs was not a task to uphold the *status quo* but to change it. Existing evidence did not, in any case, inspire them with any degree of confidence in African governments: the Asian shops were first to be looted even if the dispute was between the Europeans and the Africans or among the Africans themselves. And finally, when independence was to come, power was to be transferred to the Africans, and this was also recognised by the Asian leaders. So, it was a question of exchanging one master for the other, and who »'was to say whether the new master might not turn out to be even more difficult?

It is in this atmosphere of fear and scepticism about the future that the response of the Asians to the challenge of African nationalism must be assessed. Concerned, as they were, with the problem of security in a future East Africa, the Asians began to look around for electioneering and constitutional safeguards. Communal roll, reserved seats for the Asians in the national assemblies, and even at times qualified franchise based on education or property, and the institution of a Bill of Rights in the constitutions became common vocabulary among the Asians during this time.

In Tanganyika, the first response of the Asians to the 1954-58 British idea of creating a multi-racial society based on at equality between the races, was to accept it as the most sanguine solution to their future problems. The Asians, for a time, deluded themselves into thinking that they could share power on a basis of equality with the Europeans and the Africans in Tanganyika.

Under the leadership of a few farsighted individuals, it later dawned on them that such a formula was not practicable. If Tanganyika was to achieve independence at all, and to break her links with the sanctions machinery in London, a system based on power shared on a tripartite basis could not form a lasting settlement of the problem of the three races in Tanganyika. Besides, it was palpably unfair that the Asians with only about 1½ per cent of the population and the Europeans with still less should share out two thirds of the seats in a national assembly, leaving only one third for the remaining 98 per cent of the population.

The emergence of TANU under the wise leadership of Mwalimu Julius Nyerere made it easier for the Asians to opt out finally in favour of completely identifying themselves politically with the Africans. Although, the 1958-59 elections for the Legislative Council were based on the idea of equal representation between the races (one African, one European and one Asian member from each of the ten constituencies), and although elections took place on a limited franchise, the institution of common roll at that early stage brought victory to either the African members of the TANU or to independent European and Asian candidates who enjoyed its formal support. At the September 1960 general elections the idea of equal representation or he three races was finally abandoned, although out of 71 seats, 11 seats were still reserved for the Asians and 10 for the Europeans. Again, on a common roll, but with a widened franchise, 71 seats were won by the TANU and the TANU-supported independent candidates.

In Uganda and in Kenya too, the Asian leaders for a time toyed with the idea of electioneering safeguards for their future, namely communal roll and reserved seats in the national assemblies. In both countries the problem sparked a lively controversy and a split in the existing Asian leadership.

In Uganda, it led to the creation of a ginger group called the Uganda Action Group in the beginning of 1959. Its avowed policies were to challenge what its members called the 'old guard 'Asian' leadership, and to bring about a political rethinking of the issues currently at controversy, and to attempt to get Indians admitted to the African political parties. The leadership of the UAG consisted [mostly of young radical thinkers among the Asians who, partly because of their experiences in the U.K. from where they could view events in Uganda with a healthy perspective and partly because of a streak of genuine idealism in support of African demands, vigorously came out against communal voting roll and reserved minority seats for safeguarding the interests of the Asians. They realised it much faster than the old leadership that such safeguards had no value unless sufficient goodwill was built up between the Asian minority and the African majority. A few Asian seats in the rational Assembly voted on a communal roll would have permanently placed a thorn among the African majorities, and in the end was not good for the Asians as well.

In Kenya, the split among the Asian leadership took place at a much more dramatic moment, namely, during the eve of the 1960, Lancaster House Conference. The main points of difference again seemed to be on the question of whether to support the African nationalists unqualifiedly, or whether to demand electioneering safeguards for the minorities by retaining communal rolls and reserved seats for the minorities in the National Assembly. The more radical members of the Indian National Congress formed a splinter group called the Kenya Freedom Party in February, 1960, ostensibly with membership open to all races, but really an Indian political party designed, like the Uganda Action Group, to challenge the more conservative stand taken by the Asian representatives in the organs of the government (and also at the Lancaster Conference), and to attempt to get Asians admitted as members of African political parties. Like the UAG, the KFP also stood out in favour of 'independence now' rather than independence by gradual stage a common roll instead of a communal roll, and 'open seats' rather than reserved seats for the minorities. It is difficult to ascertain how far the Asian public was divided as between the conservative and cautious stand taken by the Indian National Congress and the radical stand taken by the KFP, since the elections in 1960-61, like all previous elections, were influenced by considerations of communalism.[2]

The Lancaster House Conference unmistakably altered the course of events in Kenya: the inevitability of African independence was brought much closer to reality than many people had thought possible. It also instituted common roll instead of communal roll; the position of the minority communities was safeguarded by the reservation of 20 of the 53 seats—10 Europeans, 8 Asians and 2 Arabs—to be filled in by primary elections within their respective communities. In addition, provision was made for constitutional safeguards of human rights and rights over property.

Both the UAG and the KFP were, thus, short-lived phenomena which had sprung up *ad hoc* at a crisis period, and were dissolved (after their aims were achieved. While it lasted the KFP functioned more like a party than the UAG and actually contested the 1960-61 elections against its time-honoured adversary, the Indian National Congress.[3] At the time of their formal dissolution, the leaders of UAG and KFP made a similar statement to the effect that there was no longer any reason for their parties to continue to exist since they could now directly become members of the African nationalist political parties.

Prospect of Asian Politics in the Aftermath of Decolonisation of East Africa

The incidence of independence has fundamentally transformed the character of Asian politics in East Africa, both in its content and its conduct. Independence has not meant simply a change of masters, as was widely believed before. With independence have come important qualitative changes in the nature of Asian politics owing essentially to two factors. The first of these factors is ideological.

The principal difference between the ideology of the colonial governments and that of the present African governments is their attitudes towards racialism. The British colonial policy hinged on racial separatism which divided the three principal races not only on a cultural and social plane, but also on an economic and political basis the Europeans occupied the apex" of the triangle; the Africans formed the base; and the Asians occupied the middle. The present governments of Kenya, Uganda and Tanzania are determined to roll back the policy of racial separatism. The Europeans could sustain their rule only by maintaining the myth of their racial superiority; the Africans do not necessarily have to assert the myth of African superiority because they have the advantage of numbers that the Europeans did not have.

The British interests in the colonies were best served by a policy of divide and rule as between different races and different tribes; the present governments believe that their interests would best be served by forging national unity between their people, whatever their racial origins or tribal backgrounds. The British had, thus, instituted separate representation for the three races in the organs of government;

the independent governments of East Africa have deprecated political representation on racial lines. This has, in principle, met the approval of the Asians, as we saw above.

Nationalisation of Citizenship

This then is the first significant change that has come about since independence. The second important change has been in the direction of the nationalisation of citizenship. Since *uhuru*, most of the Africans almost automatically ceased to hold British passports and opted out for the citizenship of their respective countries. The minority races, and significantly the Asians, were offered very generous terms for the acquisition of the new citizenships as well. That the terms are generous can hardly be disputed, if one were to compare the citizenship laws of East Africa with those of, for instance, Ceylon and Burma where large Indian minorities reside. This magnanimous attitude on the part of the East African governments may be accounted for by the fact that' the citizenship laws came as a package deal along with independence.

But, the generous citizenship laws might in part be a reflection of the recognition paid to the role of the Asians in the future economic development of independent East Africa, and in part a reflection of a genuine streak of charitableness felt by the African leaders towards a small minority race. The point about the recognition of the role of the Asians in the future economic development of the countries is mentioned particularly to explode the myth often held by minority immigrant races that hey have a right to enjoy equal status in the countries of their adoption because they 'built up" these countries. This argument unfortunately reeks of the same odour as when the Europeans in pre-independent Algeria claimed the right to stay because they 'built' Algeria. Such arguments make no impact in politics. In so far as African leaders tend to play down the past contribution of the Asians in the economic development of East 'Africa, It is evident that their offer of equal rights of citizenship is based on the contribution they are expected to make-in the future rather than as a reward for their past work.

Before we work out the impact of these political-constitutional changes on Asian politics, it may be mentioned, in passing, that the offer of equal rights as citizens to the Asians in East Africa was not effected without a certain amount of opposition from quarters who felt that the Asians did not deserve much generosity. In Tanganyika, for instance, in the months immediately following independence, there was considerable hostility, even at the parliamentary level, to permitting the Asians to sit in parliament and to enrol as members of the TANU. The reasons for such hostility are understandable not only at the emotional level—it is not easy to be equanimous with an immigrant minority race that has, rightly or wrongly, been stigmatised as having exploited the indigenous people but also at the level of strict logicality—to accord equal rights as between two obviously (economically) unequal communities palpably to lay legal foundations for perpetuating that inequality.

Demands based on equity and justice have more often been the weapon of the under-privileged. In East Africa, the concept of equal treatment could well become the tool of the privileged to perpetuate their privileges. The role of the new independent governments in the popular eyes was first to remove the existing inequalities before talking about equality. It is a tribute to African leadership, particularly of Tanganyika whose cue the others followed that the public passion in this regard wag effect controlled. The leaders who achieved independence for their own countries by raising the banner of equality and human rights could not see them denied to a foreign minority who came in their midst by an historical accident. Although, in later years, practice, specially with regard to Africanisation and promotion in the civil service, did not always conform to the law of equal treatment, one needs a little more thinking to realise that this discrepancy between law and administration is really a case of law based on a doctrinal foundation of equality bending down under the weight of the hard realities of life. From the Asian point of view, it is better that there should exist some disparity between theory and practice, than that inequality as between races should become part of the law of the land. If it is an evil, it is at least the lesser of the two evils.

The distinction between theory and practice may be utilised again to work out the impact of independence on the nature of Asian politics in East Africa. In theory, almost all the Asians could Take opted to take up the citizenships of one of the three countries in the two years of grace period given to them after independence. (In Kenya this period has not yet expired). In theory again there is nothing to prevent the Asians from joining national political parties, and from contesting elections both at the level of central government and at the municipal or regional levels. In theory, indeed, there is no reason why an Asian may not become a president or a prime minister of one of the countries. Theoretically, the Asians, therefore, enjoy a right that was not even open to them during the British rule.

Both in theory and in practice, there is no place for the Asian community as a distinct political entity in East African politics, since there is no more representation on racial lines. The Asian member in the former Legislative Council, even if elected on a communal vote, was deemed to represent the 'voice of the Asians'. The Asian member of parliament today cannot have such pretensions, for he is deemed, in a broad sense, to represent the nation, and in a narrow sense, the interests of his political party. In practice, therefore, an Asian aspiring to play a part in parliamentary politics must seek support from a political party, for there are few seats, even in the urban areas, which can be won through Asian communal support only.

A successful Asian politician today is correspondingly different from his predecessor in the British period. He is likely to be more radical in his political views, and is likely to sing the song of African socialism and to shout *'Harambee'* a little louder than the rest, or else he may not be noticed. As for the old Asian institutions like the Kenya Indian National Congress or the Uganda Central Council of Indian Association, they do not seem to have been significantly affected by independence. Of course, they have re-oriented their policies in the direction of the wind of change, but their leadership has still remained largely in the old hands, and their function not very different from before, namely, that of acting as an informal two way channel of communication between the government and the Asians, and as a forum for sounding opinions on the problems of Asians in East Africa.

For the large majority of Asians this is a period of agonising adjustments to political changes that have come with the speed of a hurricane.

Acquisition of African Citizenship by the Asians

A good number of these have not taken up local citizenship either because they are pessimistic about their future in East Africa, or because they are optimistic about their prospects in the outside world Like pious men who, if they try hard can find evidence everywhere to substantiate their theory that sin in the world is on the increase, those among the Asians who are pessimistic about the future can also find evidence to confirm their worst fears. This evidence may relate to events in one of the sister countries (like the looting of Indian shops during the *Zanziber coup d'etat* and the Tanganyika army mutiny in 1964 or to instances of alleged discrimination against Asians, particularly those in the civil services, and specially when the alleged victims had taken up local citizenship.

They are convinced that taking up citizenship would not alter the fact that the Asians could aspire to no more than second class citizenship. It is difficult to persuade them that the governments have to Africanize (in racial terms) both the economy as well as the administration in order to correct the 'racial imbalance' created as a result of deliberate British colonial policy, which the Asians largely tolerated, if not actually endorsed. Perhaps it is an under-standable reaction on the part of the Asians: it is difficult to digest rational arguments when one's promotion, perhaps even the payroll, is threatened by an allegedly discriminatory action of the government. But, since correcting the imbalance is essentially a short-term objective, there is still time to prove to the pessimistic brand of Asians that their fears were misplaced. If, however, the policy of Africanisation interpreted in racial terms becomes a long-term policy, a persistent phenomenon, then the more optimistic among the Asians are likely to get disillusioned as well.

Political Consequences of Acquiring African Citizenship

There are several economic consequences of the decision by a percentage of the Asians not to take up local citizenship. However, what we are concerned with here are the political consequences. Briefly these are: firstly, political disenfranchisement of these Asians with the result that the base of Asian voters is much smaller than their visible presence in the urban areas might indicate—this has driven an aspiring Asian politician much more in the hands of African voters; secondly, the split among the Asian minority community as between citizens and non-citizens with the result that not only has this debilitated the political strength of the Asian community, *qua* community, but it has also set up a situation in which those who have acquired citizenship are now asking for preferential treatment as against their non-citizen brothers (for example, on the question of the issue of trading licences); thirdly, the creation of a situation by which, since a large section of the Asians have retained British citizenship, the British Government has to meet their international legal and moral obligations towards the protection of lives and alien rights of nationals of a distinctly different race; and finally, since the non-acquisition of citizenship is taken to be symbolic of the Asian distrust of African governments, the acerbation of racial tension between the Asians' and the Africans, with the result that old accusations are given fresh blood. For those who have acquired East African citizenship, the problem of adjustment demands immediate attention.

Among these, a great number of people, particularly the older generation, are still emotionally ill-equipped to reconcile themselves to the changed situation, although intellectually they are prepared to integrate in the present African societies. Integration whatever form it takes, would of necessity involve a gradual whittling down of Asian ethnocentricism, and their isolationist group mentality, enforced during the British rule, of maintaining a closed society of language, religion and Old World customs and social values. This is not going to be easy, for the process may involve not only an attack on the Asians' vested interests, but possibly a breaking down of their whole framework of reference.

The extent to which the Asians will integrate in East Africa and cease to be identified as 'a problem' will largely depend on the activities of the Asians themselves. But, it will also depend on the lead provided by the African majorities. The differences between the Asians and the Africans may lessen by the emergence of common social and economic interests. But, whether the convergence of interests (for example, trade union interests) will result in cooperation or heightened competition and tension remains to be seen.

The instrumental factor here would be the attitude of the African majorities towards the racial minority. Thinking with the race, as the Nazi thinking with blood, may sometimes prove stronger than thinking in terms of economic class. In the United States, for instance, racial prejudice in the form of 'lily-white unionism' has proved stronger than the Marxist myth of class solidarity. Here, therefore, one needs to ask how African socialism would be defined, and what place a racial minority would have in it.

It is obvious that if the term is defined purely in racial terms, then the Asian community of East Africa would for ever be alienated, since it is not easy to change one's racial pigment. Then the Asian 'problem' would continue to persist, almost by definition. If there is some accommodation for the Asians in African socialism, as indeed the thinking of present African leaders indicates, then it would considerably facilitate, the eventual integration of the meagre 2 per cent Asian minority in the tasks of nation-building. And the task of nation building involves for the Asians not only their traditional functions of saving and capital accumulation for economic development, but also and importantly, helping the governments of the three countries to fill the historical gap of racial imbalance left since the colonial days. The Asians must co-operate, for instance, in credit societies, co-operative schemes and so on, and must open up their businesses to participation by the Africans. They must, in other words, consciously and actively break all forms of racial barriers even if admittedly this is easier said than done. More cannot be recommended for the subject falls out of the scope of this paper.

Conclusion

In concluding this study let us briefly address ourselves to three evaluative questions. First: how much credit should the Asians deserve for the ultimate independence of Kenya, Uganda and Tanzania? The answer, from what we have observed above, must be: very little. And it could not have been otherwise. The Asians had little or no sanctions even to support their demands for equality with the Europeans—any premature agitation for independence on their part might not only have fallen through but possibly even been misunderstood. Demands for independence became politically consequential only when the Africans made them. The Asians might have joined the freedom movement much more actively than they actually did for although officially the Asians consistently favoured constitutional progress towards self-government, the were not nearly as their African brothers, and the great majority of them had mental reservations about independence that must have neutralised the impact of their public policy. There were, of course, some who did in fact whole-heartedly join with the Africans, but these were few and far between. In any event, the credit for the independence of East Africa must unmistakably go to the African freedom movements, and, what is often not realised, to the wind of change that swept the continent following the Second World War.

The second question we may ask ourselves is: how much were the Asians an obstruction in the march towards independence? Again the answer must be: very little. It was not so much the case of the Asians determining or even influencing the pace towards independence, as the fact of oncoming independence influencing Asian behaviour. The Asians were no more than a straw in the political wind: they were not so much blowing the wind, as were being blown about. It is true that there were some reactionaries among the Asians, but they were for a large part ineffectual. It is also a true that the presence of an Asian minority had introduced tricky constitutional problems—on the question of, for instance, reserved seats, or the controversy between common roll and communal roll—but these problems were more a worry of the Asians themselves, rather than of the whole country. They had to adjust themselves to the situation of impending independence, and how best to do it was their problem.

Finally, the question: what impact are the Asians likely to make on the politics of East Africa in future? The answer is about the same: hardly any. Politically, they are impotent. This does not mean that there will not be political consequences of the fact that they still largely control the distributive side of the economy, and that they constitute an easily identifiable and relatively prosperous racial minority. What it means is that, as a community, they cannot influence the nature of the regimes that will come into power, and the kind of political-constitutional changes that may come about in East Africa. They would do well to face this reality, and to identify themselves with African aspirations, for these are very reasonable aspirations in the context of modern international relations.

NOTES AND REFERENCES

1. The Indian Government, for instance, seldom took up matters on a diplomatic level, so that the influence of India in East Africa was much less after her independence than before, for at least before, the British Raj in India was a little sensitive to the effects British laws in East Africa might have on the sentiments of their subject-race in India, e.g., on the question of immigration.
2. George Bennett and Carl Rosberg in their book *The Kenyatta Elections, Kenya, 1960-1961* (O.U.P., 1961) give a good account of Asian communal elections in Kenya. See specially p. 115-116 where they write: 'However much leaders may proclaim that it must and should end, all Asian elections in Kenya in the past... have been dominated by communalism. The first document noticed on many an Asian candidate's desk, and the first subject of conversation with the agent of any candidate, was the breakdown of the voters' roll by communities.... It always remained remarkable how Asian candidates carried the exact figures of voters of each community in their head so that they could, often most accurately, foretell the results.'
3. Although, members of KFP stood in the elections as "independents' rather than on any party 'tickets.'

7

EDUCATIONAL ROLE OF THE INDIAN DIASPORA

Development of Education in the Indian Immigrant Community

Although, the educational systems which have come into being in the three East African countries share many features in common, they also inevitably reflect circumstances peculiar to each country. That is as true of the educational systems as a whole, as of the racial segments into which they have hitherto been divided. In Asian education, this is most apparent in the extent to which educational facilities are provided by the governments, on the one hand, and by aided and unaided schools, on the other.

Government's Contribution to Education

Thus, in Tanganyika, Asian education developed on a community basis, with little aid from the government until comparatively recently. Even now most of the educational facilities are provided by aided schools in primary and secondary education. That is less true of Uganda, where the government assumed increasing responsibility, at least for secondary education, since 1932. In Kenya, a much larger proportion of the children are educated in government schools.

No more can be done here than to suggest some of the factors which must be considered in accounting for these differences; but even an enumeration of these factors gives some indication of the pressures which have shaped educational policy. One major factor is the difference in the public policies which guided the administrations in the pre-independence period. In Tanganyika, the principle that non-African education was to be organised and financed primarily the two main races concerned was enunciated early by the United Kingdom as the mandatory power. In contrast, there was a much earlier assumption of responsibility for the education of the immigrant communities in Kenya, a "Crown Colony' since 1920; the Education Department was founded in 1911 (in Uganda, only in 1925, while Tanganyika had its first Director of Education in 1920). Besides differences in public policies, account must be taken of the pressure from the Asians for expansion of education and greater financial commitment from the government. Such pressure appears to have been greater in Kenya, where education was for many decades a key issue in Asian political agitation. Since the Asian population of Kenya is almost equal to that of the two other territories combined, the strength of numbers has given a special edge and intensity to the demand.

But, there are other factors which demand equal consideration. In Uganda and Tanganyika, there has tended to be a greater predominance of the trading and self-employed in the Asian occupational structure; as will be suggested below, there has been less appreciation of education beyond literacy among these groups until recent decades. In Kenya, employment in the public sector has been more important for Asians than in the two neighbouring territories, and a correspondingly greater appreciation of the importance of education for such employment is to be expected. Finally, the style of Asian politics which developed in the three countries must not be ignored. In Kenya, the reaction against the political activities of the powerful settler minority led to the early organisation of an Asian political movement, which was able to act as a sounding-board and a pressure-group for Asian needs, in education as in other fields.

At the beginning of the century, when there were probably about 40,000 Asians in East Africa, there was little government provision for Asian education. The first Asian school in Kenya was one established by the Uganda Railway Authority, and it was taken over by the government in 1912. In Tanganyika, a small school for Asians was started after the First World War, without government assistance. A number of private schools came into existence in Uganda by 1920. Greater educational activity, private as well as governmental, became more marked in the 1920s, and it may be remarked that large-scale Asian immigration into East Africa &me in the later half of that decade.

In 1925, a small grant-in-aid was given to three Asian schools by the Uganda Government for the first time, although such expenditure amounted to only £2,500 by 1930. In Tanganyika, there were 24 Asian schools with 1,731 pupils by 1928, all entirely built and supported by the community. After 1929, the government assumed increasing responsibility, while reaffirming its policy that the administration and financing of non-African education was primarily the function of the two races. As a result of the continuation of this policy, a different pattern has emerged, as compared with the two other countries. In 1948, general control over Asian education was handed over to an Indian Education Authority (there is similar provision for the European community); and Asian education was financed in part from a special tax levied on the Asians. The contrast is visible, above all, in the predominance of the aided schools, which account for nearly two thirds of the primary school students today; in Uganda, the aided and unaided schools include three fifths, and in Kenya about half the primary school students.

The aided schools point to an important characteristic of the educational system: the continued existence of privately-organised schools which supplement (and in Uganda and Tanganyika preceded) the facilities offered by government schools. Many of these schools are operated by Asian sub-communities. In Tanganyika in 1959, for example, there were reported to be 51 Indian Public Schools, 54 Aga Khan Schools, and 16 schools associated with other communities. In 1952, in Uganda, there were 77 primary aided schools, of which 41 were Indian Public Schools, 31 Aga Khan Schools, and five 'government-controlled' (a category brought in to solve dissensions following the partition of the Indian subcontinent).

Role of Religions Organisation in Asian Education

Organisation of educational facilities on a communal basis can be paralleled by organisation of other social services on similar lines among the Asians. The pattern of immigration, whereby early arrivals attracted relations and neighbours to the land of their adoption; the paucity of government provision for social services in a newly-settled country; concentration in a small number of urban centres which brought together large numbers of each sub-community these strengthened organisation on communal lines among the Asians.

Religions organisation has been specially important in the ' education of girls. In Kenya, education is compulsory only for boys between the ages of 7 and 15 in Nairobi, Mombasa and Kisumu; but it is estimated that probably 90 per cent of boys and girls of school-going age attend school. But, in 1960, only 30 per cent of the girls receiving primary education were in government schools, compared with 68 per cent of the boys. In Tanganyika, in 1958, 14 per cent of the girls were in government schools, compared with 27 per cent of the boys. The differences are smaller in Uganda: 19 per cent of the girls, and 25 per cent of the boys, in 1960. These figures show that Asian girls have tended to be educated, at the primary level, in aided (and, therefore, often sub-communal) schools for the most part.

In the development of Asian education, it seems likely that it was primary education which was the main concern of the trading section in the beginning. Literacy and reckoning seemed sufficient, and the cost of maintaining a son at school when he could be contributing to the family income in trade made secondary education appear a luxury. It was the civil servant family, conscious of the range of bureaucratic jobs opened by further schooling, which was more concerned to agitate for improved and extensive secondary education. However, there was a growing diffusion of awareness about the importance of secondary education, especially after the Second World War. Such diffusion may show variations by territory: it may be significant that the educational reports for Uganda and Tanganyika have continued to voice complaints, even into the 1950s, about the wastage of Asian students in the secondary standards, through their being absorbed into commerce; the great dearth of candidates for teacher training from these countries has also been explained by reference to the superior attraction of commerce.

However, as the Asian and European settlements in East Africa have ceased to be enclaves in an alien land, and developed into increasingly modern and sophisticated societies, so *pari passu* has come a multiplication of roles and functions which could only be performed by those who have at least received secondary schooling. The changing nature and complexity of trade and industry have tended to make the business community as conscious as the 'service' section of the need for a higher level of educational facilities in general.

The increasingly articulated demand for more secondary education has reflected the more complex skills demanded by a developing society. It was accompanied by greater appreciation of professional and university education. The absence of local higher educational institutions and the scarcity of professional skills has meant Higher rewards and social prestige for professional men. In addition, although economic power has remained in the commercial and industrial section, leadership has tended to gravitate to professional men, whether in sub-communal affairs, or in legislative bodies.

Since the end of the Second World War, the economic prosperity of the war years, together with more generous government provision for scholarships and bursaries, led to a growing stream of Asian students going overseas for higher education. In 1945, there were 19 Kenya students studying abroad with government bursaries, of whom 11 were Asian; by 1960, there were an estimated 2,500 Kenya students abroad, of whom nearly half were Asian. Since 1956, the creation of local institution of higher education has attracted growing numbers of Asian students.

In concluding this brief survey of the development of Asian education, some remarks may be addressed to the role of education in promoting social change. The 'unintended consequences' of a western-oriented educational system upon a traditional culture, threatened with disintegration in an alien environment, constitute an important aspect of social change in East Africa. Almost within a generation, the Asian population has been wrenched from a traditional society, and has turned its sights to a western-oriented one. Education has played a key role in the transition. Any inquiry, for example, into the extent of change from the joint family to the nuclear family, with its profound social consequences, must devote attention to the impact of education, and especially of the education of girls.

It would, however, be misleading to see education as the sole mover in the transition from a traditional to a western-oriented society. In East Africa, we must consider also the urban setting of Asian settlement, exerting its influence as a forcing-house of change; the weakening of the authority of the parental culture, and the values it enshrines, because of the absence of any dense network of kinship bonds extending beyond the first generation; and, in Kenya, European settlers, small in numbers, but setting the tone of the whole society, and constituting the core of the economic and administrative structure. Given such a setting, education is one among a set of factors which can initiate a whole series of far-reaching changes in goals and values, and lead over time to important modifications in the social structure and cultural system.

Present System of Education

In 1947, an official inquiry into Asian education in East Africa was conducted by Mr. A. A. Kazimi, an eminent Indian educationist. The main conclusions of the Kazimi Report provide a convenient point of departure for analysing the present state of Asian education. These were:

1. Due to the cessation of building during the war and a continuing increase in population, all schools were overcrowded: There is terrible overcrowding even in the Government schools necessitating the practice of allowing children of certain age limits to attend school only hours a day.... The real need is for schools and more schools.'

2. The quality of the teaching staff was poor. In Kenya, only one third of the teachers in government service had a degree or any professional qualifications. Conditions were worse in aided schools. Out of 213 teachers in aided schools only 54 were matriculates, while 123 were non-matriculates. Teaching was 'poor, unimaginative and unpractical.'
3. The courses of study were too literary and the pupils had little opportunity to use their hands. The Cambridge School Certificate examination dominated everything. There was an urgent need for some provision for technical education.
4. Opportunities for higher education were very restricted. There were no local institutions of higher education. At the same time, admission to universities in the United Kingdom was barred, since the Asian schools did not provide 'advanced level' courses.

The Kazimi Report dealt with a situation which had been greatly aggravated by war time difficulties. In the years that have followed, there have been improvements over the whole range of problems mentioned above; but that does not deprive them of their significance as the points of greatest strain within the Asian educational system.

Overcrowding has continued to be a serious problem. The primary and secondary school population increased very fast in the decade 1948-58, although there has been some decline in primary school numbers since 1960 in all the three territories. The number of Asian students attending primary schools in Uganda more than doubled (109.6 per cent) in the seven years 1948-55, followed by a much slower increase of 4.36 per cent per annum between 1955-61. In Kenya, there was an increase of 77.3 per cent, between 1948-58; it had dropped to four-fifth per cent per annum between 1958-52. It Tanganyika there was an 85.2 per cent increase during 1948-58, followed by a decline from 1959. In secondary school, there was an increase of 237.2 per cent in Kenya (including a spectacular increase of 131.6 per cent between 1948 and 1949) between 1948-53, and of 96.2 per cent in Tanganyika over the same period. In Uganda, there was an increase of 240 per cent between 1948-55, followed by a slower one, 100.8 per cent, between 1955-61. Comparable figures for the other two territories were: Kenya 198.4 per cent between 1953-62; Tanganyika, 147.1 per cent between 1953-61.

Coping with an expansion of such a magnitude demanded a massive programme of building, recruitment and training; but the response of the governments concerned proved slow and inadequate. In Kenya, the Development Committee in 1946 had suggested a five-year scheme to expand schools and teacher training centres. The rapid increase in the school population, the rise in price levels, and increases in teachers' salaries rendered the original estimates out of date very soon. Buildings remained greatly overcrowded, classes were very large. A great many unqualified teachers had to be recruited, and a double-shift system was operated. It proved possible to abolish the double-shift system in Uganda by 1954; in Kenya it continued into the late fifties. The colonial government drew criticism from Asian representatives for allocating an unfair share of the revenue (proportionate to their tax burden) to the European community, while making grossly inadequate provision for the Asians. Suspicions were expressed that the results of the Kenya Preliminary Examination were deliberately 'doctored' so as to restrict the number of passes and, thus, access to secondary education to the Asian students.

In teacher training, Kenya gave a lead which was later followed by the other territories. In the past, the majority of teachers were recruited from India and Pakistan. It was gradually realised that East Africa must aim at self-sufficiency, at least as far as primary school teachers were concerned. It was necessary to establish institutions to provide teachers' training, and to supplement them by grants to students to enable them to qualify in the United Kingdom as secondary school teachers. In January 1949, an Asian men teachers' centre was opened at Nairobi, which was followed by a women teachers' training centre three years later. Neither could claim much initial success, and the main reason was undoubtedly the unattractiveness of teachers' salaries. Men teachers had to balance their choice against greater rewards and opportunities in commerce and industry. A significant number of Asian women had entered employment since the war; but in teaching they were entitled only to four fifths of the salary of male teachers in the corresponding scale. There were only 12 second-year students in the men teachers' centre by 1951, and no more than 16 girls had completed a two-year course at their centre.

Numbers improved steadily with the raising of teachers' salaries on the recommendation of the Lidbury Commission of 1954. Only one third of the teachers in government and aided Asian schools in 1954 had received any professional training; by 1957 nearly half the teachers were trained. In 1962, the three training colleges in Kenya had 261 students (65 men and 196 women).

Up to the end of 1958, there were no teachers' training facilities for Asians in Tanganyika. Students who had obtained a School Certificate were sent to the colleges in Kenya, the costs of the training being met from the Tanganyika Education Fund: for example, there were 11 students in 1958, who completed their training the following year. In March 1959, a college was opened in Dar es Salaam and 20 young men and women admitted for a two-year course for primary school teachers.

Uganda, like Tanganyika, has experienced difficulties in attracting sufficient local Asians into teaching. In 1954, 16 completed the first year of a two-year teachers' training course at the Kampala Teachers' Training College; 26 were trained by 1956. The Education Department complained in 1957 that the output of Asian teachers' training was 'very far' from providing the numbers required. The 1959 Report, noting that there had been a 130 per cent increase in the Asian primary school population since 1952, declared bluntly: 'Any further expansion will depend on a more buoyant national income and the willingness of many more young Asians to train for the teaching profession.'

The efforts of the three territories to increase the proportion of qualified teachers can be traced through the years by an analysis of the relevant statistics:

Kenya	1950	1955	1960
With university degrees	20.7	31	33
Completed secondary schooling	49.6	47	46.8
Without secondary schooling	29.7	22	20.2

Excluding those with university degrees, untrained teachers were 73.5 per cent of all teachers in 1950, and 62.9 per cent in 1955; but the figure had dropped to 46.5 per cent in 1960.

Tanganyika	1951	1956	1961
With university degrees	25.1	35.1	42.9
Completed secondary schooling	35.7	44.7	46.8
Without secondary schooling	39.2	20.2	10.3

Excluding the first category, untrained teachers were 70 per cent of all teachers in 1951, 65.4 per cent in 1956, and 46 per cent in 1961.

Uganda	1955	1960
With university degrees	49.8	38.0
Completed secondary schooling	25.2	53.1
Without secondary schooling	25	8.9

Again, excluding the first category, untrained teachers were 56.6 per cent of all teachers in 1955; they had only dropped to 52.51 in 1960.

The Kazimi Report drew attention to the neglect of technical training, and greater provision has been made, especially in Kenya, over the years. In 1949, a purely communal institution, the Mombasa Institution of Muslim Education, was established to provide technical and trade education, and it had 103 students by the end of 1953. By 1954 there were two Asian technical high schools, in Nairobi and Mombasa, with 725 students. A landmark in the provision of technical education was the opening of the Kenya Polytechnic in 1961, for students in employment who usually attend one day plus one evening per week. It includes courses in science, engineering, building, commerce and domestic science. Asians formed 33.7 per cent of its students in June

1962. In addition, the two technical high schools had an enrolment of 1935 by June 1960. There has been a Technical Institute in Dar es Salaam since 1958, and an expanding institute in Kampala.

Opportunities for higher education were greatly restricted in 1947, and the lack of post-secondary education at the schools limited the number of students able to fulfil the minimum entrance requirements of English universities. These opportunities have expanded since then due to *(a)* provision for post-secondary education; (b) government loans and bursaries for higher education; and (c) the growth of a University of East Africa, with constituent colleges in the three territories.

The first post-secondary classes in Kenya began at the Prince of Wales School in Nairobi. Kazimi had suggested that the school, which was exclusively European, should permit some Asian students to take advantage of these facilities; but the suggestion was anathema to the European community of those days. The only other solution was that of starting post-secondary classes at the Asian schools; not until 1951 were such classes started at the Government Asian School in Nairobi. Owing to the lack of hostels, students from outside Nairobi were unable to make full use of the opportunity until the end of the 1950s.

The programme of bursaries and loans against securities was expanded. In 1949, the Kenya Government awarded bursaries and scholarships to the value of £2,820; the amount had risen to £8,610 in 1960. The figures below illustrate the growth of loans and bursaries, and their distribution among the three races:

	Number of Government Bursaries held			**Expenditure**		
	1960	*1960/61*	*1961/2*	*1960*	*1960/61*	*1961/62*
Europeans	53	56	53	£8,941	9,330	10,413
Asians	62	75	80	£8,610	9,925	11,225
Africans	28	34	40	£16,505	26,390	30.085

Number of Loans for Higher Education Overseas

	1960	*1961*	*1962*
Europeans	29	33	35
Asians	63	77	72
Africans	32	35	46

There was a small provision in Tanganyika for bursaries. The triennial survey for 1955-57 reported that there were 185 Asian students in the United Kingdom, but only nine of them were in receipt of government bursaries. From Uganda, in the same year, there were 41 Asian bursars in the United Kingdom and 12 in India.

Local facilities for higher education have developed gradually. Makerere, the first institution of university status in East Africa did not attract many Asian students, probably because in its earlier stages it was meant exclusively for Africans. A report in 1952 pointed out that 'a small quota at Makerere College is available for non-Africans, but so far, very few of them have been taken up. The Asian population, therefore, relies almost entirely for higher education on universities in India and Pakistan and the United Kingdom.

Need for Higher Education

The need for a university college for all races was fully realised by the Asians, and the Kenya Asian community decided to build such a college in memory of the great Indian leader, Mahatma Gandhi. The arduous task of raising the large funds required for the purpose was undertaken by an Indian scholar. Dr. Yagnik. Meanwhile, in 1953, the Kenya Government formed an Advisory Council for Higher Education, and it was decided that the proposed Royal Technical College in Nairobi would function on a non-racial basis. The Gandhi Memorial Academy Committee thereupon decided to merge its plans into those for the new college and transferred the substantial funds it had collected to the college. As a result, the Gandhi Memorial Academy came to be incorporated with the Royal Technical College, which admitted its first students in 1956. Of the 157 Kenya students in that year, 94 were Asian, 57 African and 6 European. By 1960, the number of

Asian students from Kenya was 106. The college is now known as the University College, Nairobi, and, together with Makerere College, Kampala, and the University College, Dar es Salaam, forms part of the new University of East Africa.

The establishment of the University of East Africa has given a greater number of Asian students, in common with students of other races, access to higher education. But, it is to be expected that the majority of those seeking higher education will continue to make the United Kingdom and India and Pakistan their destinations. The relative unimportance of local institutions, as compared with those abroad, is shown by some recent figures for Asian students from Kenya and Tanganyika:

Asian Higher Education

	U.K.	*Indian and Pakistan*	*Makerere*	*Nairobi*	*Others*
Kenya					
1960/61	847	520	31	92	30
1961/62	905	800	37	87	44
Tanganyika					
1960/61	394	4	16	22	14
1961/62	477	6	20	28	18

Future Prospects of Asian Education

With the coming of independence to East Africa, many new problems have arisen in the field of Asian education; and most of the old problems remain.[1] For the Asian community the need to acquire education has increased just as the opportunities to acquire education are diminishing. Asian survival to some extent is contingent on the attainment of high technical skills. Employment at the semi-skilled or clerical level will be difficult; nor is it likely that in the future many youngsters will be absorbed in family business and shops. On the other hand, the needs of the countries for skilled manpower is unlikely to be met from Africans locally, and qualified Asians not only should have no difficulty in finding employment, but could also very significantly and positively help in the development of these countries.

There is and there may for some time continue to be, a prejudice in government and big foreign commercial firms against Asians, even though they possess the requisite qualifications. But, the world scarcity of skilled manpower and the inability of the economies to support a large expatriate staff may mitigate this prejudice. Moreover, even if these qualified Asians do not find acceptance in East Africa, it would be quite easy for them to move to other parts of the world where their services are in demand. It is, therefore, vital for the Asians that they acquire high educational qualifications, especially of a technological kind.

The control of education is primarily in the hands of the governments, and in this sense the future of the Asians is also in the hands of the governments. If the governments adopt policies which discriminate against the Asian school children and effectively reduce their opportunities for education, the future for the Asians will be terribly bleak. In the past the Asians had more favourable educational opportunities than Africans. The educational systems were organised on a racial basis, with well-nigh total segregation.

One of the most exciting challenges of independence is the integration of the educational system. Educational policies in future should no longer be tied merely to communal needs and circumstances, but should be based on the best interest of the country as a whole. Henceforth there should be no such thing as 'European Education', 'Asian Education, 'African Education', 'Arab Education'. In this process of integration, Asian advantages *vis-a-vis* the Africans must disappear. In Kenya, for example, education for Asian boys was compulsory in the urban areas between the age of 7 and 15; but this was repealed in 1963, as an instance of discriminatory practice since no such rule applied to the Africans. Also, till recently most Asian children who had obtained primary schooling could go on to the secondary school, whereas in the African educational system there was a serious bottleneck between primary and secondary schools. Integration of secondary schools will mean a re-allocation of secondary school places, and the Asian share must diminish. Asian share will diminish even if entry to the secondary schools is made competitive on an academic basis; but it is clear that the governments will introduce other kinds of control as well on Asian children.

In Tanganyika, for example, quotas are prescribed for secondary schools and an Asian child (who may be a citizen) has greater difficulties than an African child. Conditions for non-citizens are even more stringent. The result of this would be growing illiteracy among the Asians,[2] with all its consequences, or a massive effort on the part of the community to provide supplemental educational facilities. There is already among the sections of the Asian community a tradition of communal education institutions. There is no reason why this tradition should not be broadened and a collective Asian effort not be made to provide schools and scholarships. Obviously these facilities cannot be made exclusive to Asians, but a great proportion of them ought to benefit. The Asian community of East Africa has always set great store by education, and has sacrificed much so that their children might go to schools and colleges. Now, in these difficult times, they ought again to concentrate their resources on providing facilities for education.

Another range of problems is connected with higher education. In the period which immediately preceded independence, and in that following independence, 'crash-programmes' of scholarships from overseas countries have resulted in a large number of African students going abroad for higher education. The large intake in African primary schools in recent years will result in a 'bulge' in the secondary schools, and a great pressure on higher education, in future. The competition for limited places in university colleges and polytechnics in East Africa may, therefore, be expected to affect Asians increasingly in future. Thus, there are likely to be difficulties in securing admission to local institutions just when the ability of parents to finance overseas education may be decreasing.

Asian students going abroad for higher education in the period just after the Second World War tended at first to concentrate on a narrow range of subjects, specially law and medicine; later more students chose such subjects as architecture, pharmacy, optics and accountancy. At present, there is a sharp contraction in the number of those choosing law and architecture, while probably medicine, science degrees, and, especially, engineering show an expansion. The changes show the responsiveness of educational choice to the changing occupational opportunities in East Africa. In future, the choices of Asian students will obviously have to conform much more closely to the needs of developing East Africa.

Another result of the shortage of school places will be the growth of private schools. By private schools is meant those schools which have no government aid. If a school obtains any aid from the government, then it becomes liable to be ordered by the governments, and in Tanzania communal schools which receive some assistance from the government have to accept government instructions about the intake of students according to race. But, private schools have so far been free from this kind of control. The private schools have a very definite function to perform, but there are some dangers that need to be guarded against. There is the danger, for example, that these schools might become purely commercial enterprises in which educational aims are subordinated to the urge to maximise profits. Staffing will be a problem, and poor quality teaching is all too likely. There will be the temptation to admit a larger number of students than the school can cope with. Overcrowding and inadequate facilities will be the result. Thus, while the need for private schools exists, a great effort is needed to ensure proper standards, honesty and absence of exploitation; it may become necessary to take these schools out of commercial hands; and increasing government control might also become inevitable.

Other important consequences of integration of schools should be noted. The scarcity of secondary school places will result in some Asian families emigrating from East Africa if their children cannot get education here; the beginnings of this trend are already obvious. However, by far the most important consequence of integration will be on race relations. It is at this stage difficult to say what the effects will be, since integration has only just begun, but certain predictions might be made from experience elsewhere. Integrated education ought to lead to greater racial understanding; interracial friendships might grow before there is time for race consciousness and prejudice to emerge. Social contacts between the parents may not increase very much, but some African children will have access to Asian homes and *vice versa*. This could be the turning of the tide.

The integration of schools will be accompanied by some revision of the syllabus. Swahili is now compulsory in Kenya and Tanzania for all children. This fact is extremely important for purposes of social integration; language has been to some extent a barrier in the past; Swahili is becoming the national language and a pride in its use, obvious. Were the Asians to continue to display an ignorance of Swahili, they would give additional cause for suspicion and non-acceptance, and effectively reduce for themselves opportunities in government and private service. With the rise of Swahili, there is bound to be the decline of the Indian languages. This in turn will have an impact on social and cultural structure of the Asians and make social integration more possible. Even though all the governments are pledged to the principle of religious instruction, a certain amount of secularisation is inevitable; this again is relevant for Asian attitudes and behaviour.

Education is crucial not only for the Asians but for everyone else in the countries as well, for the goals of nation-building and quick economic and social development which these countries have set for themselves. Already various studies have been made to estimate the manpower requirements, especially among the high-and middle-grade personnel, entailed by the growth-rate targets.

The educational implications of these plans may be illustrated by the development plan for Kenya, which covers the period from 1964 to 1970. Basing itself on the Hunter Report of 1963, it estimates that 103,000 highly-trained people would be needed by 1971, assuming a 'normal' rate of growth. The figure would represent an increase of 45,000 over those similarly employed in 1961, as well as another 22,000 to replace those retiring or emigrating. Of the needed personnel, it is proposed to train 60,000 in Kenya. The magnitude of the expansion involved is shown by the fact that it would mean two and a half times as many Form IV school-leavers in 1970 as there were in 1963. The plan states that the government 'accepts as a second major objective in the resources field the rapid expansion of secondary level education, the assurance of university places to qualified students and the provision of managerial and technical training and increased opportunities in commerce, industry and agriculture'.

On this level, the Asian role in the educational systems of East Africa is likely to increase There is an acute shortage of teachers, especially at the secondary school levels. The attractions for qualified Africans in the non-teaching professions are too handsome, and these pose a real problem in recruiting graduate African teachers. More and more Asian graduates, on the other hand, are doing into the teaching profession. With the integration of not only the students but also the staff, increasing numbers of Asian teachers will be teaching African students—hitherto an unknown phenomenon. Africans have great respect for teachers, and it is possible that the Asian effort in the education process will help improve their image. Teaching may become the key role of the Asians. Also, the new Asian teachers will be local Asians, unlike the former generation of Asian teachers who were recruited from India and Pakistan. These new teachers are fully aware of the race tensions and Asian dilemmas; most of them are sympathetic to the cause of African progress. Theirs is a challenging task, and their opportunities are considerable.

NOTES AND REFERENCES

1. The problems which continue to overshadow Asian education in East Africa are those which the Kazimi Report noted two decades ago: overcrowding, with its attendant evils of large classes and lack of individual attention; financial limitations on building, and on training and staffing; selection procedures for secondary education, especially the K.P.E. in Kenya.
2. In the new context, the problem of Asian students who fail to enter secondary schools is part of the larger problem of *all* students who fail to do so, since the aim must be that of making best use of the human potential they provide. The difficulties which can arise in developing a common policy are shown by an

example from Uganda. There it was decided some years ago that post-primary schools should be established for such students to train them in agriculture, through rural farm and trade schools. As land is not available for Asians, such schools could not meet their needs. The Uganda Education Report for 1957 commented that, apart from those whose parents were able to provide professional training overseas, the rest of the Asian students went into trade, or such occupations as untrained motor mechanics, neglecting assistant-level job training in various government departments, and the training provided by the technical schools now open to all races.

8

CASTE, RELIGION AND THE INDIAN DIASPORA

Gujarat, the place of origin of most Indians in Uganda, is preeminently a land of, castes, and in no other part of India are the sub-divisions so minute. Although, both Hindus and Muslims took their traditional divisions with them to Africa, their significance was greatly altered, and nowhere was a traditional caste system set up. Some of the reasons for this lie in the nature of the system itself.

The English word caste has no exact counterpart in Gujarati or other Indian languages.[1] The traditional five-fold division of Hindu society into Brahmin or priestly castes, Kshatriya or warrior castes, Vaisya or merchant castes, Sudra or cultivating and servant castes, and Untouchable castes is known in India as the *varna* or colour system. Each division is associated with a symbolic colour, and the Brahmin, Kshatriya, and Vaisya are called the white or twice-born castes in contrast with the Sudra or black castes who are excluded from ritual privileges belonging to the twice-born. The Untouchables are thought to be altogether outside the system.

In this sense, the caste system is of great antiquity; and the details of its proper arrangement in a hierarchy, with the Brahmin as the highest ideal of human life, possessing the greatest amount of sanctity, supported by warriors and merchants, each respectively less honourable, and all dependent in their turn on one another and on the humbler work of the cultivating and servant castes, have been worked out for centuries in the mythological, philosophical and theological works of Sanskrit literature. These are revered in all parts of India and provide an ideal of proper behaviour for Hindus everywhere.

If, in contrast with this view, caste is considered not as an historical arrangement of *varna or* as a traditional ideal, but is examined as an aspect of the actual social system in any district in India, then he real unit of the caste system is not one of the five *varnas, but jati,* which are very small endogamous groups practising a traditional occupation and enjoying a certain amount of cultural, ritual, and judicial autonomy'.[2] The number of *jati* in the whole of India is very large, and it has been estimated that there must be about two thousand in each linguistic area.[3] They themselves are often sub-divided into yet smaller exclusive groups by locality, occupation, eating and drinking regulations, and rules of marriage. The hierarchy of groups which prevails in a district is a balance of many factors which is unlikely to be the same even in adjacent localities.

In any district of India it is the local arrangement of sub-castes and the systematic relations of inter-dependence of *a jati* group with the others above or below it which matter in the daily lives of the inhabitants. Except for those who are indisputably Brahmins or Untouchables, people may even be uncertain of the *varna* to which their *jati* belongs; and the *varna* classification often acts as no more than an ideological scheme which cuts across the many local caste systems of India, and which, therefore, allows a stranger in a district to relate himself roughly to the local hierarchy.[4] In Africa *varna* does not even serve this purpose, for there are no local hierarchies, and it is only on his return to India with sufficient wealth and influence to improve the ranking of his whole *jati* that an immigrant, in an attempt to raise his own personal position, is at all likely to concern himself with *varna.*

Caste categories, comprising people of the same *jati* name in a number of local hierarchies also appear to have had few functions. Indeed *jati* (local sub-castes) with the same name might be differently ranked in neighbouring hierarchies. Often the only common feature in a caste category (besides its common name) was a belief that all its members had a common origin.[5]

Caste System

The caste system has been described and defined in many ways, though attention has mainly been directed to the separate castes and their attributes rather than to their place in a system of economic, political and ritual relations. For Hutton, a caste was an endogamous group, often with an ascribed occupation, and ranked in a hierarchy.[6] A man was born into a caste, and unless expelled from it he could not alter his status. His relations with people in *jati* above or below him were regulated by the idea of pollution. He could pollute or be polluted by contact with someone of another caste in eating or drinking, in ritual, in sexual or other contexts. Brahmins were most susceptible to pollution; and, following the Brahmins' view of the matter, Western writers have usually considered them to be the keystone of the caste system.

Hocart, also following Hindu views, regarded the ascription of occupations to castes as perhaps their most important feature, and looked on it as a division of both sacred and profane labour, the ideal model of which was provided by a king's court. Priests, scribes, soldiers, goldsmiths, barbers, washermen and so forth were as much needed in a village as in a palace; and their relations were, therefore, best considered 'as a degradation of the royal style'.[7] In village life in many parts of India grandiloquent titles reflecting this/style' are commonly applied to people of the humblest castes.[8] It should be noted, however, that though a man born into a potter sub-caste, for example, had the right to practise that occupation, he might not choose to do so; but whether he did or did not, he and his fellow members had the right to exclude anybody else from practising it.

The justification of this division of labour is both legendary and religious. The sage Manu, who is said to have founded the system, wrote that the castes were like the parts of the body, all of which are essential for a healthy life.[9] In the belief of orthodox Hindus a man is born into a particular *jati* and *varna* because, according to the doctrines of *karma*, his birth is the reward or punishment for observing or failing to observe the moral rules *(dharma)* of *his jati* and *varna* in a previous life. A man reaps as he sows, and his condition in this life is the measure of his moral progress and his standing with supernatural powers. Any attempt to alter his status can only lead to dangerous ritual impropriety: to maintain the caste system is, therefore, a moral and a religious duty.

It follows from this belief that *jati* must be ranked in a hierarchy of *varna* categories in which the Brahmins, who are closest to the sphere of the sacred, and who ought to devote their lives to ritual propriety, necessarily have the highest place; in which Untouchables, who are furthest from the divine, and who are, therefore, allotted the most polluting and ritually damaging occupations, consequently have the lowest prestige. Every *jati* is distinct, and its peculiar rights and duties are complementary to and not competitive with those of all *other jati*.[10] A caste system, then, is one of a division of labour from which the element of competition in economic, political, and ritual relations has largely been excluded.[11] For socio logical analysis the inter-dependence of *jati* is more fundamental than the cultural details of their separateness and arrangement in an order of rank.

In East Africa, the economic and political system in which the immigrants lived did not permit the complementary, uncompetitive division of social labour characteristic of and essential to a caste system. The communities which they formed on the basis of caste or caste categories were always in competition with one another. By organising *jati* as competitive communities, the immigrants were acting against the principles of caste.

Empirically, society in India was made up of many small-scale hierarchies of *jati* each of which was a self-contained system. In them relations tended to be multiple, in that two individuals very frequently filled a number of roles in relationship to one another, whether they were of the same caste or not. A landlord might, for example, own some of a peasant's land. He might also be his political and economic patron, and, because of the caste system, be at the same time in a special ritual or service relationship with his tenant. Summation' or evolution' of roles of this kind is characteristic of small-scale and not large-scale societies.[12] In India the immense numbers of separate caste systems were all small enough and the roles in them sufficiently well defined for individuals in them to know enough about one another to make sure that nobody went beyond the limits of what was allowed. *Some jati* regulated the behaviour of their members by a council; others, like the Patidar sub-caste of Gujarat, relied on a close-knit system of marriage alliances to ensure proper behaviour. The Patidar, too, like other *jati* in Gujarat, frequently entertained one another at feasts of different kinds, and thus ensured conformity to the rules of the caste on pain of exclusion, not merely from entertainments, but from other more important forms of cooperation.[13]

Ideally, the ranking of *jati* was immutable and no individual could move from one sub-caste to another. In fact the arrangement of sub-castes was sometimes altered, but the change was in the status of the whole group and not of individuals. For the members of a sub-caste to improve its standing they had either to persuade all the other members to become stricter Hindus and follow the local Brahmin ideals more closely, or they had to separate themselves from those who refused to conform and become a new *jati* with a higher ranking because its behaviour was more orthodox. Another method of improving a sub-caste's position was for its members, either through wealth or political adroitness, to ingratiate themselves with the rulers of the secular state in which they lived. The wealth and influence which they gained in the larger political sphere brought them local prestige, and, if they wished, provided grounds for a claim to higher status in the local hierarchy.[14]

In general, the gains won by the first two of these three methods were the more certain and enduring, for the members of *jati* who acquired power and prestige by following the secular ideals of their political rulers might find that they still had to consolidate their position in their local caste system by adopting stricter Brahmanical practices at home. In Africa most immigrants attempted to gain wealth first and then honour and prestige on the basis of European ideals or those of the Westernised classes of India; but members of one *jati* at least, the Bhatia in Zanzibar, became progressively stricter Hindus during their stay abroad, and over a period were able to raise their standing in India.[15]

Although, Hindus regard the caste system in terms of ritual purity, it is nevertheless not primarily a religious system, but is a part of the secular order. The wide range of theological and philosophical ideas and practices which comprises Hinduism is largely independent of the caste system. Alongside and cutting across the caste divisions are many purely religious cults and sects whose members may or may not consider caste differences to be important in their religious lives. Some of these sects have been taken to Africa, but they have not given rise to corporate communities of an importance comparable with those based on caste or Muslim sectarian divisions.

Hindu Religion

The Hindu religion is remarkable in its complexity. It is also very old, and the range of beliefs and practices within it is so wide that Hindus have seldom attempted to define it.

The current terms, Hinduism and Brahmanism are of European origin, the only Hindu general term for 'religion' being *dharma,* defined (Macdonnel, *Sanskrit English Dictionary,* London, 1893, s.v.) as established order, usage, institution, custom, prescription; rule, duty; virtue, moral merit; good work; right, justice, law.[16]

In effect, Hinduism is what Hindus do and believe, and a Hindu is a man who generally follows the rules of conduct and ceremonial... laid down for him, particularly regarding food and marriage, and the adoration of the gods.'[17]

Of all the larger religions Hinduism, is outstandingly syncretic; and though Brahmins have for many centuries attempted to bring order into the thousands of local and village religious and magical practices throughout the length and breadth of India, they have never attempted to do so with the help of an ecclesiastical organisation. They have relied principally on a common stock of sacred Sanskrit texts, and the habit of making pilgrimages to and studying at a few well-known centres to keep a measure of uniformity at least among Brahmin sub-castes. In spite of their efforts the diversity of belief and practice everywhere is immense. On the one hand there exist local deities in villages, who may or may not be fully assimilated to the Brahminic pantheon that is venerated by most Hindus, except Jains.[18] The worship of these local gods is accompanied by what has been called element worship, tomb worship and stone worship; and disease, animal, river, sea, hill, grain and plant worship.[19] There also exist practices of omen-taking, spirit medium-ship, ancestor worship, witchcraft and sorcery. These beliefs and practices vary from region to region, and within a district they may differ not just from village to village, but from caste to caste as well.

The heterogeneous practices of Hinduism take many forms, which for convenience, may be grouped under three heads:

1. Ceremonies of worship mainly directed to deities *(puja)*;
2. Ceremonial readings or recitations from sacred texts *(katha)*; and
3. Pilgrimages.

These observances may be organised around the agricultural or the religious calendar; they may be followed to avert or cure misfortune; or they may be undertaken in fulfilment of a vow. Sometimes they are for the benefit of an individual and his domestic group or they may be for the wider public good, serving castes, villages, or even wider groups.

In East Africa, Indians settled in towns as traders, and large sections of ritual connected with the maintenance and welfare of the traditional rural groups from which the settlers came fell into disuse. Much domestic religion connected with rural life also became obsolescent, and only a few of the many Hindu sects which flourished in Gujarat were successfully transferred to Africa. Perhaps because communication with India was easy and frequent, centres of pilgrimage did not appear in East Africa, because those who really wished to make a pilgrimage could return to India without too much difficulty. Connected with this too may be the secular outlook of most of the immigrants, though secularism and relative neglect of the older forms of Hindusim was not peculiar to Indians in Africa. For more than a century after the British conquest of India a succession of religious leaders had re-examined received traditions in the light of Western ideas, and had founded a number of neo-Hindu cults and sects which had most of their following in the rapidly growing towns of India, and which did not place so much stress on pilgrimage and the older forms of ritual. A few of these neo-Hindu forms of worship were taken to Africa.

Hindu Sects

A sect usually denotes a dissident group which secedes from a main body of believers and sets up its own exclusive organisation. No single ecclesiastical body has ever included all or even most Hindus, and cults which have arisen in Hinduism have always been founded on an interpretation or elaboration of existing views which scarcely ever laid claim to an exclusive salvation or membership. Adherence to a Hindu cult does not, therefore, present its adherents with the problems of orthodoxy and heterodoxy which confront Muslim or Christian sectarians, and membership does not mean that a man or woman, even within the same domestic group, is obliged to neglect other parts of the Hindu pantheon or to forgo other forms of Hindu worship.

'The chief objects of modern Hindu worship beginning with the Epic age are the Trinity: Brahma the Creator, Vishnu the Preserver, and Shiv the Destroyer',[20] and cults arise when a teacher takes an aspect of one of these deities and embodies his teaching in a permanent organisation, which if it survives frequently invests the founder with divine attributes. In Gujarat most such cults are Vaishnavite (following Vishnu), though there are others devoted to Shiva (Shaivites) and to Shakti or Energy. Divine energy is most commonly worshipped in the form of local goddesses known as *Mata*, or mother, who, in common with a multitude of subsidiary deities, are assimilated to or associated with the principal Hindu gods.

Hindus believe that Vishnu, in the aspect of Preserver, has been incarnated nine times and that a tenth is to come.

These incarnations or *avatars,* together with the details of belief and practice of his worship, as well as that of Shiva and other deities, are described in the Sanskrit epics and *puranas.*[21] Other sources of belief and practice are the *tantra,* which were composed to give prominence to the worship of the female counterpart of Shiv;[22] but in northwestern India, where the worship of *Mata* goddesses is widespread, the more extreme forms of tantric worship found in other regions are uncommon, and were not taken to East Africa.

At the beginning of this century, there were approximately nine million Hindus in Gujarat, and it was estimated that the members of Vaishnavite cults were four times as numerous as those of Shaivite cults.[23] The majority of Vaishnavas worshipped Vishnu in his incarnation as Rama; only half as many worshipped him as Krishna. The castes and the districts in which the worship of Krishna was strongly entrenched were however those which contributed largely to the East African migration. The followers of Shiva, on the other hand, drew their strength mainly from Brahmin and low castes, few of whom went to Africa.

Serious devotion to the religious life, especially after a man has reared a family, has always been esteemed by Hindus. To become an ascetic was the ideal way for a man to free himself in this life from the vicissitudes of re-incamation and the trials and tribulations of caste, for a holy man is a man without caste. Any religious leader in Hinduism is, therefore, likely to attract a following, and if he wishes it, found a new cult.

Vaishnavites defined themselves by their relationship to their founders. In Gujarat and East Africa the most important Hindu cult is the *Vallabhacharya* cult, devoted to Krishna. It was founded in South India, and its doctrines and organisation were modified by a teacher, Vallabh (1479-1531), who was sixth successor to the founder and who gave his name to the cult.

The seven chief seats or *gadi* of the cult are temples privately owned by male patrilineal descendants of the seven grandsons of Vallabh. Vallabh himself is believed to have been an incarnation of Krishna, and his divine qualities are held to have been transmitted to the present incumbents of the *gadi,* who are known as *Maharaj,* and who were formerly permitted the ceremonial perquisites of secular princes. Two of the seven seats are in Gujarat; and the main places of worship and pilgrimage are the privately owned *gadi.* Each seat is independent of the others, and unlike analogous Muslim sects, the cult as a whole has no overall inclusive organisation.

The British conquest of India in the eighteenth century and the influence of European ideas produced a social and intellectual ferment among Hindu leaders, which led to the formation of new cults. Some of these were traditional in form, like the Swami Narayan sect which grew up among the Vaishnavas of Gujarat in the early part of the nineteenth century; others were more closely modelled on European ideas and forms of organisation, as with the neo-Hindu Arya Samaj sect, and were often closely associated with the growth of industrial cities and the development of nationalism. The scholarship and influence of the Brahmins compelled any reformer of Hinduism either to work with or against them. The position of the Brahmins and the caste system had often been attacked in the past, but the authority of the sacred Sanskrit texts, unlike that of the Brahmins, was seldom challenged; and in the nineteenth century the founders of neo-Hindu cults rejected only parts of the sacred canon, however much they might feel free to modify caste discrimination and other parts of Hindu social and religious organisation.

The earliest neo-Hindu cult was the *Brahmo Samaj,* founded in 1828. In opposition to orthodoxy its founder taught strictly monotheistic beliefs and rejected doctrines of divine incarnation. A more influential sect was the *Arya Samaj,* founded in 1874. It too taught monotheism and regarded only the Sanskrit Vedic writings as divine scriptures containing all knowledge. Caste divisions and Brahminic ideas of pollution were held to be wrong, but as the founder's words on this subject were ambiguous, the precept was not always strictly observed. The sect is organised into local congregations, which anybody over the age of eighteen may join, but those who are not 'twice-born' Hindus require initiation. Each congregation is governed by elected officers, and may send delegates to provincial assemblies, which in turn send delegates to the central council for India. The founder of the sect is not believed to be a divine incarnation. Arya Samaj buildings and congregations exist in most of the larger towns of East Africa, and the Provincial Assembly is at Nairobi.

The circumstances and ideas which produced these neo-Hindu sects also produced educational and political movements, which in the person of Gandhi were united with religious Hinduism. He did not found a cult or a sect; but his views on caste and theological and social reform were closely allied with those of the neo-Hindu movement. In India people followed him as a political leader; many followed him for religion as well. In Africa the immigrants accepted some of his ideas; they could venerate him as a saint and hang his picture in their houses as an ikon; at the same time they could safely accept his political and social ideas, for they had only a limited relevance for Indians in Africa. In giving devotion to Gandhi they could feel that they were both traditional Hindus and modern men of the world.

Hinduism in Uganda

In East Africa, most Hindus thought little about religion. One of them said: the gods are unwilling to cross the sea. Most of them, I think, stayed in India. The women brought over a few that are important to them; but for me, it will be time to pray to God when I go back to India. Only rogues in Kampala bother to pray. When ' a man goes bankrupt or gets into trouble with the police he goes to the temple crying Bhagwan! Bhagwan! [Lord! Lord!], and promises to go on a pilgrimage to the Ganges if he gets out of his mess. The contrast between the apparent unimportance of religion to the Indians of East Africa and what seems to be a pre-occupation with it in South Africa, Mauritius and Fiji[24] is very marked.

In East Africa, Hindu religion tends to be relegated to the sphere of women. The caste system was not successfully established anywhere overseas by Indian emigrants. Wherever they went, except in East Africa, the settlement was mainly one of coolies recruited for agricultural labour; and the conditions of settlement were usually such that caste could not remain sufficiently important even to form Aasis for the development of caste communities, as happened in East Africa, where it was always reasonably easy for ordinary and not very rich people to return to India on visits or for good. Indentured coolies usually arrived with virtually no material possessions and small likelihood of returning home. Unlike the traders in East Africa they lived in agricultural settlements and they and their children cultivated land, as had their ancestors before them.

Among their immaterial possessions were their gods and their habits of worship. In their new environment many of the 'dangers were similar to those they had left at home in their villages, and the gods were, if anything, more needed. For most it would have been useless to vow a pilgrimage to the Ganges, and it was not long before new saints and shrines were discovered. In East Africa a man could safely vow a pilgrimage to India, knowing that it was not impossible to fulfil at a convenient time, if he felt that it was really necessary. He could also safely ignore his gods for the duration of his stay abroad, if he believed that he could make amends in later years. As a very large number of people believed that their visit to Africa would not become permanent, they did not urgently need an elaborate public religion.[25]

The man who thought that the gods had not crossed the sea to Africa was mostly thinking of what he called 'the old religion'. Orthodox Hinduism—the old religion—in contrast with the neo-Hindu developments of the nineteenth and twentieth centuries was usually known in East Africa as the *Sanatan Dharma,* a name which had come in effect to cover all traditional Hindu religion.

In rural India, much traditional religion had been concerned with the caste system in general, and the constituent castes in particular; it also had functions in maintaining the ritual health of the village as a whole and of the households and the individuals in them. In Uganda the caste system did not exist, though caste communities did; the traders, whether they lived in large or small settlements were essentially urban and commercial in outlook. In these conditions in a foreign country the public functions of rural Hindu religion did not apply, and not much of the older ceremonial was adapted to the newer units of organisation in Africa. The ritual care and safety of individuals and smaller units, such as the family and household (which had also undergone alteration), also appeared to be less urgent than it was at home, though 'domestic religion' remained very important in Africa.

In Uganda, three religious institutions in 1955 still specifically concerned the Hindu community as a whole. The first of these was the *Sanatan Dharma Mandal* or temple in Kampala, which, because of its situation and the influence of its leading members, acted as an informal centre for much of the organisation of the 'old religion' in the country. The second was the neo-Hindu *Arya Samaj* with a formal organisation that covered the whole of East Africa and provided religious services for any Hindu in situations where orthodoxy did not appear to have an answer. The third institution was the annual festival of *Divali*—the beginning of the calendar year. *The Sanatan Dharma Mandal.* The Hindu temple in Kampala was registered as an association with the Land Office and had appointed trustees who were eminent men, and who usually belonged to different castes. It was managed by an annually elected committee, roost of whose members were influential citizens with access to the Protectorate administration.

All kinds of worship—prayers to Lord Vishnu, Lord Rama, Lord Shiva and other Gods and Goddesses mainly Amba Mata, Hamunanji and Ganesh [son of Shiva] take place in the Temple. The followers of Swami Narayan do not usually pray at the Temple but they do come to the Temple to attend occasional religious functions because Swami Narayan Sect is only a Branch of Hinduism and most of them do believe in Lord Krishna and other Gods.

The Mandal employs a Brahmin as Priest to perform all religious ceremonies in the Temple permanently. The same priest always officiates even though the worshippers may be vaishnavites or shivites or other sects. The priest is not engaged as Schoolmaster; his only duties are to look after the Temple and to attend to the worshippers.

It might be added that the Sanatan Dharma Mandal has already started putting up Temples with high domes without using iron. They are being erected on the site of the old Temple to be demolished completely. There are going to be separate Temples for Lord Shiva, Lord Rama, Lord Krishna and Goddess Ambamata.[26]

The Mandal Committee financed and managed a large school as well as a rest house for visitors to the town. It partly maintained a public library of Gujarati and Hindi books, and in as far as it provided religious and secular services for all Hindus, it did to that extent represent the local and even the whole Hindu community of Uganda acting as a group. But,, as we saw earlier, the offer of rent-free sites for places of worship for the 'major religions in Kampala had very nearly broken the unity of the Sanatan Dharma, and had shown that though orthodox Hindu cults and sects were able to cooperate tolerantly in most situations, the ties that held them together were fragile.

The Arya Samaj

One organisation included all *Arya Samaj* congregations in East Africa, and provided facilities for all Hindus willing to disregard caste regulations and orthodox beliefs. But, even in East Africa such people were a minority, though few found difficulty in using the Arya Samaj when the reasons were strong. One man said: If you are religious and want to marry a woman out of caste, of course you will go to the Arya Samaj. They don't mind When at the end of the Second World War it became difficult to find school places for children and the Arya Samaj built a school in Kampala, few parents objected to the sect's theology, though more refused to send their daughters to the school because it was coeducational. Exclusiveness in Hindu society is institutionalised in the caste system and not in religious cults or sects, which often have overlapping memberships. They, therefore, do not provide as good a foundation for the development of competing communities as do castes or exclusive Muslim sects.

The Dwali Festival

Religious festivals are celebrated at several points in the year of the Hindu calendar, but in India one may be more emphasized in this district than in that, and one caste may ignore or hardly notice what all others celebrate. In Uganda only *Dwali* the last four days of the Hindu year (which fall in late October or early November), was celebrated publicly by all Hindus. In Gujarat it was particularly a bankers' and merchants' festival,[27] whereas in Uganda it was a public holiday observed by almost all Indians, Muslims as much as Hindus. The religious content of *Divali* in East Africa was not great, but to observe it was appropriate to a Hindu and was a mark of his status.

Certain other less formalised aspects of Hindu religious thought were also important in East Africa. To revere the Vedas and hold strong beliefs concerning the unique spiritual value of Indian civilisation, especially as embodied in Gandhi, was a pervasive element in the outlook of most Hindus. In appropriate situations the idea of Indian civilisation allowed all Indians to feel a sense of community in the face of Europeans or Africans. By its nature Hinduism is not and cannot easily be a missionary religion, and most Hindus do not wish to spread it outside India; but even the most materially minded traders in Africa supported all kinds of visiting mendicants from India, some of whom, in contrast with the settlers, consider it 'their sacred duty to spread the light of this neo-Hindu Dharma in every nook and corner of the world.[28] Although, few Hindus in Africa considered it their duty to Hindu Dharma, the knowledge that it existed assured them that they were inferior to nobody. Their religion taught them that any discomforts and inequalities they suffered were merely 'the illusions of the world'. Hindus everywhere were one in possessing the revelation of the Vedas.

In Gujarat some castes organised themselves as corporate groups by the use of councils; others achieved a measure of uniformity by means of marriage regulations or by particular religious observances, such as the 'fire worship' of the goldsmiths, or by possessing tutelary deities. Some built special caste halls as well. In East Africa many of the new caste communities, especially when they were sufficiently numerous, built halls at convenient centres for recreational and ceremonial purposes where the correct rituals on such occasions as a marriage or a death, which might affect a man's standing in India, could be performed. But, in general neither traditional nor reformed Hinduism played an important part in the development of the caste communities.

The individual and domestic functions of religion, on the other hand, retained much of their importance in Africa. The Indian women who emigrated possibly had a greater need of their gods and supernatural protection than did their fathers, their husbands and sons. Both sexes regarded Africa as potentially dangerous and unhealthy. For men, after the early days of difficult pioneering, the main hazards were those of trading; for women the risks were those they knewathome although much mitigated by a better climate and medical services and a prosperity greater than any they had known in India. In Gujarat the calamities of life tended to fall more heavily on women than on men.

The risk of death in child-bed faced most women over the age of twelve, and the loss of her sons, who were a woman's only real safety, was a constant fear. Barrenness or life-long widowhood were catastrophes familiar to all women, whose personal security lay in the sons they bore and in the clothes and the jewels they could acquire and keep. All her life a woman remained a legal minor, first under the guardianship of her father, then of her husband, his brothers, or possibly her sons or husband's nephews. In these circumstances she could not easily feel safe without priests and experts in casting horoscopes and reading omens. She also needed spirit mediums to discover and placate spirits or ghosts that afflicted the household. Even in the easier circumstances of Africa she felt the need for a minimum of family worship, and in that the cooperation of her husband was essential.

In the early days, few women came with their men to Africa, and many of those who did died. When improved conditions allowed people to live longer than in Gujarat and to rear larger families, the risks and uncertainties of life still bore more heavily on women. Although, they were not legal minors in Africa, nevertheless they still depended almost entirely on their fathers and husbands. A widow and her children might be far from any of her relatives, and the traditional protection of her husband's joint family seldom existed outside India. Her children might be sent away from Africa when they were quite young, and she often never saw them again. Where her husband might feel safe in ignoring the gods, she hardly could.

The principal rituals of domestic religion in Uganda were concerned either with the household and its safety or with the life cycle and health of individuals. Where the presence of the men of the family was needed for these ceremonies, the women were usually able to make them take part for the sake of the household as a whole. By strict orthodox standards the performance of both public and domestic religion was often barely adequate, partly because of ignorance and partly because competent experts were rare. Few of those who lived in Africa were able to maintain themselves solely by the practice of their religious vocation.

In the Sanatan Dharma all priests were Brahmins. In Gujarat they belonged to a number of Brahmin sub-castes, each ministering to one or more non-Brahmin castes. Family priests of this kind, supported wholly or in part by offerings and fees for ceremonies, hardly existed in East Africa, and those devoted to the exclusive service of a particular sect or deity at a temple were few and far between.

To be a priest in the Arya Samaj sect, a man did not have to be a Brahmin, but did in theory need to be registered with the Provincial Council. As fully trained priests were few in number, anybody of good repute and familiar with the rituals might officiate at ceremonies in small and isolated congregations.

Ascetics, either itinerant or resident at shrines, were not found in East Africa. Since there were always situations, such as affliction by ghosts or other spirits, which neither Sanatan nor Arya Samaj priests were always able to handle, there also existed a number of other ritual experts, as, for example, spirit mediums. These people might belong to any caste. They had entered into a special relationship with a deity (usually a *mata* goddess) who was able to possess them, and who by using human mediums was able to give advice and help.

By their own standards, the organisation of Hindu religion among the settlers in East Africa was deficient in many respects, but it did provide them with the minimum of ritual services. The women were able to feel that they were not in serious danger from culpable neglect, and the available religious support was enough to allow the men to feel that they could later, and in more favourable circumstances, repair any harm that might come from their behaviour in Africa.

Conclusions

The traditional caste system in India was a hierarchical division of social labour. It was peculiar in the rigidity of the relationships of inter-dependence among the component groups, and in the extent to which they were explained and justified by religious concepts. Although, an ideal pattern of the caste system was recognised in all parts of India, the actual arrangement of castes and sub-castes in a hierarchy varied from one district to another.

Neither the ideal model nor an actual example of the caste system was taken to East Africa. Moreover some of the changes that occurred in East Africa had already taken place in the towns of India to which rural castes had migrated. The reasons may be summarised as follows:

1. The settlers in Africa were unable to reproduce the social system of any district in India because they were a minority in a large non-Hindu population, and because they themselves came from widely separated districts in India. Even if there had been the full range of castes needed to establish a local caste system in any part of Africa, it would have been difficult to agree on a hierarchy. Nobody was willing to accept any position for his own caste except that which it held in his home district.
2. The economic and legal systems in East Africa did not permit division of labour according to the rules of caste. A man who did not want to practise his traditional occupation was not allowed to stop others from following it. Most immigrants came to Africa for trade and not for their caste occupations; but certain caste services, such as washing, barbering, shoe-making, were essential to the system and were

frequently performed by non-Hindus, who by definition were out-castes and polluting. In brief, the large-scale social system in which the immigrants gained their living made full observance of caste rules impossible.

3. Finally, the ease with which India could be visited meant that though the immigrants were unable to construct a caste system in Africa, they were obliged to maintain the identity and exclusiveness of their castes, notably in arranging correct endogamous marriages, so that on their return home they could once more assume their proper place in the local system.

This need for caste exclusiveness was so strong that it became one of the most important structural principles in organising Indian social life in the East African territories.

Other factors, however, were necessary for the emergence of independent communities related to one another and the wider society in Africa in ways quite different from those of the small-scale caste systems of rural India. These factors have already been discussed but are recapitulated for the sake of completeness.

1. No caste community ever emerged as an organised group until there were enough members for effective action.
2. Although, several castes came to Africa with experience in organising caste councils for supervising the behaviour of members, and accustomed to building, maintaining and using caste halls and funds, a caste in Uganda did not usually organise itself into a community unless its members felt their interests seriously threatened by other castes or sects. The emergence of the Ismaili Muslims as an organised community usually provoked other sects and Hindu castes into following their example.
3. The favourable political atmosphere in all parts of East Africa encouraged the multiplication of communities, because among other things they provided positions for politically ambitious men, from

which they could advance their own interests as well as those of their community. As a rule this aspect of the matter was not fully appreciated until a number of communities had emerged.

In the light of these circumstances, we can see why caste was one (of the main principles of organisation among Indians in Uganda. What is not so clear is why communities did not crystallise around Hindu sects, as they did around those of the Muslims.

In considering the Hindu religion in Uganda, the failure to develop a caste system meant that a large part of the public religion connected with the system also failed to develop. I suggested, too, that other features of public religion did not establish themselves in strength because of the ease of communication with India. Nevertheless, religious cults and sects were transplanted to Uganda, and, allied with one another in the Sanatan Dharma, were sufficiently strong in Kampala to maintain activities of considerable social and economic value. At the same time it should be observed that these activities were begun when the Indian community was still relatively small, before the development of separate caste communities.

Finally, even had the Hindu traders in East Africa wished to support large and highly organised cults and sects, the practical regulations would have made the task difficult. No alien was admitted unless he could fill a post that was for the benefit of everybody. European officials did not find it easy to appreciate the value of priests and ascetics and contemplatives without occupation; and most professionally religious men in India hesitated when confronted by the ritual impurity of Africa. But, the critical factor which made caste rather than sect the basis of community membership among Hindus in East Africa was undoubtedly the fact that in India exclusiveness was institutionalised in the caste system and not in religion. The leader of a Hindu cult movement could never rely on the undivided loyalty of ordinary members. Unlike their Muslim counterparts Hindu divine leaders were never able to offer exclusive salvation to their followers or everlasting damnation to unbelievers. For a Hindu salvation depended upon correct caste behaviour and the discovery of religious leaders suitable to his station in life. In Africa, communities emerged as exclusive, competitive corporations, and Hindu religious institutions did not supply a good foundation for such associations.

Islam

In the belief of all Muslims, Muhammad, who founded Islam in the seventh century AD, was the Seal, the conclusion of a long line of '.prophets charged with revealing the divine purpose of the world to men. Muhammad's particular mission and its attendant religious-authority ended, therefore, at his death. During his life he was also secular leader of the believers, and this authority did not end when he died. The Sunni section of Islam, which comprises the majority of Muslims, believes that he did not appoint a secular leader to succeed him; the Shias believe that he bequeathed both secular and religious leadership to his cousin and son-in-law, Ali, and his descendants by Fatima, the prophets daughter, until the day of final judgment and the establishment of the millennium. The doctrinal division on this point between Sunni and Shia is fundamental and goes back to the days soon after the death of the prophet. Out of this Shia belief arose doctrines concerning the person of the Imam or religious leader which increased the rift between the Shias and the Sunnis; for the latter hold that the only legitimate leader of the faithful is the secular leader or caliph elected by the faithful themselves. The word *imam* is used of a prayer leader by all Muslims, and also of the founders and leading jurists of the different schools. In addition it is used by some and especially the Shias, for the leader of the whole Muslim community, whom the Shias insist must have been divinely designated and whom they regard as impeccable and infallible. In detail their attitude varies from sect to sect: the Zaydis are the most moderate, although even they consider their Imams as possessed of divine light substance, the 'sole and permanent channel of sanctifying prerogatives and illuminating inspirations', while the Ismailis go even further.

In the factional disputes about leadership which took place after the prophet's death, Ali did not at first succeed in becoming caliph of all Muslims, though in the eyes of Shias today he was Muhammad's only successor, and was both caliph and imam. Eventually he became caliph for Shias and Sunnis alike; but to the latter he is still merely the fourth caliph, and he and his wife and their descendants are invested with none of the mystical qualities attributed to them by Shias. Ali was assassinated during his tenure of office, and his sons and immediate descendants suffered misfortunes at the hands of Sunni rivals who seized the caliphate. Thus, at a time when Islamic law and theology were rapidly developing in the cosmopolitan cities of Damascus and Baghdad, successive generations of Shia Imams and their followers were living in political eclipse. The differences between orthodox and heterodox theology which arose in this situation made doctrinal reconciliation between Sunni and Shia virtually impossible and undoubtedly poisoned social relations whenever the two divisions came intimately into contact. At the same time, it is easy to over-emphasise the differences and to overlook the similarities, both of belief and organisation.

For Muslims society exists so that men may live correctly and have a proper relationship with God in the ways revealed by the prophet and the interpreters of his revelation as embodied in the religious law or *shariat*. Consequently for a believer to live in a secular or a non-Muslim state can at best be only a compromise with unfortunate worldly circumstances. Ideally the basic social unit in all parts of the Muslim world is a congregation united physically and metaphorically behind a leader in prayer. The ritual differences between one Shia sect and another are often hot much greater than those among the orthodox Sunni schools, whose congregations, it has been noted 'in the ordinary law-books cannot pray behind the imam of another'. Shia sectarians too judge orthodoxy and heterodoxy by a man's relationship to the sect's imam. In addition, all Muslims acknowledge five imperative religious duties: the witness of God's unity and the prophet's mission, prayer, alms-giving, fasting and pilgrimage. A sixth duty, *the jihad* or the waging of war against wrong belief, is often added. For Shias the duty of recognising and obeying the imam is paramount and encompasses all other duties. To escape damnation a man must find and acknowledge the Imam of the Age.

Sunni Divisions

According to tradition the prophet said:

> The Jews are divided into seventy-one sects, and the Christians are divided into seventy-two sects, and my people will be divided into seventy-three sects.

Discussion of this saying by Muslim scholars has turned not so much on the meaning of sect as on the enumeration of dissident groups and the likelihood of their damnation. If we regard a sect as a group of dissenters who cut themselves off from the main body of believers and set up their own exclusive ecclesiastical organisation, then the division between Sunni Muslim and Shia groups is clearly sectarian. On the other hand, the division of Sunni Muslims into Schools of Law is less clear, and orthodox opinion about their status differs.

The Schools of Law are systematic but differing interpretations of the Koran, the traditions, and the past and present opinions and consensus of the Islamic community put forward by the founding jurisprudents whose names the schools bear. All, in contrast to Shia sects, are considered orthodox by the Sunnis, and, according to some of their theologians, a Muslim may pray behind anyone whether pure or sinner. But, others disagree, and for this reason certain Western scholars have also considered the Schools of Law to be real sects.

Although, opinions differ on the degree of exclusiveness which the schools impose on their adherents, it seems that in the main they are never completely exclusive groups, with separate organisations and inflexible demands on their followers which put them into sectarian opposition to all other Sunni Muslims.

Shia Sects

Dissenting Shia sects have never been able to deny the need of an infallible, impeccable imam descended from Ali and the prophets daughter, for these doctrines were developed in Shia theology at a very early date. Instead they disagreed on the rightful successor to the office and the certainty of his nomination as imam by his predecessor. The reigning imam, by reason of his innate qualities, has the right to designate any male of his patrilineal lineage to succeed him, and the divine incarnation with all its attributes, first embodied in Ali, passes at his death into the new imam. As a rule Shia imams have followed a principle of primogeniture, but a nomination made by the imam may be withdrawn at any time before his death; and on occasions the late imam's intentions have not always been clear, thus opening the way to dissent.

The first split in the Shia ranks took place on the death of the sixth imam, who lived in Baghdad during the eighth century. As was the custom, he nominated his eldest son, Ismail, to succeed him, but subsequently changed his mind and appointed another son, Musa, in his place. The reason for the change is not clear, but probably arose from the imam's doubts of Ismail's political acumen. The Sunni rulers in Baghdad regarded the Shias with suspicion, and after the sixth imam's death the Shias were gradually forced to conceal their religious preferences, while their leaders went into hiding.

On his death, the Shias divided. The larger group accepted Musa as their seventh imam and the rest adhered to Ismail. The successors of Musa lived in Baghdad under the growing hostility of the authorities, and in AD 873 the last of the line, the twelfth in succession from Ali, vanished without trace. In the belief of his followers, known as the *Ithna 'Ashariya'* or *Twelver Sect* and today constituting the majority of Muslims in Iran, the imam deliberately went into concealment, and still lives undying, unknown and unnoticed. When he re-appears the Day of Judgment will be at hand.

In AD 969, the adherents of Ismail's successors conquered Egypt, and the imams again became secular and spiritual rulers. On the death in Egypt of the nineteenth imam the Ismailis split into two main groups, the *Nizarian* or *Eastern Ismailis* and the *Mustalian* or *Ismailis,* which persist until today. Nizar, the elder son of the imam fled to Persia and from his following is derived the *Shia Imami Ismailia* sect with the Aga Khan as its present imam. The younger son, Mustali, remained in Egypt and became the twentieth imam of the present *Daudi Bohora* sect. In AD 1130 the twenty-first Nizarian imam was murdered and in the belief of his followers left a young son in the care of a council of lieutenants, the

Da'is, who took him into concealment and nothing more was heard of him'.

The Doctrine of the Imamate

Of all the Shia sects today only the Shia Imami Ismailis believe that a known, revealed imam still walks among men. For them the Imam of the Age is Mowlana Hazar Imam His Highness Karim Aga Khan, the lineal descendant of Ali and Fatima, the forty-ninth imam. Most other Shia sects have evolved the doctrine of 'the concealed imam' who is awaiting a suitable time to reveal his living presence once more. In each sect the details of the doctrine differ. For the Ithnasheri the twelfth imam has never died; for the Daudi Bohora he is concealed but in each generation lives and dies as an ordinary man before his attributes pass on to his successor; and for the Shia Imami Ismailia he is a publicly known living man. For all Shia sects the office of imam is central, and a members relationship to it defines orthodoxy and heterodoxy and institutionalises the exclusiveness of membership.

At the creation of the world, it is said, God prepared a divine ray of light which generation by generation is incarnated in the Imam of the Age. For men to think of electing an imam is, therefore, blasphemy. He was revealed by God when the prophet designated Ali and his descendants as his successors. For this reason, too, the imams are perfect sinless beings. The imam must be obeyed without question, not only because he is infallible, but because he is also the executor of the word of God revealed by Muhammad.

The Shias very early elaborated the doctrine and practice of *taqiya* or permissible dissimulation of real belief, and required all followers to observe it as a religious duty. After the death of the sixth imam they were often obliged to conceal both the imam, if he was a known living man, and their own religious views, maintaining at the same time an organisation of local mosques and lieutenants who stood between them and their hidden leader. When Islam was taken to India, Shia doctrines, which had been elaborated in the Near East, provided a congenial background for converts. Sacred leaders of Hindu sects, also thought to be divine incarnations whose holy attributes were passed patrilineally, were prominent features of Hindu society, especially in Cutch, Sind, and western India generally, where Ismaili missionaries were most successful.

The doctrines surrounding the imam were not difficult for converts to accept; and the practice of *taqiya* allowed missionaries to clothe their message in ambiguous, half-Hindu terms that did not require converts to completely alter their traditional beliefs and practices. A devotional book, *Dos Avatar,* attributed to a missionary of the fifteenth century and still in use, was written to demonstrate that Ali was the long-expected tenth incarnation of the God Vishnu, whose worshippers were particularly numerous in western India. In ways such as this Hindu beliefs and practices were intimately woven into the ritual and secular life of Shia sects in India, and have remained so to the present day.

Shia Sects in India

The establishment of Islam in India began soon after the death of Muhammad. The monsoon winds which had taken Arab and Indian traders to East Africa also brought Arabs to the coast of western India; and from the seventh century onwards, by land and sea, Muslim traders, soldiers, refugees and slaves arrived, especially at the ports of Gujarat, Kathiawad and Cutch. Most came singly and were absorbed into the general Hindu population. Some were missionaries who set out to convert the humble; others proselytised the rulers, who occasionally forced large sections of their subjects to adopt their new religion. Among these Muslim immigrants from the Near East were Sunnis and Shias of all kinds.

The Shia Imami Ismailia Sect

According to Shia Imami Ismaili tradition the first missionary of their sect to India was sent from Persia by the imam early in the eleventh century, soon after the division into Eastern and Western Ismailiism. In 1840 the first Aga Khan and the forty-sixth Nizariah imam, great great-grandfather of the present imam, the fourth Aga Khan, fled from Persia after an unsuccessful rebellion against the throne.

He suffered many vicissitudes and ultimately took refuge in Sind. Here he helped the British in their annexation of that country and in the second Afghan war. For his services the government of India awarded him a pension and the rank of hereditary prince prefixed to his Persian title Aga Khan. He was prevented from returning to Persia and eventually settled with his retainers among the Shia Imami Ismailis of Bombay, whose living imam he was.

As Imam of the Age, the Aga Khan expected absolute obedience from all his followers; but for some years before his arrival in Bombay the organisation of the sect there and its relationship with the imam had been in an unsettled condition. In western India generally most Khoja Ismailis, as Shia Imami Ismaili adherents were usually called, acknowledged the Aga Khan as their imam, paid him tithe offerings and had made visits of pilgrimage to him in Persia. At the same time they also observed Sunni practices. In Bombay they were married by Sunni officials and were buried according to Sunni rites. These customs, they said, had been adopted in times of persecution and were allowable under the doctrine of *taqiya*. As early as 1829 the followers of the Aga Khan in Bombay were disputing the payment of tithes to him.

In order to overcome this opposition, [he] sent to Bombay [a] special agent... accompanied by a very energetic lady, the Aga's maternal grandmother, Marie-Bibi, who herself appears to have harangued the Bombay Khojas in Jamat Khana assembled, and with very considerable effect.

In spite of his grandmother's oratory, the Aga Khan in 1830 was obliged to order his agents to file a suit against the malcontents in the High Court of Bombay. The case was subsequently withdrawn and the dissenters were excommunicated; but the grievances were not settled, and in 1866 the dispute was again brought before the court.

In presenting their case, the dissenters maintained that the Khojas in Bombay were in fact Sunni and always had been so. The Aga Khan, they alleged, was an interloper who had persuaded the officers of the congregation to misappropriate funds and hand them to him for his personal use, when they ought to have held them in trust for communal purposes. In bringing a suit against the Aga Khan and the treasurer and the accountant of the Bombay congregation, the dissenters asked the court to direct that an account should be taken of all communal property and that it should be declared trust property held for the religious and charitable benefit of the community by the treasurer and the accountant. They also asked the court to settle a scheme for the periodic and regular election of these two officials and requested a direction to the Aga Khan to cease his interference in the management of the trust property and the affairs of the community generally.

Mr Justice Arnould in a remarkable and learned judgment decided in favour of the Aga Khan, whom he held to be historically and in fact the acknowledged Living Imam of the Khojas in Bombay and of Shia Imami Ismailis elsewhere. He also held that all communal property belonging to the sect was vested in the imam for his own absolute use, without any responsibility of trusteeship. Finally he held that the Bombay congregation was a Shia Imami Ismaili body, in no way Sunni.

The effects of this judgment on the organisation of the sect and on its relations with the rest of society in India and other places where English law prevailed were far-reaching; a hundred years later the consequences were still being worked out. In delivering his judgment, Mr Justice Arnould described the organisation of the sect in India at that date.

Wherever a Khoja community is to be found, however small, its organisation is the same: it has a *famat* a *famat-Khana,* a *Mukhi* and a *Kamaria.* The Jamat is the congregation of the people', the assembly in council of all the adult male members of the Khoja community in that place. The 'Jamat Khana' is the council-hall or guildhall of the community. The 'Mukhr is the treasurer or steward, and the 'Kamaria' is the accountant... these two functionaries... are not, according to the usage of the Khoja community, elected for any ascertained and fixed period, but appear to hold their office [if they wish so to do] as long as they give satisfaction.... Besides these local *mukhis* and *kamarias'* proof was given that in Sind and Kattywar, it may also be the case elsewhere, provincial kamarias are appointed by and hold office under the imam....

The duty of these functionaries is to collect and forward for transmission to the imam, wherever he may chance to reside, the contributions raised on his account by the Khoja community.

In many parts of the Ismaili world, similar organisations survived in the twentieth century. The members belonged to local congregations which were largely independent of one another, though in theory all were ranged behind the imam in prayer. Each congregation was answerable direct to the Aga Khan. In some places, as Mr Justice Arnould observed, a wider though very loose administrative organisation might also exist, often directed by hereditary chiefs.

A considerable measure of local responsibility prevails, questions of marriage and divorce for example are entirely the concern of the local representatives of the Imam... the actual day-to-day administrative work of each local community is done by the Imam's representative and local chief.

In East Africa and India, the organisation of the sect subsequently departed far from these traditional forms.

The success of the first Aga Khan in establishing in a court of law both his Imamate and his absolute legal ownership of communal property immediately placed him in a position different from that of other sacred leaders in India, whether Muslim or Hindu; and he and his son and his son's widow, a most powerful character who administered the imamate during the third Aga Khan's minority, established a large personal fortune for themselves. It was this fact which allowed the third Aga Khan during a very long life (1877-1960) to rule his followers with more detachment and benevolence than other financially pressed sacred leaders found possible. The decision of the first Aga Khan to settle in Bombay was not only a wise and happy personal decision, but it had an admirable effect on the religious and communal life of the whole Ismaili world. It was as if the heavy load of persecution and fanatical hostility, which they had to bear for so long, was lifted. Deputations came to Bombay from places as remote as Kashgar, Bokhara, all parts of Iran, Syria the Yemen, the African coast and the then narrowly settled hinterland behind it.

In the words of the official biographer of the late Aga Khan, his grandfather, the first Aga, became a familiar figure to the people of Bombay.

He consoled himself for the loss of the Persian throne by becoming one of the leading supporters of the Turf.... The Aga Khan, having heard of the Prince of Wales' intention to visit India, sent a commission to invite the Prince to honour him with a visit.

When the visit took place, the two men very much enjoyed one another's company. Both were fat and exchanged hunting stories. The same biographer wrote:

The present friendship formed with the Royal House of England has not only continued but strengthened and the present Aga Khan's steadfast loyalty and attachment to the Throne of England has won for him the high regard of the Sovereigns of England.

At the death of the first Aga Khan in 1881, his son, the second Aga Khan, succeeded to the imamate but died in 1885. His heir, the third Aga Khan, was then a child, eight years of age. Besides receiving an Ismaili and a Western education, the imam was also taught to take his place in upper class society of Bombay. Of it he writes:

The viceroy and vicereine, Lord and Lady Dufferin, were... people of kind and gentle sensibility, warm hearts and graceful manners. A tone thus set could not be ignored, and Indo-British relationships in general were of this pattern. There was agreeable and unstrained social mixing at receptions, on the race course, or on the polo ground.

In 1897, the Aga Khan visited Europe for the first time. In England he was invited to dine with Queen Victoria. He also made the acquaintance of the Prince of Wales and was introduced to the English governing classes, among whom so much of his subsequent career in international politics was to be laid. As he grew older he returned less and less to India and his mother, a woman quite as formidable as his ancestress, Marie-Bibi. His social and political career in Europe, which was founded on the fortune built up by his immediate predecessors and which set him so far apart from other sacred leaders in India, was as important in the development of the sect as the success of his grandfather in the law courts. Combined with his role as imam his position as a European politician and aristocrat was crucial in helping him re-organise the life and welfare of his followers in ways that would not have occurred to the first Aga Khan.

In this process, it was important for the imam not to disturb his traditional position. A follower in Uganda explained the imam's place in his theology in the following words:

Our Imam, His Highess the Aga Khan, is like your Jesus Christ. Even Hindus believe that God will never leave the world deserted, and we believe that God, that is Vishnu, descended to earth in Ali and has never left us. When the Imam dies the Light moves on to his son: it follows the sacred blood—like the King. The King never dies.

Substantially the same view of the infallible, impeccable imam, whose person it is proper to worship and pray to, is expressed in the following leaflet published in English by a small East African congregation in 1950:

His Highness the Aga Khan an Extraordinary Personality. In the reign of Queen Victoria.

Her Majesty Queen Victoria had held a Levy, which was attended by the Consuls of all Countries, and His Highness the Aga-Khan was also invited at the occasion. When the Aga-Khan went there, the Queen herself went to receive him at the door and welcomed him with great respects and *made him sit on the Throne of their Pope*. As soon as the Aga-Khan sat on the throne, the Queen said to all the Consuls, What is the reason of your surprise, and what are you all thinking of?' The Consuls replied 'up to now many Indian Kings have come to Europe but you have given more honours to Aga-Khan, and even made him sit on the throne of our Pope; what is the reason of this?' The Queen in reply said, 'You are all wise, prudent and learned, and you know better than I the reason of this. In short, *I must tell you that we have never seen our religious leader Jesus Christ and, without doubt, the Aga-Khan is our same leader, and considering this I have made him sit on our Pope's throne.'* On hearing this all Consuls were greatly surprised and wired to their respective countries about the above fact. Consequently the Rulers of France, Germany, Italy, Belgium, etc., sent telegrams to Aga-Khan from all over, requesting him to give them honour of visiting their countries, which the Aga-Khan accepted.

Extract from: (*Saint Gazette 22* July 1898.)

On this foundation of trust and belief, together with his experience and knowledge of the Western world, the Aga Khan was able to persuade his followers to re-organise the sect and to discard much of their Hindu inheritance.

The Daudi Bohora Sect

According to Daudi Bohora tradition the first Mustalian missionary to preach in India came from the Yemen in AD 1067. When the infant twenty-second imam went into seclusion in AD 1130, the missionary programme and general supervision of Mustalian affairs was given to the ruler of Yemen, a woman, whose tomb is still a place of pilgrimage. Before her death she appointed, in AD 1151, a successor to the supervision of the sect, with the title of *Dai al mutlaq*. He was the first of the imam's representatives in sole and absolute charge of the sect, and his successors still fill the gap left by the concealed imam. The present *Dai al mutlaq* lives in Gujarat and is the fifty-first holder of the office.

Because the Bohoras believe that the Imam of the Age lives concealed and may at any time reveal himself, the *Dai* has never been able to claim the full powers attributed to an imam. Nevertheless, the office has attracted many of the qualities of the imamate. The incumbent has the right to nominate his legitimate successor, a power which has at different times led to the formation of new sects. Unlike the Aga Khan, no Dai has ever succeeded in establishing a right to the absolute personal ownership of all sectarian property. An attempt was made in the High Court of Bombay in 1922, and on behalf of the Dai, counsel asserted: 'Mulla Sahib was in effect God, or for all practical purposes God, and this suit was sacrilege'. When challenged, he modified the claim, but argued that the Dai's authority was tantamount to that of the concealed imam. God first delegated authority to Muhammad, who passed it to the imam, who in turn delegated it to the Dai. For this reason he too is an infallible, sinless being.

Since 1866, English legal ideas on corporations and trusts had altered, and judges were reluctant to follow the precedent of the Khoja case. In the Bohora case the judge ruled that the ownership of mosques was vested in the reigning Dai but was not his personal property. Nor did he have the right to alienate or permanently close them. Gifts made for the benefit of the sect were to be held by the Dai on trust, though he was under no obligation to appoint co-trustees.

The decision was a compromise which satisfied neither side. It did not enable the Dai to stamp out dissent nor did it allow him to accumulate a fortune like that of the Aga Khan, thus giving him the opportunity to organise the welfare of his sect with detachment and benevolence. It gave the Dai powers to exercise very close control over the religious and social activities of all members of his community', but they were primarily restrictive powers and hampered constructive developments. A college for training officials had been founded at Surat in 1807, and the challenge to the Dai's authority came from men trained in it. In resisting them he steadily lowered its educational standards and appointed relatively uneducated but loyal followers to all ecclesiastical offices. The Dai's failure to establish himself as an absolute ruler and his need to maintain traditional forms and taxes to support his position meant that he himself always tended to hold conservative views at a time when an influential section of his followers wanted change. It also meant that in Africa the majority of his followers were the least willing of the-, Shia Muslims to adapt themselves to altered circumstances.

The Shia Ithnasheri Sect

The twelfth imam of the Ithnasheri sect went into concealment in the year AD 873. For seventy years afterwards, the period of the Lesser Concealment, he was represented by *Vakil* each of whom nominated his own successor. The last one refused to name a successor because persecution had scattered the sect and made formal organisation dangerous. This was the beginning of the Greater Concealment which still continues.

Since that time the Ithnasheri sect has never developed a comprehensive organisation. The unit of organisation is a mosque and its congregation. In Iran, where the sect is the state religion, religious and much civil law is administered by judges *(mujtahids)*, but within the limits of civil and religious law each congregation is still virtually independent. In India, during the last years of British rule, an attempt was made to form large-scale Ithnasheri institutions, but as they had no direct control over the congregations their influence was not great.

The Ithnasheris came to India, like other Shias, as individuals and in small groups, but do not appear to have systematically sent missionaries. In the Near East they had long concealed their beliefs by the practice of *taqiya,* and many of them have continued to do so until the present day. A small number migrated to East Africa and set up independent congregations there, and, as in India, have always resisted the formation of effective centralised institutions.

Conclusion

In the census of Gujarat made in 1899 Muslims were divided into 'foreign Muslims' and 'local Hindu Muslims', The 'foreigners' were separated into twenty-one named classes, all of whom were Sunni. The 'local Hindu Muslims' were divided into seventy-eight categories, of whom sixty-five were Sunni, nine were Shia and four could not be placed in either division. All 'foreign' Sunni Muslims inter-married, but 'local Hindu Muslim' converts, even when they were Sunnis, tended to be endogamous, as they had been when they still belonged to Hindu *jati.* They also preserved their former caste names and occupations and remained within the general caste structure of society with little difficulty. Within the Sunni community they were indistinguishable, except for small differences of dress, their marriage regulations, and certain minor modifications of the laws of inheritance of the Hanafi School of Law to which the majority belonged.

The relationship of Muslims to the caste system was from the beginning of almost no significance in East Africa, though former caste affiliations were sometimes remembered and provided grounds for expressions of personal dislike. The Shia sects in Uganda comprised 72 per cent of the Indian Muslim population. The total Sunni population numbered approximately only three thousand, and it was too small and evenly divided to allow the emergence of separately organised communities such, for example, as the small 'foreign' group of Sunni Buluchis from Gujarat. Sunnis worshipped at the same mosques and followed Hanafi law. Most Indian Sunnis were Punjabi or Urdu speakers, and this was an important distinction, but their numbers were insufficient to allow them safely to act as a permanent separate group.

Indian Shia Muslims came to Africa as distinct and organised sects, most of which had a long tradition of trading and connections overseas, which partly accounts for their outnumbering the Sunni immigrants in Africa. Unlike the Sunnis, who all worshipped in the same mosques, the Shias, as such, had no institutions for common activities. In theory all Muslims, Shia and Sunni alike, acknowledged their unity; but in practice they were deeply divided. In the early days, when the Indian community was small, their interests as Indians and traders were usually more important than their division into Hindus or Muslims, and there were very few occasions when Muslims felt the need to act as united Muslims or Sunnis or Shias.

NOTES OF REFERENCES

1. In Gujarati, the formal term for sub-caste *is gynati;* the more colloquial *jat or jati,* In its widest connotation the word means kind or species, and in this general sense is used of plants or animals without connotations of hierarchy, specialisation of occupation, ritual purity, or other limitations of its meaning which apply when it is used of the caste system.

2. M.N. Srinivas, *Religion and society among the Coorgs,* Oxford, 1952, p. 24.

3. G.S. Ghurye, *Caste and Race in India,* London, 1932, p. 27.

4. M. N. Srinivas, *Religion and Society among the Coorgs,* p. 24. *Varna* may also be used by the members of a *jati* who reject its place in the local hierarchy. By maintaining that the *varna* which is attributed to it locally is incorrect they may, if other circumstances are favourable, be able to assert successfully that it should be placed in a higher *varna* and thus alter the ranking of the *jati* group.

5. Census of India, 1911, UN. VII, Bombay, Part I, Report, p. 284; for an account of the Lohana caste category in Kathiawad, Cutch and Sind,

6. J.H, Hutton *Caste in India* Cambridge, 1946, p. 49.

7. A.M, Hocart, *Caste: A Comparative Study,* London, 1950.

8. M. Marriot, 'Little Communities in an Indigenous Civilisation, Village India', *American Anthropological Association,* vol. 57, no. 3, part 2 (1955), p 190.

9. Sir William Jones (tr.) *The Institutes of Manu,* London, 1825.

10. C. Bougie, *Essais sur le Regime des Castes,* Paris, 1908.

11. E. R. Leach, 'Aspects of Caste in South India, Ceylon and North West Pakistan', *Cambridge Papers in Social Anthropology.,* no. 2 (1960), p. 5.

12. S.F. Nadel, *The Theory of Social Structure* London 1957, pp. 64-72.

13. *Bombay Gazetteer* vol. ix, part I (1901), p. xxvi.

14. D. Pocock, "Movement of Castes', *Man,* vol. lv (May 1955), art. 79.

15. D. Pocock, "Movement of Castes'.

16. W. Crooke, 'Hinduism', *Encyclopaedia of Religion and Ethics* James Hastings (ed.), Edinburgh, 1908, vol. 6, p. 699.

17. A. Lyall, *Religious Systems of the World,* London, 1889, p. 14,

18. Strictly speaking Jains are not Hindus, though in East Africa they are counted among the Hindus as opposed to Muslims, Jainism is a monastic religion which, like Buddhism denies the authority of the Veda, and is, therefore, regarded by the Brahmins as heretical. The Jain church consists of the monastic order and the lay community. H. Jacobi 'Jainism', in *Encyclopaedia of Religion and Ethics.*

19. *Bombay Gazetteer* vol. ix, part I (1901), p. 348.
20. *Ibid.,*. 531.
21. *Ibid.*, p. 532.
22. *Ibid.*, p, 532.
23. *Ibid.*, p. 530.
24. H. Kuper, *Indian People in Natal,* Natal, 1960; B. Benedict, *Indians in a Plural Society* London, 1961; A. Mayor, *Peasants in the Pacific,* London, 1961.
25. The name *Sanatan Dharma* in this sense is recent. In the early part of this century a Hindu college at Benares published a series of pamphlets to combine Hindu religious and ethical training with Western education suited to the needs of the time'. The title *Sanatana Dharma* was chosen for the series 'after full discussion as best representing the idea of the fundamental truths presented. It has become somewhat of a sectarian name in parts of India, but it is here taken as meaning the eternal religion' *(Sanatana Dharma,* Benares, 1919. pp. v-vii).
26. Private communication from Mandal Committee Member, 1957.
27. *Bombay Gazetteer,* vol. ix, part x (1901), p. 82.
28. *All India, Arya (Hindu) Dharma Sewa Sangh, Brief Report,* Delhi, (undated) p. 1.
29. J.N.D. Anderson, *Islamic Law in Africa,* London, 1954, p. 367: 'Khalifa Caliph of Successor. This term was used by Sunnis of the head of the Muslim community until the abolition of the Ottoman caliphate. In the orthodox view, however, the *Khalifa* must be of the Qurayshi blood, and possessed of a number of other attributes: but he was the upholder, not the interpreter, of the law; the ruler not the pontiff of the community.'

9

ROLE OF THE INDIAN DIASPORA IN THE RISE OF NATIONALISM

Nature of Asian Politics

Asian politics in Tanganyika, Uganda and Zanzibar during the post-war years were somewhat different from politics in Kenya but followed the same general course to an early post-war division among Asians, a close rapport between the more radical Asians and the African leaders in the struggle for independence, and a post-colonial dissolution of this relationship. In these territories, political issues never attracted the attention of resident Asians to the same degree as in Kenya, and they pertained more to local subjects of interest. In forming their decisions on these issues, the political leaders acted, with few exceptions, independently from those in Kenya.[1]

Despite some attempts, primarily by trade unionists in Kenya, to establish coordinating organisations, the politicians in each territory, for the most part, went their separate ways. The course of Asian political history, however, was essentially the same for all the Asians on the new whole supported the African nationalist movement but divided on the issue of the appropriate time for, independence. In the new national governments, despite the fact that some were 'exceedingly helpful to the countries' future leaders, the Asians were permitted no important participation.

In the meantime, during the late colonial and early post-colonial years, the Asian politicians were unable to mitigate the policies of socialism and Africanisation that were destroying their economic opportunity. As in Kenya, their economic decline coincided with their political decline.

Tanganyika

Immediately after the war which interrupted political activity, the Tanganyika Africans formed many new branches of their Dar es Salaam "African Association and began to call for independence. In 1946 Julius Nyerere abandoned a teaching career to assume the presidency of the Tabora branch and, demanding independence without any unnecessary delay' and denouncing closer union, he quickly acquired a position of leadership throughout the country. In 1953 he was to become president of the Dar es Salaam organisation which had been renamed the Tanganyika African Association.[2]

In 1950, the Asian leaders of Dar es Salaam responded to the post-war nationalism by forming a new political organisation, the Asian Association. Designed to replace the older Indian Association, the new organisation was more overtly political and more concerned with African interests. Unlike its counterparts in Kenya, it was a colony-wide organisation with branches in the other urban centres. It also retained its Muslim members. Among the twenty founders were the businessmen Amir Habib Jamal, Akberali Abdulhusem Adamjee and Dahyabhai Kalyanbhal Patel, the barristers Kantilal Laxmichand Jhaveri and Mahmud Nasser Rattansey, and the accountant and company director Jayantilal Keshayp Chande, Leading the liberal wing of Asian politics in Tanganyika, they were distinguished men representative of all age groups and nearly all segments of the Asian community. In 1951, when a United Nations mission visited Tanganyika, the Asian Association presented a petition that revealed a political consciousness far more enlightened than that which then prevailed in Kenya. It requested not only a common roll, but also a universal adult franchise and independence within twenty years.[3]

During the fifties the Asian liberals assumed an important rolc in the nationalist movement. As explained in Chapter 11

Asians had provided some assistance to African politicians in earlier years, but it was not until the post-war era that Asians and Africans began to merge their Interests In a drive for independence. Beginning in 1950, leaders of the Asian Association began to meet frequently with Africans, including Nyerere to consider formation of a new African political organisation. They helped to institute the Tanganyika African National Union (TANU) in 1954, and afterwards to further its progress. Some of the initial TANU meetings were held in have home despite the fact that Asians were barred from membership. Two Asian brothers, Surendra and Randhir Thaker also devoted their printing works to issuing the TANU weekly *Mwafrica* and in 1959 established their own newspaper. *Nguramo* (Thunder) as a voice for African independence.[4]

In promoting African interests, these Asian leaders provoked opposition not only from the government but also from many in their own community. When they began to support TANU in their newspaper, recalled Surendra, 'eighty to ninety per cent of the Asians hated us', and the government often sent police and CID agents to their office.[5] Shortly after the Asian Association began a close co-operation with African nationalists, nearly all the Ismaili members suddenly withdrew from the Association apparently on the advice of the Aga Khan. Why the Aga Khan took this step, which destroyed the possibility of Asian unity, became a subject of dispute among the Asian leaders. Some said that he wanted his followers to dissociate from any one community' and thought 'Asian" a racist term, others that it conformed to his general policy of concentrating on economic development as opposed to politics, and still others that he believed that the Ismailis' future was best secured by a perpetuation of British rule.[6] It was common knowledge that the Aga Khan and Sir Edward Twining, Governor from 1949 to 1958 were close friends.

Although, he began his administration with a favourable impression of the Asians, the new Governor soon deprecated the role of radicals such as Jamal. Rattansey and Jhaveri because of their association with the African nationalists. Twining staunchly opposed a rapid advance to independence. In 1952, he proposed a new constitution based on a parity of legislative representation for Asians. Africans and Europeans.

In opposing the proposal, the Asian leaders revived their nine teen-twenties slogan of native paramountcy' and they were soon joined In this call by the Africans. Apparently in an attempt to placate their more conservative members, however, the Asian Association requested a common roll only for Asians and Europeans.[7]

The division in the Asian ranks became evident in February 1955, when Nyerere, with assistance from the Asian Association flew to New York to present the case for independence to the United Nations. In opposition to Nyerere, Twining sent Iqbal Chand Chopra, a Punjabi Hindu barrister who had been newly appointed to the Executive Council, to state before the United Nations that from the Asians' view, the country would not be ready for independence in another twenty-five years. When Nyerere informed the Asian Association of this, the Association, which by then was led by the radicals, immediately dispatched a telegram refuting Chopra's claim to speak for the Asian community and asserting that Tanganyika was ready for independence 'now'.[8]

In 1956, Twining took the lead by announcing a general election for 1958-59 and initiating the United Tanganyika Party (UTP) with a platform of multi-racialism, a common roll and again a parity of representation in opposition to TANU's platform which by then included a common franchise and 'one man one vote'. Among the Asians supportive of the DTP were Abdulkarim Yusufali Alibhai Karimjee, the wealthy and Influential Bohra businessman who was Mayor of Dar es Salaam. Madatall Moolil Nazarali, an Ismaili leader, and Dr. and Mrs. Kussann Mohamad Khakoo, prominent Muslims. To some in the Asian Association, these men and Chopra were known as Twinmg's 'Asian stooges'.[9] At the time Twining is said to have promised Rattansey, then president of the Asian Association, favours if he left the Association and dampened us agitation.[10] In the preceding year during a luncheon. Twining had advised the legislative councillor Shyam T. Thanki to stop associating with 'this riff-raff—meaning Nyerere.[11] There were rumours that the Aga Khan donated money to the UTP but apparently he did not openly urge his followers to support it.[12]

In the two-stage elections of December 1958 and February 1959, although it did not permit Asians to become party members, TANU endorsed ten Asian candidates, some of whom faced African opponents. To the gratification of the Asian Association, TANU won by an overwhelming margin, and all three candidates put forward by the Association—Jamal, Jhaveri and Rattansey—were elected.[13]

After the elections the UTP was dissolved, TANU led Tanganyika rapidly to self-government and as in Kenya, the Asians within a short time were virtually excluded from politics. Tanganyika became self-governing in December 1961 and a republic with Nyerere as President one year later. In April 1964 it combined with Zanzibar in the formation of Tanzania. Meanwhile, in the wake of the 1958-59 election, many of the disaffected Asians had rejoined the Asian Association and be-' come enthusiastic supporters of TANU. The rewards to those who faithfully supported TANU, however, were minimal. Nyerere's first Cabinet, following the election of August September 1960, comprised seven Africans, four Europeans and only one Asian, Jamal. Nyerere's later Cabinets were to reveal a similar token representation of the Asians.

During 1962-63 after TANU removed its restrictions on non-African membership more than half the members of the Asian Association, from 1,500 to 2.000 joined TANU. Subsequently Rattansey and a few other Asians were successful in running for office. Three were briefly honoured: Karimjee during 1959-62 was Speaker of the House, the Hindu businessman Manilal Mathuradas Devani became the Mayor of Dar es Salaam and D.R. Patel a Deputy Mayor.

The Asians' economic decline paralleled that of their politics. Although, some Kenya Asians doggedly persevered in commerce beyond the sixties, far less were able to continue in Tanzania where the official actions affecting the mercantile sector were much more severe.

Until promulgation of Nyerere's Arusha Declaration in February 1967. Tanzania, like Kenya, continued the British policy of encouraging private business while steadily expanding government control. During its first year, 1962, the government greatly increased the number of co-operatives and began to establish parastatals, commercial and industrial companies in which it retained a controlling interest. One of its first parastatals was the Co-operative Supply Association cf Tanganyika Ltd. (Cosata) which served as a wholesaler to the consumer cooperatives. In 1964 it replaced the development agencies inherited from the colonial period with a parastatal National Development Corporation (NDC) which, with far more money (£1 million) than its Kenya counterpart, offered financial assistance to African traders and industrialists and encouraged Joint management between Africans and Asians. The NDC formed an investment holding company, the Tanzanian African Finance Co. Ltd. (TAFCO), to promote partnership with the government in commercial and industrial ventures. Although, these measures represented, on the whole, further restraints on individual initiatives, Nyerere after five years of experimentation decided that the continuing private enterprise was the root cause of Tanzania's disappointing growth in GDP and the widespread corruption in the co-operatives.[14]

Arusha Declaration

Among the drastic changes announced in the Arusha Declaration was a programme of nationalisation in which the government assumed either total ownership of or a majority interest in the principal instruments of production. The programme affected Asians in all sectors of the economy but mainly in commerce. In addition to taking over the key industries, mining and processing of agricultural produce, the government nationalised banking, insurance and a large portion of the import-export business. Importing, distribution and much of the retail trade were assigned to a new State Trading Corporation (STC) which absorbed Cosata and set up a network of retail co-operatives. The STC exported commodities obtained from new parastatal companies, government agencies, marketing boards and co-operatives. The aim attained through a gradual increase of government participation, was a complete socialisation of the economy. The result was a rapid decline of private business affecting Asians, Europeans and Africans alike. Although, Nyerere professed adherence to a non-racial policy, his efforts to eliminate the middle class had racial implications. Asian shops all over Tanzania were closed. By 1970, only 3 or 4 per cent of all imports were still handled by private firms.[15]

Although, they enjoyed a higher status than in Kenya, the Asians quickly realised that they had no future, economic or political, in a society that was multi-racial in name. But, monoracial in operation. In the initial years, however, not many left Tanganyika for this reason. Chopra, who had been most conspicuous in his co-operation with the Europeans, was among the few. He retired to Geneva with his British wife. Those who remained, perceiving that their political organisations no longer served a useful purpose, terminated them shortly after independence. The leaders in Dar es Salaam devoted the proceeds from the sale of the Asian Association's property, augmented by gifts from Karimjee and others, to establishment of the non-racial Shaban Roberts Secondary School.[16]

Uganda

Though similar in fundamentals. Asian politics in Uganda differed in important respects from the politics of Kenya and Tanganyika, the Before independence most, Asians in the other territories assumed a wait and see posture in the conflict between Africans and Europeans while small minorities sided with either the British or the Africans In Uganda, however, were very influential. Moreover, unlike in Kenya and Tanganyika, the British government, in the wake of its dispute with the Kabaka and the existence of a strong traditional resentment g against the Ganda by other Africans, did not clearly support any one party.

The Asians involvement in the nationalist movement began in 1952 when Milton Obote returned to se tup the Lango branch of the UN, long-standing differences over the problem of separatism and the course to independence increased. In 1956 the most conservative Ganda, mainly Roman Catholics, were instrumental I establishing a second political organisation, the Democratic Party (DP). During these years, as the Uganda Asians' foremost statesman. Sir Amar Nath

Maini, has pointed out, 'the Asian community never got down to any stematic discussion and analysis of the implications of independence so as to decide upon and concerted approach to it.[17] After 1952, however, the Central Council of Indian Associations, the Central Council of Muslim Associations and the Kampala Indian Association all sought co-operation with African politicians and supported the UNC's general multi-racial platform.[18]

There was one exception to this Asian pattern in Uganda. In 1958 a score of young Asian intellectuals including Gurdial Singh. Rajat Neogy and Natoo Karia—in Maini's view. Young Turks' with Dr. Muljibnai Motibhai Patel as their guru—formed the Uganda Action Group (UAG). Their principal aim was to explain to the African on the street the Africans, and Asian aspirations to 'collectivise and channelize', and to mobilise both communities for independence.[19] Associating with the more militant Africans, they contributed to Obote's rise and to the breakaway from the UNC in 1959 that led to the founding of his Uganda Peoples' Congress (UPC). Afterwards most of the Asians in the UAG above all Gurdial Singh, worked closely with Obote and the UAG vigorously supported the UPCs demands for independence under a common roll and universal adult franchise.[20] In the first general election of February 1961 the UPC lost to the DP which by this time had displaced the fragmented UNC as the most popular African party.

During the ensuing year as Uganda prepared for self-government, the DP's Benedicto Kiwanuka headed the temporary government, the UNC was split further and the more extreme Ganda formed a separatist party, the Kabaka Yekka (KY). Early in this hectic year. Just after the election, the UAG dissolved itself and its leader joined Obote's UPC. Membership. Meanwhile, the more conservative Asian leaders,' such as Dr. M.M. Patel who led the Kampala Asian Association, and the two Ismailis Sherali Bandali Jaffer and Galamhussein Kassim-Lakha who were prominent in the Central Council of Muslim Associations followed a middle course in avoiding support of any one party. A few, including the Ithnasheri woman politician, Sugra Haiderali Allidina Visram, Joined the KY.[21] The second general election, April 1962, which provided the basis forfeit government, was in effect a victory for the radical Asian as the UPC won the most seats and, in a coalition with the KY took over the government of Uganda.

After independence, though accorded a more active political role than in Kenya and Tanganyika, the Uganda Asians quickly disappeared from the mainstream of politics. Those who had worked the hardest for the African ascendancy received no meaningful recognition of their efforts Kiwanuka's Cabinet included only one Asian, Chandulal Kalidas Patel, a barrister, legislative councillor and Mayor of Jinja who became Minister of Commerce and Industry. Obote's coalition Cabinet was composed of thirteen members: eleven Africans, one Briton ad Narendra Manubhai Patel, a prominent Kampala barrister, as Deputy Minister of Internal Affairs. As in the other territories, it was the more conservative Asian politicians who attained the few posts of honour. In 19612, for instance, Maini was elected Speaker of the East African Central Legislative Assembly and in 1963 N.M. Patel became Speaker of the Uganda Parliament.[22] Asian polities, however, could have no separate existence. The Asian political organisations were dissolved shortly after October 1962 when Uganda achieved independence.

The Asian politicians in Uganda were unable to stem the tide of socialism and Africanisation that undermined their economic well-being. Initially, while encouraging African businessmen, Obote emphasised co-operatives much to the detriment of independent business. By 1966, for instance, marketing co-operatives were being allocated 75 per cent of the cotton crop. In 1967 after introducing a new constitution which vested power in the office of the president, Obote intensified the take-over of commercial and Industrial concerns and began to regulate the economy through parastatals. He failed, however, in his aim to raise farm prices by substituting parastatals for the remaining Asian wholesalers, retailers and artisans with the result that there was widespread rural unrest culminating in the assassination attempt of 1969.[23]

Obote reacted with what became known as the 'move to the left'. As a first step he abolished all political parties except his Uganda Peoples' Congress. On May Day 1970 he proclaimed a Common Man's Charter which involved not only nationalisation of the banking system, but also an assumption by government of a 60 per cent ownership in all the means of production.[24] Obote then proceeded to reassert government control over the co-operatives, which since 1963 had been virtually autonomous, and to sponsor a Trade Licensing Act that stipulated an annual fee of Shs. 500 and a minimum capital of Shs. 80,000 for the conduct of business. He also appointed a Commission for Africanisation of Commerce and Industry, and the commission introduced an Immigration Bill requiring all non-citizens to apply for entry permits. The purpose of the Bill, explained by the Minister of Commerce and Industry, was to make sure that Africans go to the top of as many companies as possible'.[25]

Uganda's move to the left was deceiving. Unlike Nyerere, Obote apparently realised in time that the economy was still dependent on the Asians. Although, he nationalised many of the larger companies, he negotiated with the leading traders and manufacturers with the result that none had to yield a 60 per cent share to the government. His measures to drive the Asians from the import-export and wholesaling trade were permitted to remain ineffective, and the Trade Licensing Act proved as severe a hardship for the aspiring African businessman as for the Asian petty trader. When he perceived that many Asians were leaving the country, Obote announced that he was considering granting citizenship, and hence the right to trade, to 30,000 Asians.[26] The contradictions between his policies and actions created widespread unrest, increased African resentment against the Asians and became a major cause of the military coup of January 1971. It was Obote's successor, Amin, who, with his expulsion order of 1978, was to terminate all Asian enterprise and what remained of Asian politics.

Zanzibar

On Zanzibar the pattern in the other territories was repeated as the Asians divided with the approach of independence. The division began during 1954-56 when the Arabs began a boycott of the Legislative Council and formed the Zanzibar Nationalist Party (ZNP) calling for Muslim unity under Arab leadership. In response, the immigrant and indigenous Africans formed the Afro-Shirazi Party (ASP) with a platform of immediate Independence under the control of the African majority. The situation became complex when each of these parties split. In 1959 the Zanzibar and Pemba Peoples' Party (ZPPP) was established by moderates in the ASP who favoured multi-racialism, and in early 1963 a few extremists advocating close ties with China left the ZNP to form Umma (The Masses). As in Uganda, the British government, which retained control of both internal and external affairs until June 1963, did not openly take sides. The choice for the Asians was essentially one of joining either the Arabs or the Africans. In this situation the Ismaili, Hadji Ladak, and many Asian youths worked actively for Umma, but apparently none for the ZPPP and some Asian leaders like the venerable Ahmed Abdulrasul Mohamed Lakha, who was a legislative councillor and president of the Chamber of Commerce, avoided taking sides and attended any and all meetings to which they were invited.[27]

Most Asian political leaders wavered between the two major parties. The ZNP had the support of the Ithnasheris the more conservative Asian newspaper. *Samachar* and the Muslim Association. After the election of July 1963 when the ASP formed a coalition government with the ZPPP it was considered 'the safe party to back'.[28] The ASP was supported by the *Zanzibar Voice* and the Indian National Association, and thus by both Hindus and Ismailis, Although, Asians could not be ASP members, four of them ran for office pledged to ASP support. Among the many Asians who campaigned for the ASP, the most active were Rastom Sidhwa, secretary of the Chamber of Commerce and chairman of the Town Council, and perhaps Vaghjibhai Shankerbhal Patel the long-standing secretary of the Indian National Association, president of the Arya Samaj an d legislative councillor. After the ASP coup of December 1964, to the disappointment of these men, not one not even Sidhwa, the most "indefatigable worker, was honoured with office, and apparently all the leaders left Zanzibar.[29]

After the coup all Asian activity en Zanzibar, economic as well as political, was virtually non-existent. Only about twenty Asians were killed, but almost all the rest lied to the mainland.

About sixty stayed on, and by 1989 their number had dwindled to approximately fifteen. They were mostly old people who were no longer active economically and had no Voice in the new Zanzibar politics.

NOTES AND REFERENCES

1. Morris, *Indians in Uganda* (Chicago: University Press, 1958), p. 179.
2. John Iliffe, *Modem History of Tanganyika* (Cambridge: University Press, 1979), pp. 426-33.
3. K.L. Jhaveri, intv. by Gregory, 20 Feb. 1973; and by Honey, 16 Mar. 1973, Dar es Salaam. Brief biographies of all these men are in E. G. Willson, ed.. *Who's who* in. East Africa, J 965-66 (Nairobi; Marco, 1966).
4. Surendra Bhanushanker Thakar, intv. by Honey, 8 Mar. 1973, Dares Salaam; and by Gregory, 16 Mar. 1971, Syracuse. For early African political organisation, see Daisy Sykes Buruku, Townsman: Kleist Sykes', ch. 5, *Modem Tanzanians:* a *Volume of Biographies,* ed. John Iliffe (Nairobi: East African Publishing House. 1973). pp. 101-12.
5. Thakar intv., 16 Mar. 1971.
6. Among those who did not withdraw were Hussein and Jamal For background on this period, see Cranford Pratt, *Critical Phase in* Tanzania, *1945-68: Nyerere and the Emergence cf a* Socialist *Strategy* (Cambridge: University Press. 1976); and Andrew G. Maguire, *Towards 'Uhura' in Tanzania:* the Politics *of Participation* (Cambridge: University Press, 1969). Dr. Gulamhussein Mohamedali Daya. 25 Jan. 1974; H. Dharam, 19 Oct 1973, S.B. Thakar, 8 Mar. 1973; Abdulia Hassam Kassam Tejpar, 27 Mar. 1973; E.S. Udwadia. 28 July 1973—all intv. by Honey. Dar es Salaam.
7. Iliffe, *Modem History,* p. 476.
8. Udwadia, intv. For a biography of Chopra, see Shantt Pandit, ed., *Asians in East* and *Central Africa* (Nairobi: Panco, 1963), p. 118.
9. S.M.A. Kitabwalla, intv. by Honey, 24 Mar. 1973, Dares Salaam. A.Y.A. 1973; and by Honey. 20 Mar. 1973, Dares Salaam.
10. Dharani intv., 19 Oct. 1973.

11. Reminding Tuning that the British had called Nehru riff-raft, Thanki predicted that Nyerere would soon be made the head of an independent government Thanki said he was sucking with a winner. Thanki, intv. by Honey. 9 Sep. 1973, Dar es Salaam.
12. Baldev Krishna, intv. by Honey, 19 Apr. 1974. Dares Salaam.
13. Iliffe, *Modem History.*, p. 561, For an Asian perspective of political events July 1958-March 1961, including the election, see Sophia Mustafa, *Tanganyika Way: a Personal Story of Tanganyika's Growth to Independence* [London: Oxford University Press, 1962). The *Sunday News* (Dar es Salaam), 20 July 1958, presented biographies of the candidates.
14. Issa G. Shivji. Class *Struggles in Tanzania* (New York: Monthly Review Press. 1976). pp. 73-7. For an Asian view of the new organisations, see 'Dar es Salaam Merchants' Chamber: Presidential Address Delivered by the Chamber's President, Mr. M.M. Devani, at the Annual General Meeting... 28 March 1964', file 10. 'Other Chambers. 4. Minutes, Circulars', Mombasa Indian Merchants' Chamber records. Syracuse University microfilm 1922, reel 3.
15. Julius K. Nyerere, Freedom *and Development: a Selection from* Writings and Speeches. *1968-73* (Dares Salaam: Oxford University Press, 1973), pp. 312-4. *Tanzanian Second Five-Year Plan for* Economic and. Social *Development 1st July. 1969- 30th June,* 1974: vol. I, Genera! *Analysis* (Dar es Salaam: Government Printer, 1969), p. 12.
16. Jhaveri intv.. 10 Feb. 1973; also M.M. Devani, intv. by Gregory, 19 Jan. 1973, Nairobi, and 17 Feb. 1973, Dares Salaam.
17. Sir Amar Maini, 'Asians and Politics in Late Colonial Uganda: Some Personal Recollections ch 8, Expulsion of a Minority: *Essays on Uganda Asians,* ed. Michael Twaddle London: Athlone, 1971), p. 117.
18. Maini, intv, by Gregory, 22 Nov. 1984, London.
19. *Ibid.*, Rajat Neogy. Intv by Gregory, 8 Feb. 1974, Syracuse.
20. *Ibid.*; also Natoo T. Karia, intv. by, Gregory. 13 July 1973, Porbandar; and Raminlal Gokaldas Suraiya, intv. by Gregory, 21 June 1973, Bombay The complexities of Uganda party formation are lucidly explained in D. A. Low, *Buganda in Modern History* (London: Weidenfeld & Nicolson. 1971), esp. ch 6; and David E. Apter, *Political Kingdom in Uganda: a Study in Bureaucratic Nationalism.* (Princeton: University Press 1961).

21. Neogy, Karia, & Suraiya interviews: and Maini, Asians', p. 124. Brief biographies of Jailer, Kassim-Lakha, M.M. Patel, and Visrarn appear in Wilson. lido's Who, pp. 32. 41, 96, 117.

22. For biographies of Maini and of C.K. and N.M. Patel, see Wilson, Who's pp. 63, 94, 96. For the Cabinets, see Facts on. *File. 1961* p 87. 1962 p. 184.

23. In his seminal work on Uganda polities Jan Jelmert Jorgensen has described these changes as beginning with Obote's interim' constitution of April 1966: *Uganda, a Modern History* (N.Y. St Martin's 1981), pp. 230 ff. See also Uganda, *Report of the* Commission, of Enquiry into the *Cotton Industry* (Kampala: Government Printer, 1966). pp. 24-5. Mahmood Mamdani, *Politics and Class Formation in Uganda* (London: Monthly Review Press. 1970) pp. 260-2. E.J. Stoutjesdijk. *Uganda's Manufacturing Sector: A Contribution to an Analysis of Industrialisation in* East Africa (Nairobi: East African Publishing House. 1967) pp. 34-5.

24. The charter was published as Dr. A. Milton Obote, Common Man's *Charter* (Entebbe: Government Printer, 1949).

25. Uganda, *Parliamentary Debates,* 23 July' 1970, pp 198-201. Yash Tandon, 'Pragmatic Industrialist'. ch. V, *Jayant Madhvani,* ed. Robert Becker and Nitin Jayarit Madhvani (London: W. & J. Mackay, 1973), pp. 17-8. For a comprehensive description of the 'move to the left', see Jorgensen, *Uganda,* pp. 332-7.

26. Mamdam, *Politics,* pp. 280-1, Sultan Jaffer, intv. by Bennett, 9 Apr. 1973. Nairobi. Jorgensen has described Obote as allying with Asian civil servants, manufacturers and wholesalers to counter the Canda 'hegemony' in domestic affairs. Obote's regime, he asserts, encouraged the Asian mercantile class to turn to manufacturing. Together, 'the UDC [Uganda Development Corporation, the government's chief nationalising agency], Madhvani and Mehta groups formed the big three, the core of industrial capital in Uganda'. Jorgensen, Luanda, pp. 249, 252.

27. Ahmed A. M. Lakha, intv. by Honey, 15 Jan. 1974, Dar es Salaam. Some attention is given to Asians in Michael Lofchie, *Zanzibar. Background 10 Revolution* (Princeton University Press, 1965).

28. Mrs. Abdul Rahman Mohammed, intv. by Honey, 16 Jan. 1974. Dares Salaam.

29. Others were Hussein Jess Bhaloo, R.D. Bhimji. Jethaliladhar, Nabherarn Panachamb, Iswarlal Ravai, D.M. Shah, Gulamhusein Ismail. Ebrahim Kassum, A.H. Viljee, and Muraiji Visanji—names provided by V.S. Patel, intv. by Honey, 8, 10 Jan. 1974. Dar es Salaam, Fora biography of V.S. Patel, see B.G. Vaghela, *East Africa Today: Comprehensive Directory of British East Africa with* Who's who (Bombay: Overseas Information, 1959), p. 691; for Sidhwa, see Wilson, Who's Who p. 92. V.V. Patel intv. 8. 10 Jan. 1974, Ahmed A.M. Lakha. Mrs. A. R. Mohammed, Akbar Vellani, all intv. by Honey, 13. 14 Feb. 1974, Zanzibar. Also Roshanali Hassanali Master, Intv. by Honey, 11 July 1973, Dares Salaam.

10

DECOLONISATION AND THE POLITICAL PROSPECTS OF THE INDIAN DIASPORA

After World War II, African nationalism, which the Asians had to generate and had generally supported in the inter war years, became a vital force in East African history and produced a serious split in the Asian leadership.[1] For the first Asians had to fake seriously the question of how fast East Africa should proceed to self-government with rule by an African majority. While some Asians clung steadfastly to the principle of African paramountey, others, alarmed by the increasing emphasis on African interests and the violence of Mau Mau, began to revise their fundamental political goals towards delaying independence and creating constitutional safeguards for their future. In the end, the fears of the more conservative Asians were realised. 'Africa for the Africans' was to spell the end of Asian politics.

Nationalism received a great impetus from the war which, brought new forms of economic and social restriction, enhanced the political power of the European community and generated a new European drive for self-government and closer union. Nearly twenty per cent of the adult male Africans served in the East African Forces. In Somalia, Ethiopia. North Africa/ Madagascar, Burma and India, they associated with many peoples, were exposed to new cultures and saw that the racial discrimination so prevalent in East Africa was not a universal phenomenon. They acquired technical skills, advanced in literacy and gained a political consciousness. Out of the war, as Rosberg and Nottingham have explained, came 'a new politics—mass political movements under a leadership determined to replace colonial rule with African majority rule'.[2]

Early Post-War Association with African Leaders

The new nationalism was first expressed in Kenya. In October 1944 to replace the banned KCA, a number or Kenya Africans, including James Gichuru. Harry Thuku and John Kebaso, formed the Kenya African Union (KAU). Though constrained by government to change its name to the Kenya African Study Union, the organisation two years later resumed its original name and rapidly became the foremost African political organisation Initially KAY called only for a more equitable distribution land and a removal of all forms of distribution In June 1947 shortly after his return from Britain, Kenyatta replaced Gichuru as president and, to avoid government suppression, retained a moderate platform.[3] A more extreme nationalism found expression in a militant trade unionism and a new vernacular press.

During the initial post-war years, African and Asian leaders were drawn together in opposition to the continuing war-time restrictions and the new European movement for autonomy. It was the Asians who took the initiative. At a large Asian meeting in November 1944. W.L. Sohan, secretary of the Nairobi Indian Association, stressed the need for Asian-African co-operation. Asians leaders then invited representation from the Kenya African Study Union at the next meeting of the Congress, and the president, Gichuru, became in October 1945, the first African ever to attend an open session. At a mass meeting in July 1946, organised by the Nairobi Indian Association in protest against eventsm South Africa, four prominent Africans—Peter Mbiyu Koinange, Muchochi Gikonyo, W.W.W. Awori and Henry Gathigira—were among the speakers. Three months later during an interview with the Asian press, Kenyatta accused the government of trying to separate the two communities and urged that in the future they work together on a 'completely equal footing'.[4] At the next session of the Congress in September 1946, which several African leaders attended, resolutions were passed urging the appointment of an African to the Executive Council and an increase of African representation in the Legislative Council.[5]

There is some evidence indicating that Asians in these early f post-war years provided financial support for the African or oganisations. In October 1945 Governor Mitchell advised the Colonial Office that the Kenya African Study Union was being 'encouraged and financed by the Indian community'.[6] In July 1946, at a joint meeting of Africans and Asians to celebrate the departure of an African deputation to London, the Congress president presented a large cheque as an Asian contribution towards the costs. After the war, G.L. Vidyarthi's Colonial Times Printing Works published several of the new vernacular newspapers and in some instances provided financial backing.[7] Asians were careful, of course not to let their support of African nationalists appear in their financial records.

The initial African-Asian co-operation was augmented by a number of new issues. Apartheid in South Africa, as already noted, was one problem Closer union and European self-government, emphasised by the two imperial publications—Colonial 191 and Colonial 210 —was another. A third issue was the Mombasa strike of January 1947 followed by Makhan Singn and Fred Kubai's joint union, activity. Other issues that drew Africans and Asians together were the proposed finger-printing bill of 1947, separate electorates, the Europeans' Kenya Plan of 1949 and the Europeans' opposition to the Tanganyika constitutional reform of 1950. The Congress and KAU issued a joint statement condemning the finger-printing proposals a result of the Kenya Plan and the proposed Tanganyika reform, the two organisations arranged the exceptional Kaloneni Hall meeting of April '1950 where thousands of Africans and Asians congregated to hear their leaders denounce the settlers and colonial rule. In an extraordinary resolution, the first of its kind in East Africa, the meeting called for immediate independence.[8]

The move towards extremism had two important consequences. One was the imposition of new suppressive measures and the arrest of the more militant leaders. In May 1950 Makhan Singh and Kubai were arrested, and their organisation, the East Africa Trade Union Congress, was declared illegal. Among several new restrictions imposed on trade unions was a law prohibiting strikes in essential services. With similar action the government curbed the press by arresting Vidyarthi. Karoon Ahmed and other journalists, and enacting a law permitting confiscation of offending presses. To thwart African-Asian political co-operation, the government in April 1952 prohibited the Congress and KAU from holding joint meetings or jointly sponsoring meetings.[9]

The other consequence of the rising extremism was a serious division in the Asian leadership. It was Makhan Singh who at Kaloneni had proposed the resolution for independence. At that meeting, A.B. Patel and another Asian barrister, D.N. Nene, spoke against the resolution. The difference of opinion at Kaloneni about the future course of Kenya was but the latest manifestation of a division that had become evident two years earlier in a meeting of the Congress Standing Committee. Ahmed, the journalist, had denounced the Congress leaders for their long-standing conservatism and demanded a 'progressive policy' of democratic rights of all people'.[10] In a *Colonial Times* editorial. Ahmed had advocated that the Legislative Council be reapportioned to include one European, three Asians and 140 Africans. During a legislative debate in August on a trade union bill, Patel took the opportunity to dissociate himself publicly from the more extreme Asians. He intimated that Makhan Singh and Ahmed were receiving financial aid from communists abroad.[11]

From before the war until his retirement in 1956. Patel was the leader of a conservative faction, sometimes referred to as the moderates, which included Anant J. Pandya, Dr. Mohamed Ali Rana and Kassamali Rajabali Paroo of Mombasa, and Shivabhai Gordnanbhai Amin, Chumlal B. Madan, Devi Dass Puri, Sir Eboo Pirbhai and N.S. Mangat in Nairobi. Pandya, who was born in 1917 and became the most influential of these men, threw himself into politics and social sendee after qualifying as a barrister at Lincoln's Inn. After his father's death in 1942 he quickly assumed his father's position as a leader of Kenya coastal society and in 1956 succeeded A.B. Patel in the Legislative Council. Unlike Patel, Pandya was able to adapt to African nationalism and after independence, to remain in the legislature as the most popular Asian leader. He moved from a conservative to a liberal position. The other two in Mombasa, Rana and Paroo, both Muslims, were far more conservative and were soon to withdraw from politics.[12]

The conservatives in Nairobi—Amin, Madan, Puri, Pirbhai and Mangat—were individualists. Amin, like Pandya, a barrister from the Inns of Court who was involved in many social and philanthropic endeavours, was the least conservative of the four. Before immigrating to Kenya in 1926, he had followed Gandhi in civil disobedience. He became a leader of the Congress and, beginning in 1942, a member of the Legislative Council. After independence he was to join Patel in an ashram in Pondicherry. Madan, a Punjabi Hindu who was born in Kenya, qualified as a barrister of the Middle Temple and successfully combined politics and law. He was in the Municipal Council from 1937 to 1948 and then in the Legislative Council. With his appointment to the Supreme Court in 1961 as a Puisne Judge, he was to become Kenya's first permanent Asian judge. Subsequently, he became the Acting Chief Justice. Like Pandya, he was one of the few Asians able to remain in office after independence. Puri a Hindu from India's Northern Frontier Province, had worked for the railway and then, as a businessman, become a prominent landlord and industrialist. He was twice president of the Congress, three times president of the Federation of Chambers of Commerce and Industry of Eastern Africa and a leader of many other organisations. Like Madan, he moved in 1936 from the Municipal Council to the Legislative Council. Pirbhai president of the Central Muslim Association and the leading Ismaili in Kenya politics, began in 1952 an eight-year term as a nominated member of the Legislative Council.[13]

Mangat, in contrast to the others, is an enigma. He began his political career as a radical and finished it as a reactionary. A Sikh and a barrister who became president of the Kenya Law Society, he was a powerful speaker with a forceful personality. He had entered politics in the late twenties as a supporter of Isher Dass and, in 1933 after joining the Congress, was elected to the Legislative Council where he subsequently supported Dass on a number of issues favourable to the Africans. During the early fifties, unlike most Sikhs, Mangat remained in the Congress. It was then, apparently, that the events of the emergency provoked a drastic change in his political views. He began to court a close association with the Europeans and to denounce African nationalism. Shortly before independence, when it was discovered that someone in the Congress executive had been reporting the closed-door deliberations to the government, Man-gat was suspected.[14]

Although, regarded as conservatives among the Asians, these men with the possible exception of Mangat, were not collaborators with the government and Europeans. Within the entire colonial spectrum of political opinion, they probably should be considered as liberals. Concerned primarily with achieving equality for their own community, they were often in bitter conflict with the colonial officials and the settler representatives. With the rise of a militant African nationalism, they began to doubt the efficacy of the long-sought common roll and complete equality as solutions to the racial problem of East Africa. Exhibiting a more accurate foresight in some ways than the extremists did they were apprehensive of the Asians' future under an African government. Thus, they began to oppose a rapid transfer of power. Of course, the government welcomed this development and bestowed its honours on this group. Patel was awarded a C.M.G. in 1949. Pirbhai was knighted in 1952, Madan and Mangat became Queen's Counsellors and Puri was able to add to his King's Silver Jubilee Medal of 3935 a King's Coronation Medal (1937) and a Queen's Coronation Medal (1954).

At the oilier end of the spectrum of Asian politics was an assortment of humanitarians known as the radicals or extremists. Foremost among them were Makhan Singh who is discussed more fully in the chapter on trade unionism. Ahmed, who is described in the chapter on journalism, and Pio Gama Pinto, a man of similar breadth who, because of his unique role in the mainsteam of Asian politics, deserves description here. Though born in Nairobi. Pinto had been raised in India where he had taken his primary and secondary education/ served briefly in the Indian Air Force, and then helped found the Goan National Congress and campaigned for the liberation of Goa. To avoid arrest, he had returned to Kenya in 1949 at age twenty-two. He quickly became associated with other young radicals in the East Africa Indian National Congress and by 1951 was its general secretary. Meanwhile, in employment, he had turned' from clerical work to writing for the Colonial *Times* and *Daily Chronicle*. From the early fifties until his assassination in 1965, he was to be primarily a journalist, but he also was to assume a very important role in labour organisation and politics. He threw himself into the nationalist movement and became closer than any Asian to the African nationalist leaders.[15]

Pinto, Makhan Singh and Ahmed were Marxian socialists. Equating colonialism with capitalism, they regarded the European officials and settlers and the Asian businessmen as the privileged bourgeoisie, and the Africans, together with the Asian clerks and artisans and other minorities, as the exploited proletariat. They envisioned a classless state governed by the workers and devoid of all economic, social, and racial discrimination.

Another group of humanitarians derived their egalitarianism from religious principles. In their view all peoples were equal in the divine scheme and, to be true to one's religious principles whether Hindu, Muslim, Sikh, Jain or Christian, one had to believe in and strive for a complete equality. Such a person was Kantilal Punamchand Shah. He had come from a village near Jamnagar in 1941 at age nineteen and worked his way through various enterprises to Kanti & Co. a wholesale enamelware business on Nairobi's Bazaar Street In 1947 he became president of the Indian Youth League and, the follow year, caused the word 'Indian' to be dropped from the title to attract African members. Subsequently, he became chairman of the Indian Chamber of Commerce, secretary of the Nairobi Indian Association and a leader of the Congress. In 1961, he was to help found the Kenya Freedom Party and enter the Legislative Council. Unlike most Asian politicians, he retained a simple Indian dress and wore a Gandhi cap.

There were also some humanitarians whose egalitarianism does not appear to have been based primarily on either Marxist or religious principles. They exhibited a natural sympathy for the oppressed and a deep resentment against the injustices of colonial rule. Within this category, it seems, were Chanan Singh. Fitzval Remedies Santana de Souza, Indravadan Tribhovandas Inamdar and Ambu Haribhai Patel. Chanan Singh, a Punjabi Hindu, came from India in 1923 at age fifteen to work as a fitter on the railway. He soon took up journalism, saved his money, and studied law at Lincoln's Inn. After 1945, he combined careers of journalism and law, entered politics and became one of the foremost leaders in the Congress. Nairobi Indian Association and Indian Youth League. Studying Sanskrit. Persian, French and German and speaking Gujarati as well as Punjabi, he gained recognition also as one of the foremost Asian scholars. Like Chanan Singh, de Souza attained distinction as a barrister, journalist and scholar. Born in Bombay in 1929, he was brought to Zanzibar as a child by his father, a medical doctor, and in 1942 to Kenya. After qualifying at the Inns of Court, de Souza practised law wrote for radical Asian newspapers and became very close to African nationalists. In 1961, he was to obtain a Ph.D. in economics from the University of London. Inamdar the youngest of the three, was born in 1931. He too studied at the Inns of Court and made law his principal profession. After the war lie engaged in many literary and benevolent activities in Mombasa and developed a sympathy for the oppressed. Like Chanan Singh and de Souza he was to be drawn to the side of the African nationalists by the events of the emergency.

Apart from the conservatives and radicals were several individuals who followed an independent course, voting with one side or the other depending on the issue, and who should probably be classified as liberals. In Nairobi, they included J.M. Nazareth. Zafrud-Deen, Ibrahim E. Nathoo, Arvind B. Jamidar and Bachulal Tribhovan Gathani. Nazareth, the Nairobi Goan, became president of the Congress during 1950-52 and soon earned a reputation as a very capable, highly independent legalist who never compromised.

Zafrud-Deen, son of Shamsud-Deen. had assumed his father's position after the war as the leader of the Muslim community. A Sunni born In 1909 and educated in Lahore, he entered the Nairobi Municipal Council in 1949 and two years later the Legislative Council. In 1954, he was to become president of the Kenya-Muslim League. Nathoo, an Ismaili businessman, was another prominent Muslim who was first elected to the Legislative Council in 1948. Jamidar, an advocate, legislative councillor and Congress leader, was to found the Kenya National Party. Gathani differed from these others in being an influential commercial as well as political leader. Coming from Gondal in 1928 at age eighteen, he developed a number of industries in printing and road transport and served successively as president of the Nairobi Indian Association. Nairobi Chamber of Commerce, and the Federation of Indian Chambers of Commerce and Industry.

Early in 1952, as political agitation, trade union activity, and militant journalism intensified, the division among the Asians over separate electorates and African nationalism led to the creation of a new political organisation. Nazareth, Ahmed, Pinto, K.P. Shah, Chanan Singh, Makhan Singh, de Souza, D.K. Sharda and several other Asians joined Joseph Murumbi and a few fellow Africans in forming the first non-racial political party the Kenya League Dedicated to the attainment of equal political rights without distinction as to race sex language or religion', the League held weekly planning sessions in the Desai Memorial Library. With KAU it sponsored a mass meeting in Kaloleni Hall at which African and Asian speakers called for 'one man one vote' and a common roll with no reservation of seats. The Kenya League, however, was to last only a few months. It was proscribed in June 1933 when KAU and all African political parties were banned. It was soon revived under another name, the Anti-Federation League, but that too was banned. It was then renamed the United Nations Association. By then, however, the organisation had lost its force.

Eventually, a number of its members were to form the nucleus of a much more important organisation, the Kenya Freedom Party. One of the main activities of those in the League was to break the segregation barrier in the Nairobi hotels and restaurants. Joining Africans to form a group of forty to sixty, de Souza, Pinto and some others in the League set out each week to enter premises that until then had catered exclusively to a European or Asian clientele. On several occasions they were arrested by police—de Souza two or three times, as he recalled—but in the end with each of the hotels and restaurants, they prevailed. The joint adventures led to a spirit of comradeship among the Africans and Asians. De Souza and Pinto began to share a house with Murumbi and Awori—all four were still single—and to plan together Kenya's liberation.

Reaction to the Man Mau Revolt

The Mau Mau rebellion and the state of emergency declared in October 1952 heightened Asian concern over the future course of Kenya and intensified the differences among Asian political leaders Early in the emergency an Asian trader was brutally murdered and his wife and children slashed with *pangas*. An Asian trading centre was attacked by an armed gang. Although, Europeans and African loyalists were the principal targets. Asians also, particularly traders in remote areas, were among the early victims. During the next few years nearly one hundred Asians were to be slain as compared to about one hundred Europeans and over ten thousand Africans. The fact that more Asians were not killed has been attributed to Pinto's close association with the rebels and the political leaders.[16]

> Had he not been able to enter the secret conclaves of the freedom fighters unnoticed, and had he not won the trust of leaders such as Stanley Mathenge, Jomo Kenyatta. Senior Chief Koinange and Tom Mboya for his sound and clear advice, thousands of Indians may well have been murdered and their property looted. Nehru and, later, Indira Gandhi, knew what Piu [Pio] Pinto had done for the Indians in those tumultuous days.

Whether the Asian deaths that did occur had been directed by Mau Mau or whether they were merely a result of the general increase in lawlessness during the time is still a moot question. What is clear is that the initial violence evoked a strong negative reaction in the Asian community.

Asian political leaders and organisations were initially almost unanimous in denouncing the violence. The Aga Khan expressed his opposition in a letter to the London *Times*. During a debate in the Legislative Council. A. B. Patel declared. The Asian community is strongly in favour of taking very drastic steps for dealing with the present situation. Chanan Singh stated that the 'strongest possible measures should be taken to stamp out lawlessness'.[17] The other two Asian elected members, C.B. Madan and I.E. Nathoo expressed similar views. All four later supported a government motion to impose the death J penalty for administering an oath in support of Mau Mau. The Indian Association of Thomson's Falls, where many Europeans were attacked, resolved. This Association notes with grave concern and anxiety present incidents in this district.... They condemn African actions and request Government for immediate drastic action'.[18] All the major Asian political organisations, including the Congress and the Federation of Indian Chambers of Commerce and Industry, pledged their loyalty to the government.

When the emergency was declared, the Congress was under the able direction of Gathani. Since the beginning of the war the Congress had been weakened by factionalism and lack of sustained leadership. As president from 1952 to 1954. Gathani reorganised and revitalised the Congress and emphasized topics on which the Asians could agree, such as closer union and immigration. With the majority in the Congress, he deplored any form of violence and supported the following statement which was issued by the Congress in December 1952.[19]

The terrorist tactics and methods used by some of the Africans deserve to be condemned as they have done the greatest possible damage to the cause of the African people as well as the country as a whole.... People of all races are bound to support the Government in the task of finding and punishing all those people who commit crimes of violence.[20]

Near the end of Gathani's administration, in March 1954 the Conservative Secretary of State for the Colonies, Oliver Lyttelten, proposed a new constitution for Kenya. Although, he subsequently claimed that he had given the colony its first multi-racial government, he made no significant change. His only contribution towards increased African and Asian participation was the establish multi-racial executive body the Council of Ministers, in which non-European unofficial representation was equal to European.

The Lyttelton plan was enthusiastically accepted by AJB. Patel and the other Asian legislative councillors, both Hindu and Muslim, by the Aga Khan and by a majority of the Congress at its July-August open session. Foremost among the Congress minority opposing the plan were Chanan Singh and other members of the late Kenya League. The plan was flatly rejected by the Africans who, unlike the Europeans and Asians, had not been consulted by the government. The Africans refused to participate and withdrew from the Legislative Council Mathu charged that the Asian councillors had joined the Europeans and the government in a conspiracy against the Africans, Later at a public meeting in Nairobi of five hundred Asians, A.B. Patel sought to heal the breach by explaining that the Asian leaders had staunchly supported African interests during the negotiations. The majority at the meeting, however, rallied behind Gathani, the late Congress secretary. Speaking for Chanan Singh who could not attend, Gathani criticised the Lyttelton plan, Patel and the new Congress leadership.[21]

At this time when it was becoming obvious that Mau Mau was not merely an outbreak of transitory indiscipline, but a deep-seated nationalist revolt, the Asians were unable to establish a coherent, liberal platform. Most were too preoccupied with "business to have much interest in politics, but if the majority of those who were so interested had swung solidly over to the African side and supported the subsequent African move to independence, much of the future resentment against the Asians might have been avoided. Only one politician had the charisma, respect and following to provide this essential leadership but unfortunately at the critical time, when he was at the height of his political career and there was a unique opportunity to ally with the African leaders, A.B. Patel withdrew from politics and moved to Pondicherry to devote the rest of his life to religious contemplation. He left a void and, in his absence, the Congress and the Asian majority were steadily drawn even further from the Africans by a leader with very different views.

From 1954 to 1958, perhaps the most important four years in its history, the Congress was dominated by Mangat, Gathani's successor. Under his leadership the Congress became more conservative and even reactionary as it sought a rapprochement with the Europeans and the government. In March 1955 it issued a 'Statement of Policy' advocating equal representation of the three main races in the central and municipal governments and the introduction, but only 'in stages', of a common roll.[22]

Mangat called very few meetings of the executive and standing committees and the Congress quickly declined as an influential force in Kenya politics. Many of the conservatives, including Amin, lost interest and drifted away. In his second presidential address. August 1956, Mangat shocked many of his supporters by advising the Asians to end their '50-year feud with the European community' and abandon the goal of a common roll and universal franchise. To reduce the Europeans to the same level as the Africans he warned, 'is to court our own disaster. It would be a tragedy, for us of all people, if the British lion in Kenya dies of an ass's kick'.[23]

Mangat was still president in 1957 when Lyttelton's Conservative successor, Alan Lennox Boyd, introduced further constitutional change, in March at the new Secretary's direction. Africans for the first time were permitted to elect representatives loathe Legislative Council. In November, announcing a policy of partnership under a system of communal election, Lennox Boyd, introduced a new constitution in which 21 elected Europeans in the 84-member Legislative Council would be balanced by 14 elected Africans; 6 Asians and Arab. In the Council of Ministers there would be a similar balance of 2 Africans, 2 Asians and 4 Europeans. Although, the Kenya Muslim League and Muslim legislators quickly signified their acceptance and the Africans and the Nairobi Indian Association as readily proclaimed their rejection, the Congress hesitated for five months, until the end of Mangat's office, before declaring the new constitution unacceptable. While demanding increases in both Asian and African representation, however, the Congress, as the new president S.G. Amin explained, was not prepared to accept African majority rule for at least ten years.[24]

The fact that many Asians as early as 1952 were concerned over the rise of a militant African nationalism is illustrated by the zeal of a considerable number to participate in the suppression of Mau Mau. When the emergency began, there were 2.173 Asian Home Guards and 696 Asians in the Kenya Police Reserve any Arians soon volunteered to assist with essential technical tasks but A.B. Patel and some other leaders urged that the government employ Asians in a combat role and I proposed a national conscription. Accordingly, the government in May 19583 decided to register all Asian males between ages eighteen and twenty-three and establish three or four self-contained Asian combat units as part of the Kenya Police Reserve. The first unit of thirty-two Asians—Sikhs, Hindus and Muslims including a dairyman, draftsman, a big game hunter, a former soldier, and many clerks—was assigned in November 1953 to Kiriaini Police Station north of Fort Hall, 'one of the worst areas in the District.' Conscripted for two years, the men had been trained for six weeks and were led by a European officer They were described as 'all keen and fit and taking well to the new life'. They went out on patrol day and night, laid ambushes and, at the end of the first week, won official praise for killing two Mau Mau.[25]

Despite the eager participation of some Asians in combating Mau Mau and the conservative stance most of Asians appear to have sympathised with the African freedom fighters. The latest Intelligence Reports, noted a surprised Colonial Office official in March 1953, 'suggest that active Asian opinion in Kenya is not anti-Mau Mau. By then, a number of Asians were beginning to support the insurgents and during the later years many became involved. The artisan, Jaswant Singh Bharaj a revolutionary skilled in many crafts, manufactured guns in his Nairobi shop for freedom fighters and donated them together with a variety of materials, such as piping for gun barrels. The Nairobi insurance underwriter and company director. Jashbhai Motibhai Desai, and his wife cared for wounded Africans who came secretly to their home. Desai also advised Mbiyu Koinange to escape arrest by flying to London and then paid his air fare. Dr. Vithaibhai Raojibhai Patel treated wounded Kikuyu after dark in his Nairobi dispensary. Pinto hid Mugo Muratha, the Klambu-Dagoretti

Mau Mau leader, for six months in his home and, as indicated by the government's charges on his arrest and the testimony of one of his Asian associates, probably supplied guns and ammunition. The lumberman Yacoob-Deen at his saw mill in Karatina served Mau Mau food, clothing and medicine.[26]

Other Asians provided more indirect types of aid. The advocates A.R. Kapila, F.R.S. de Souza. Sayeed Cockar and Jaswant Singh were prominent among a number of Asians who defended Mau Mau detainees in court. The journalists Pinto, Ahmed. Pranlal Purashotam Sheth and D.K. Sharda vigorously supported African interests in the Colonial *Times, Daily Chronicle, Africa Sumachar* and the short-lived Tribune. The printer Ambu H. Patel published pro-African leaflets and books and looked after Kenyatta's daughter, Margaret, while her father was in prison. Not all those who assisted Mau Mau escaped punishment. Bharaj was sentenced to be hanged, given a revised sentence of life imprisonment, and then detained for nearly five years. Pinto followed Makhan Singh into detention, Jaswant Singh was deported. Sharda and Yacoob-Deen had to flee to India, and the Asian press, as explained in Chapter VIII was muzzled.

India's Humanitarian Influence

The Asian extremists were encouraged in their support of Mau Mau and African nationalism by the newly-independent Government of India. In April 1953 on the anniversary of the Amritsar shooting of 1919, Nehru remarked that the Africans of Kenya, Central Africa and South Africa were being persecuted and denied fundamental rights. In Kenya, he said, there had been wholesale oppression of the Africans while a handful of white settlers had usurped all the land. Indian sympathies he asserted, were entirely with the Africans in their struggle against exploitation, repression and colonialism. As early as 1937, Nehru had defined the policy of the Indian National Congress towards Africa. The Congress holds by the principle he stated 'that in every country the interests of the people of that country must be dominant and must have first consideration'. He counselled the Asians to merge their interests with those of the Africans.[27] Reflective of the new emphasis was Nehru's dissolution of the Ministry of Overseas

Indians in 1947, Subsequently Nehru repeatedly referred to the Asians—a reference very disturbing to Asian conservatives—as mere 'guests' of the Africans.[28]

Nehru had an able spokeman in Apa B. Pant as the first Indian High Commissioner for East and Central Africa. Pant arrived in Kenya in August 1948 on the first anniversary of India's independence. Born in 1912 into a princely family, he had participated in India's freedom struggle and become personally acquainted with Gandhi. After attending Oxford University and Lincoln's Inn to qualify as a barrister, he had persuaded his father, the Raja of Aundh, to take the exceptional steps of resigning his throne and transforming his kingdom into a republic of village democracies. Pant had then begun a distinguished career as a diplomat, author and philosopher. He came to East Africa, as he later noted, with 'Gandhian dreams' and a dedication to nonviolence democracy and humanity.[29]

In his new office Pant moved the Asian leaders into a closer rapport with the Africans. On arrival in Mombasa and later in Nairobi he was greeted by crowds of ten thousand. 'Never in the history of Kenya', it is said, 'were such scenes of tremendous enthusiasm previously witnessed in Nairobi'.[30] At his first public address, he was preceded by Mangal who stressed how helpful the Commissioner could be in assisting the Asians achieve equality with the Europeans. Pant startled his audience by asking. 'What have you done for the Africans'? Within a short time, he was arranging weekly outings, including picnic's and dances, for the Asian and African politicians, and he insisted that their entire families participate. Since the segregation in hotels and restaurants precluded in lei-racial meetings. Pant urged the Asians to invite Africans into their homes.

Pant and his wife Dr. Nalini Devi together with his First Secretary. A.R. Rehman, set an example for others to emulate. Pant's office and residence became multi-racial forums for discussion of many topics. At a public meeting chaired by James Gichuru he evoked considerable criticism by leaping to his feet and shouting, 'I would have no objections if my daughter married an African!' With Nehru. Pant arranged for

Government of India scholarships for the higher education of Africans in India. India', he told them 'to see our mistakes so you can avoid them'. He also encouraged fund-raising by Asians for African schools and other educational assistance. Pant, however, cautioned the Asians throughout East Africa against exchanging their British citizenship for Indian as many were wont to do after India's independence. The fact that so many Asians a generation later, following their exodus from East Africa, were able to establish new homes in Britain must be ascribed to Pant's foresight.

The Asians in Pant's circle included prominent businessmen and social leaders as well as politicians. J.M. Desai, who was already well know for his hospitality to Africans, and Suryakant Chhaganbhai Patel, another prominent businessman who had founded the Nyanza Hardware Stores and become an important trader and financier, were especially close to Pant. Others in the initial group were the advocates Kapila and de Souza the insurance agent and playwright Vinay J. Inamdar and the pharmacist-photographer John Karmali. After 1954 a new generation joined including K.P. Shah, Zafrud-Deen, Chunilal Kiparam, Ambu H. Patel, Rajnibhai Patel, Kakubhai Patel and Dr. Krishnalal Vithaldas Adalja. Even the more conservative politicians Mangat, Pirbhai and Nathoo participated in the social functions, and A.B. Patel and Amin helped collect funds. Foremost among the donors were the wealthy industrialists Nanji Kalidas Mehta, Muljibhai Prabhudas Madhvani and Pvleghji Pethraj Shah. In Uganda Pant inspired Dr. Muljibhai Motibhai Patel and Chandubhai Kalidas Patel and in Tanganyika M.P. Chitale and LK. Patel to initiate a similar association with Africans.[31]

The African response was gratifying. Desai, the most noted for entertaining, has estimated that his guests —Africans. Asians and Europeans—numbered each year from two to three thousand. Pant became especially close to Kenyatta, Chief Koinange and Mbiyu Koinange, all of whom were frequently in his home. He was formally adopted as Chief Koinange's son before the Kikuyu elders and he was subsequently made an elder of both the Kikuyu and Luo peoples. In 1952 when the young Kabaka. Mutesa III fled from Uganda, he came to Pant's home for refuge and when Mutesa finally appeared in public, it was at a picnic in the highlands arranged jointly by Pant and Kenyatta. One hundred cars transported the Asian and African guests to the lavish event. A number of the African leaders including James Beauttah. Oginga Odinga, Mbiyu Koinange and James Gichuru accepted Pant's invitation to spend prolonged periods in India. The response to the Government of India's offer of scholarships created a problem for the High Commission. Pant and his staff had to review more than two hundred applications each year.[32]

Pant continued a close relationship with Africans during the emergency. Mau Mau, he later recalled 'burst on us as a surprise'. From New York, where he was addressing the United Nations at the time, he immediately flew back to Kenya. Although, he sympathised with the freedom fighters. Pant deplored the violence. On a visit to India, he engaged in a heated argument with Nehru who believed that the Africans had no alternative. During the emergency Pant's association with African leaders was limited, but he continued to see the older leaders, such as Odinga and Gichuru, who were still free and became acquainted with Tom Mboya, Joseph Murumbi, W.W.W. Awori and others in the new generation.

Initially, Pant had had a friendly relationship with the Governor, but in time, misunderstood by Mitchell, he was suspected of encouraging violence and aiding Mau Mau. Pant was kept under constant surveillance by the government apparently without good reason, but at one time a freedom fighter was apprehended hiding in his lavatory. Also, some among Pant's acquaintances were actively engaged in the armed struggle. 'We all pretended' recollected de Souza, that we did not know our African friends were Mau Mau. Eventually, according to Pant a document was forged showing that he had encouraged violence, and on the basis of that document, through Mitcheirs insistence. Pant in 1954 was recalled by Nehru and posted to Sikkim.

Pant had been venerated by the Asians and his departure was to them a serious loss. In his presidential address to the Congress in July 1954. Mangat expressed the common sentiment: 'His charm, grace, erudition, simplicity and sincerity were captivating and a sense of pride to everyone who had the capacity of appraising such priceless things'.[33]

Pant's and Nehru's obvious sympathy with the Africans in their struggle for liberation prompted the African leaders to appeal to India for aid. In July 1953, a group daring to designate themselves only as 'Kenya Africans', submitted a letter through Pant to Nehru with copies to the Governor of Kenya, Queen Elizabeth II, and the presidents of the United States, Egypt. France and the Congress of People against Imperialism. The " authors described the denial of economic and human rights to Africans under colonialism and the Kikuyu's sufferings as a result of the emergency. The emergency was proclaimed by European settler, they declared, to enable them to kill as many Kikuyu as possible. They could not express, they said, the horror then prevailing in African families. An appeal was made to India to arrange with the other recipients of the letter a revision of British policy resulting in an amnesty, a release of all detainees, and a redress of African grievances.[34]

Move Towards Independence

Despite Pant's and Nehru's accomplishments in promoting African-Asian friendship and unity among the Asian leaders, the division among the conservatives and radicals increased after Pant's departure. Events reached a climax near the end of the decade as the African leaders, refusing to accept any compromise that might perpetuate European rule, clung to a platform of a common roll and 'one man one vote' and refused 'to participate in the new government inaugurated by Lennox would in January 1959 when the Congress leaders procrastinated in implementing a boycott of all government offices. "Nazareth and twelve others walked out and the four elected Asians in the Legislative Council began their own boycott. It was then that Michael Blundell, representing a more liberal group among the settlers, formed the New Kenya Group, soon known as the New Kenya Party (NKP), which affirmed the need for British control and a communal roll involving separate electorates.

Shortly afterwards, Madan declared his support for and joined the NKP, and Zafrud-Deen. as president of the Muslim

League, declared, without pausing to consult the membership, that the League was supporting the NICP. It was the African and Asian disaffection from the government, however, that prompted Lennox Boyd to announce in April 1959 that the leaders of all communities would soon be invited to London for a conference on Kenya's future.[35]

During the eight months preceding the conference, there were important changes in Britain and further fragmentation among the communities in Kenya. In October 1959 Lennox Boyd was succeeded as Secretary of State by the Conservative lain Macleod who at once toured East Africa and, though his views were not immediately discernible, decided on a speedy revision of imperial policy for all the dependencies. One week after Macleod took office a new Governor, Sir Patrick Renison, 'proclaimed the end of the seven-year-old emergency. Three months later the Prime Minister, Harold Macmillan, was to embark on a visit to West and South Africa and deliver his Wind embark on of Change speeches. Meanwhile in Kenya, in July 1959, six Asians in the Legislative Council had combined with one European and ten African members to form a multi-racial Kenya National Party (KNP). The Asians, who at that time in their careers wear as liberals, were Jamidar, the group leader, Nazareth, Pandya. Zafrud-Deen, K.D. Travadi and Dr. S.G. Hassan. Among the African members were Masinde Muliro, who became the chairman, Ronald Ngaia and Daniel Stressing the need for a democratic government, the organizers called for a new constitution based on universal suffrage, a common roll and majority rule.

The more conservative Europeans also formed a new party in opposition to the KNP. The United Party (UP) was an all-European, ultra-conservative body that emphasized European control, abolition of the Legislative Council, and separate governing systems for the racial communities.[36] Within this same period the Asian liberals dedicated to the development of a non-racial, independent Kenya had their confidence in the good faith of the African leaders shaken by a number of events. In August 1959, apparently at the instigation of Mboya, who had intentions of forming an all-African party, the meetings of the KNP began to be forcibly broken up by Africans, some of whom waved 'Down with Asians' placards.

During the same month Mboya, Odinga and other prominent Africans who had not joined the KNP began the Kenya Independence Movement, a political party in all but name, which soon announced that its membership would consist only of Africans. In September, the KNP's application for membership in the Pan-African Freedom Movement of East and Central Africa was refused and although Julius Nyerere denied the charge, the KNP attributed the refusal to the KNP's multi-racial a character. In succeeding weeks, the African members proceeded to convert the KNP into an all-African organisation with the result that by December all the Asians had been expelled or constrained to resign. One of the new points in the KNP's platform that particularly disturbed the Asians was that all land in Kenya was to be 'held in trust for the African inhabitants'.[37]

Cries of 'Africa for the Africans' began to be heard through much of Kenya, and in December Asians driving cars in Nairobi were pelted with stones, others were beaten on sidewalks one Asian was slain, and several were injured in what some called an anti-Asian riot. Meanwhile, although Africans had readily accepted a common roll in a municipal election in Mombasa where they had a majority, they had objected to it in Kisumu where they were a minority.[38] In addition to all these reasons for Asian apprehension in late 1959, there was the chaos in the Congo.

The first Lancaster House Conference of January 1960 has been described as undoubtedly the most momentous conference in tile history of Kenya because it shattered the power of the European settlers and set Kenya firmly on the road to independence.[39] Fifty legislative councillors—Africans, Asians, Europeans and Arabs—met in London with the Governor and Macleod to draft a new constitution. Because of the events preceding the conference, however, the liberals and conservatives who comprised the Asian delegation—Nazareth, Pandya, Zafrud-Deen, Hassan, Nathoo and Somabhai Shiva-bhai Patel—were of one mind when the deliberations began. All had serious reservations about a rapid transfer of power to an African majority. Although, Hassan was the Asians' nominal leader, Nazareth took the lead by explaining the Asians' reservations and proposing a plan with safeguards that ultimately became the basis of the settlement.[40]

During the subsequent proceedings the Asian members with one exception voted solidly with the Europeans in favour of communal representation, reservation of seats and constitutional guarantees for minorities. The exception was Nathoo who surprised the other Asians by joining the African bloc in opposition. Nathoo later explained that the Nairobi street fighting three months earlier had convineed him that Africans dearly believed the Asians, like the Europeans, were standing in the way of their independence.

The conservative stance of the Asian delegation led to the formation of a new political party. In January, shortly after the conference began, thirty-one extremists in Nairobi issued a statement calling for immediate democratic government and Kenyatta's release, a common roll and universal adult suffrage. After learning of the vote they cabled to London to urge the Asian delegates to reconsider their position and support the statement. In February, while the conference was still in session the group of thirty-one, disappointed with the delegates response, formed the Kenya Freedom Party (KFP).

Dedicated to the principles enunciated in the statement and open to all peoples, the party's central aim was 'to represent and educate Asian public opinion.[41] Its initial officers included Chanan Singh, president: I.T, Inamdar and the Muslim barrister Abdul Rauf, vice-presidents; K.P. Shah secretary; and I.K. Mehta, treasurer. The others among the thirty-one were Asians except for the Anglican clergyman, Andrew A.G. Hake. Africans would have been Included, but the government had prohibited their Joining a non-racial party. All the members were radicals, a composite of humanitarians and pragmatists, perhaps even some opportunists, who believed that all Asians and Europeans should cast their lot with the Africans. Their first act was to draft a Bill of Rights and to send it to Ronald Ngala, leader of the African delegation in London. Borrowing from the LTN's Universal Declaration of Human Fights, the document stressed the rights that were of particular interest to the Asian community, that is, to acquire nationality, be free from racial or religious discrimination, engage in any trade, occupation or profession, and own and occupy property.

The Macleod constitution of February 1960, which followed the deliberations in London and represented a compromise among the dissident groups, was to be an interim, measure until Kenya could be self-governing under African rule. It instituted for the first time an African non-official majority Macleod reduced the Legislative Council to 65 members of whom 33 would be elected on a common roll to open seats, 20 would be elected communally to reserved seats, and 12 would be elected to national seats by the Legislative Council. The twenty communal representatives would consist of 10 Europeans, 8 Asians and 2 Arabs, and the twelve national members of 4 Africans, 4 Europeans, 3 Asians and 1 Arab. The revised Council of Ministers, reduced from sixteen to twelve members reflected the new emphasis on African representation Macleod also removed the ban on colony-wide African parties, and eight months later he issued a Bill of Rights which, unlike the one proffered by the KFP upheld some forms of discrimination such as racial covenants in grants of land.[42]

The constitution was readily approved, by the Congress, the Muslim League, and Blundell's NKP and accepted with reluctance by the Africans and more militant Asians were disappointed in the delay of independence, the communal franchise and the reservation of seats a few days after publication of the constitution, Odinga, Gichuru and Mboya initiated the formation of the Kenya African National Union (KANU), and a week later Ronald Ngala. Masinde Muliro and Daniel arap Moi led in the formation of a rival party, the Kenya African Democratic Union (KADU).

While KANU represented the larger ethnic communities and stood for a strong centralise government KANU favoured the smaller groups, and a regional emphasis. To the disappointment of the Asian radicals, KADU announced that their membership would be African Both accepted the new constitution and prepared for the general election. Though sharing the Africans opinion of the constitution and critical of

Macleod's Bill of Rights, the KFP also decided to enter the election.[43]

The momentous events of 1960 prompted the Congress to forsake the conservative policy that it had followed since 1952. At its open session in October 1960 the Congress elected a new president, the barrister Satish Chandra Gautama, and drafted a radical platform. Echoing the demands of the KFP it supported African demands for independence and Kenyatta's release, called for universal suffrage and a common roll and renounced reserved seats and minority safeguards. The Congress also decided to nominate a slate of candidates for the election. The decision of this all-Asian organisation to contest for seats was opposed by the radical wing of the Congress—many KFP members were still in the Congress—on the basis that it contradicted the idea of national unity Implicit in a common roll, and eighteen of the thirty-four delegates from the Mombasa Indian Association, led by the KFP vice-president Inamdar, walked out. Before the open session Nazareth had also left the Congress and, shunning all political organisations, had become, as he said, 'a party of one'. Mangat had quit politics entirely and, retiring to India, was soon to be slain in a family quarrel.

Early in 1961, the Congress chartered an airplane to send a deputation to confer with Kenyatta in detention at Maralal Among the Jour Asians were Gautama as Congress president and Pandya as the leading legislative councillor. They sought a preview of Kenyatta's ideas and were surprised to find that he had been reading books on Hinduism.

While the politicians were sorting out the future of Kenya, the humble bookbinder who had been prominent in Pant's circle, Ambu H. Patel was working assiduously for the release -of Kenyatta. Emigrating in 1944 from Badhran at age twenty-five with scarcely any education but with a deep reverence for Gandhi. Patel for five years had been variously employed in Uganda. He then had taken special training in bookbinding in London. Returning to East Africa in 1952, when the emergency began he set up the Western Book-binders Co. in Nairobi. Appalled at the treatment of Africans, he decided to dedicate himself to the release of Kenyatta, have adopted Jomo

Kenyatta as my Baba (father)', he later remarked', 'and ail other Africans as my brothers and sisters'. Beginning in 1952, he 'lived, worked, and breathed every moment of the day, for Baba's release and Kenya's freedom'.[44]

The means Patel chose for liberation was to arouse public opinion. He first gained the support of a group of Asians including K.P. Shah and the young advocate, V.V. Patel, then, obtaining the approval of Odinga, Mboya, and Muliro, formed a 'Release Jomo' Committee and solicited funds. Sixty-four Asian individuals and companies, in which the Shah community was prominent, subscribed each from Shs. 50 to Shs. 500. With the money, Patel printed and airmailed one thousand circulars to "great men' in over one hundred countries and appealed to them for moral support. Discovering that many of the letters were withheld by postal officials. Patel had to disguise his name. Later circulars went out under the signatures of Odinga and other Africans. While collecting testimonials from world leaders, Patel printed a variety of posters and drove 4,500 miles to display them all over Kenya. Beginning with a meeting of several hundred Africans at Kiambu, he also arranged mass demonstrations in the reserves. By 1961, not only the politicians, including the Congress president Gautama, but the people as a whole were clamouring for Kenyatta's release. Patel was aided in his cause by the political events of early 1961. The 'Kenyatta election' of January-March 1961 which produced the first African government, was won by KANLL.

Although, they had a substantial majority, the KANU members refused to accept ministerial responsibility until Keriyatta was released. When KADU, led by Ngala, formed the new government, the KANU members sat in opposition.[45] The election was the last occasion in which there was a sharp division among the Asian politicians. The Asian reserved seats were won by three Congress candidates. Pandya, Jamtdar and the Kisumu advocate Dharam Bir Kohli. Together with three KFP representatives, K.P. Shah, Chanan Singh and Anjarwalla, and two Muslims. Zafrud-Deen and Nathoo. National seats were taken by de Souza, representing the KFP, Jan Mohamed, an Ismaili businessman from Machakos, and S.S. Patel a Nakuru advocate. After the election Pandya, Kohli,

Jamidar, Patel, Zafrud-Deen, Nathoo and Mohamed—all the liberal Hindu and Muslim Asians—moved to the government side of the legislature with the KADU Africans, while de Souza, K.P. Shah, Chanan Singh and Anjarwalla—the KFP representatives joined the KANU Africans in opposition. Jamidar, appointed Minister of Works, became the only Asian minister.

End of Colonialism

After the election the Kenya, Africans advanced rapidly to self-government. Kenyatta was released in October 1961 and quickly assumed the presidency of KANU. Twelve months later, KANU and KADU remove their racial restrictions on membership. Meanwhile, in February 1962 after another change in the Colonial Office, with-Mad end succeeded by Reginald Maudling, a second Lancaster House Conference worked out the main provisions for self-government. The decided on a two-chambered legislature consisting of a Mouse of Representatives and a Senate. Certain safeguards for African and non-African minorities were incorporated in the Senate and a Bill of Rights. At a third conference in September and October 1962, the last details were settled. During this time the Asian conservatives had tended to follow Mangat and Nazareth in withdrawing from politics, the liberal Hindus led by Pandya and the Muslims of Zafrud-Deen's League had taken membership in KADU whereas the radicals, including de Souza and K.P. Shah had joined KANU. The members of the KFP had dissolved their organisation and entered KANU as soon as it was permitted by the party K.P. Shah was elected treasurer of the KANU Nairobi branch. In the next genera election in May 1963. KANU won an overwhelming majority in both Houses, and a month later Kenyatta became the first Prime Minister of an internally self-governing Kenya. In December, the country attained full independence as a republic within the Commonwealth, and Kenyatta became President.

As many conservatives had predicted, the Asians were accorded no significant place in the new African government. Kenyatta chose for his first ministry in June 1963 fourteen Africans and one European. With Mbiyu Koinange. Mboya, Odinga, Murumbi, Gichuru, Kiano, and the eight others sat

Bruce R. McKenzie, the new Minister of Agriculture and Animal Husbandry. The Minis try of Labour and Social Services went not to the veteran trade unionist, Makhan Singh but to E.N. Mwendwa an African who had contributed very little to Kenya's labour history. Although, de Souza became Speaker of the House, there was no ministry for him or for K.P. Shah and any of the other KFP leaders who had championed ah Independent Kenya under African rule. Nor was there any honour or recognition concerning the services of Ambu Patel. J.M. Desal or Kapila. Only two Asians were appointed to posts in the new government. Jan Mohamed became Kiano's parliamentary secretary, and Chanan Singh was one of three who received a similar appointment with Kenyatta. Highly valued for his legal knowledge and writing ability, Chanan Singh was entrusted with drafting many of the writings and speeches attributed to Kenyatta, Mboya and the Chief Justice.

After independence a number of Asians, including Pandya and Mohamed, continued for a time to win legislative seats, but only one, Pio Gama Pinto, as Bildad Kaggia has remarked, 'had the confidence of the people'. As is evident in other chapters. Pinto was a man of many talents, an outstanding journalist and one of the most important trade unionists as well as a politician. Beginning in 1949, he moved from a series of clerical posts into Journalism and trade unionism, adopted socialist views, and gradually became involved in the nationalist movement by preparing memoranda and statements for KAU. While active in the Kenya Study Group and Pant's circle with de Souza, Chanan Singh and other young Asian radicals, he formed a close association with the African leaders. Although, he remained free during the first two years of the emergency. Pinto, as explained, secretly assisted Mau Mau in various ways. Arrested In 1954 in Operation Anvil, then detained for six years mostly with 'hard-core' Mau Mau on Manda Island and finally at remote Kabarnet, he won the hearts of his fellow prisoners as a man of 'decent, straightforward, fearless and honest' character.[46]

On his release in October 1959. Pinto resumed his active role in politics as well as Journalism and trade unionism. He joined Ambu Patel's 'Release Jomo' Committee and worked with the Africans for a victory in the 1961 election. It has been said that his contribution towards KANU's victory was 'greater than that of any other single person'. As described in Chapter VIII. Pinto then founded the Pan African Press and launched *Sauti Ya KANU* (Voice of KANU). Meanwhile, adept at shorthand and typing, he was taking down, typing, and distributing the minutes of the KANU meetings. He was never close to Mboya because of trade union rivalries, but he became a valuable ally of Odinga, Kubai, Achieng Oneko and other KANU leaders. Murumbi, who co-operated with Pinto in his publishing ventures later recalled. 'It was through his inspiration that entered politics'.

Though never seeking position for himself. Pinto was induced by KANU leaders to run for a seat in the 1963 election. He won easily over an African rival, obtaining a national seat chosen by members of Parliament, and was to be re-elected in 1964. After independence Pinto became increasingly critical of the Mboya faction within Kenyatta's government. He organised a Back-Benchers Group, formed committees within it, and urged that the committees be utilised in advising the corresponding ministries. For those, who did not share his views in politics and trade unionism. Pinto was a powerful adversary. In February 1965 he was shot dead—the first politician so eliminated during the Kenyatta administration—by assailants who were never apprehended.

Pinto's removal was but the most glaring of many events that convinced the Asian leaders that they had no political future in independent Kenya. In November 1962 when KANU opened its membership to all races, the Kenya Indian Congress dropped the name Indian' from its title. Thc new Congress, however, attracted no non-Asian members and no longer served a useful purpose. With the Kenya Muslim League it rapidly disappeared from the mainstream of Kenya politics. Its last open session, the twenty-seventh, was in 1962, and Pandya, elected at that session, proved to be the last of the presidents.

At a meeting with Pandya and Gautama in August 1966—the last occasion at which the Asians were ever consulted—Kenyatta signified that the Congress should be abandoned. Although, it continued with some activities into 1965, the

Congress did not enter any candidates in Kenya elections after 1961. The Nairobi Indian Association, which shared the Congress office, died out with the Congress. The Nakuru organisation ceased to function after 1962, and the one in Kisumu lasted into 1965. The Mombasa Indian Association, which apparently had the longest life, terminated in 1969 when Pandya, who with Ngala shared the leadership of Mombasa politics, finally lost his seat to an African.

During these same eventful post-war years, culminating about 1967. Asian commercial organisation and enterprise, the support of which had been a principal reason for Asian political activity, suffered a similar decline. After independence the Kenyatta government, with considerable guidance and aid from expatriate staff, adhered to two contradictory policies inherited from the colonial era. Promoting the 'managed economy', it proclaimed African socialism as the goal, reinforced the cooperative movement, added new government agencies, increased the regulations on commerce and raised taxes and fees. At the same time it endeavoured to foster the rise of the independent African businessman.[47]

Africanisation of the Economy

Among the East African nations Kenya was the foremost in encouraging African entrepreneurship. In 1964, it formed the Industrial and Commercial Development Corporation (ICDC) which considerably augmented the financial aid to African traders. By 1966 the ICDC had issued nearly £90.000 in loans and £30,000 in credit guarantees to about 170 African wholesalers and retailers. Meanwhile an ICDC subsidiary, the National Trading Corporation, forced Asian retailers to purchase their stock from African suppliers and put pressure on breweries and factories to sell only to African distributors.[48]

Citizenship for Employment

The policy of Africanisation evident in the ICDC actions was augmented by measures requiring citizenship for enterprise, the sharing of ownership and management with Africans, and increased participation by government. In 1967, Kenya passed legislation requiring citizenship for employment and the conduct of business. All non-citizens had to apply for re-entry permits and dependents' passes. Greatly increasing the Asians insecurity, the laws prompted an exodus from Kenya beginning in December 1967. In subsequent years the non-citizens failed to obtain trading licences and work permits, and many who applied for citizenship met delays and obstacles. A large number of those who remained in business were served quit notices and their premises were assigned to Africans.[49]

The demise of the chambers of commerce was symbolic of the end of Asian commercial enterprise. In January 1964 the Federation of Indian Chambers of Commerce and Industry in Eastern Africa, led by its president, Anant Pandya, and its honorary secretary, Mohan Madan, took steps to refashion the Asian chambers along multi-racial and national lines. In January 1964 the Federation gave up its office and henceforth functioned as a part of the Nairobi Indian Chamber of Commerce (NICC). Shortly afterwards the NICC changed its name to the Nairobi Central Chamber of Commerce and Industry (NCCCI).[50] Other Asian chambers throughout Kenya, in fact throughout East Africa, followed by dropping the word 'Indian' from their titles and proclaiming a multi-racial membership.

African Reactions

These initiatives were unacceptable to the Africans. Commercial leaders among the Africans refused to join the Asian organisations and instead formed their own Kenya Chamber of Commerce and Industry (KCCI) and then opened the membership to Asians and Europeans. But, Kenya's new Minister for Commerce and Industry, Dr. Julius G. Kiano wanted a multiracial organisation closely associated with the government. At his initiative the KCCI was reorganised and registered in May 1965 as the Kenya National Chamber of Commerce and Industry [KNCCI). Among the officers were the KCCFs president. Francis Nduati Macharia, and the European commercial leader, Sir Derek Erskine, but there was no Asian. Two months later Macharia, as president, called a meeting of all the Asian and European chambers to insist on dissolution of the non-African organisations and their replacement with local chapters of the KNCCI.[51]

The Europeans, led by Erskine, resisted and had to be threatened into compliance by Kiano, but the Asians, apparently more aware of the full significance of the power change readily complied. By the end of 1965 nearly all the European and Asian local chambers had been absorbed by new chapters of the KNCCI. The NCCI, the last of the Asian organisations and the vestige of J.B. Pandya's once powerful Federation, vacated its office in March 1966 and formally dissolved in November 1968. Commercial organisation in Kenya, and indeed in all East Africa, was by then exclusively an African entity.

NOTES AND REFERENCES

1. Mboya, *Fredom and After* (Boston: Little. Brown, 1963), p. 178.
2. Carl G Rosberg and John Nottingham. *Myth of Mau Mau Nationalism in Kenya* (New York: Praeger. 1956), p. 188. See also Anthony Clayton and Donald C. Savage, *Government and Labour in Kenya, 1895-1963* (London: Frank Cass, 1974). pp. 232-4; and John Middleton. 'Kenya: Administration and Change in African Life, 1912-45', ch. VII, *History of East Africa,* vol. H, ed. Vincent Harlow and E.M. Chilver (Oxford: Clarendon. 1955), pp. 386-7.
3. Rosberg and Notttingham, *Myth,* pp. 214-5.
4. Colonial *Times* (Nairobi), 12 Oct. 1946, p. 6; 18 Nov. 1944, p. 4; 13 Oct 1945, p. 1. 'Kenya Colony Intelligence Security Summary, July 1946', p. 3, India Office Library, L/P&J/8/248. Koinange was the son of the Kikuyu Senior Chief. Mbiyu Koinange; Gikonyo was a member of the Nairobi Municipal Council; and Awori was an officer of KAU.
5. *Colonial Times,* 14 Sep. 1947. pp. 7. 13.
6. Mitchell. 'Confidential Report No. 8', 9 Apr. 1946, C.O. 533/537.
7. 'Kenya Colony Intelligence & Security Summary. July 1946', p. 3, India Office Library. L/P&J/8/248.
8. *East African Standard, 8* Aug. 1946, p. 6: 25 Apr. 1950, p. 5.
9. Seidenberg, *Uhuru and the Kenya Asians: the Role of a Minority Community in Kenya Politics, 1939-63* (New Delhi: Vikas, 1983), pp. 105-8.

10. 'Minutes of the 8th Meeting of the Standing Committee... 5th Feb., 1948', file 'Minutes of the Standing & Executive Committees 1945-50.

11. Colonial Times. 6 July 1946, p. 4. *Kenya Legislative Council* Debates. 12 Aug. 1949, vol 33. col 145.

12. Shand Pandit, ed. Asians in East and Centra! *Africa* (Nairobi:? Panco. 1963), for biographies of Pandya (p. 203) and Paroo (pp. 206-7), and E.G. Wilson, ed. Who's *Who in East Africa, 1965-66* (Nairobi: Marco, 1968) for Rana (p. 127). Pandya and Pirbhai were intv. by Gregory.

13. Pandit, Asians, includes biographies of Amin (p. 106), Madan (p. 175) and Purl (p-236).

14. Mangat has been Ignored in biographies, but see Seidenberg, *Uhuru,* pp. 131. 137, 141: and Nazareth, *Brown* Man, pp. 172-66 passim.

15. Anon., *Pio* Goma *Pinto: Independent Kenya's First Martyr, Socialist and Freedom Fighter,* pamphlet (Nairobi: Pan African, Feb. 1966). pp. 5-6.

16. Pant. *Undiplomatic Incidents* (Hyderabad: Sangarn Books, 1987), p. 27. The statistics are from Sir Evelyn Baring (Governor) to High Commissioner for the U.K. in New Delhi, confidential telegram, 29 Dec. 1952, j file 'Position of the Asian Community in Kenya during the Emergency, 1952-53, C.O. 822/465. See also Seidenberg. *Uhuru,* p. 111.

17. Baring to High Commissioner, 29 Dec. 1952. Times (London), 3 July 1953, p. 7.

18. Baring to High Commissioner. 29 Dec. 1952. Baring to Secretary of State for Colonies, confidential telegram, 21 Jan. 1953, file Position of the Asian Community'.

19. Baring to High Commissioner, 29 Dec. 1952.

20. *Kenya: Proposals for Reconstruction of the Government,* Cmd. 9103 (London: HMSO. March 1954).

21. Resolution 6, The KIC... Presidential Address by Mr. N.S. Mangat... 31st July, 1st & 2nd Aug. 1954, with the Resolutions, p. 40, file 'KIC: Presidential Addresses & Resolutions, 1932-62'. Congress supplemental records, reel 1. *East African Standard,* 11 Mar. 1954, pp. 1, 5; 151. Mar. 1954, p. 1: 25 Mar. 1954, pp. 1.4.

22. The KIC (Successor to the EAINC) Statement of Policy. 12th Mar., 1955 pp. 3 6 file 1955, March-April. EAINC records. SU microfilm 1929, reel 13. Nazareth. *Brown Man,* pp. 179-82.

23. 'Presidential Address by N.S. Mangat... 4th, 5th & 6th Aug. 1956'. File 'Kenya Indian Congress: Presidential Addresses & Resolutions, 1932-62 Congress supplemental records, reel 1.

24. E. *African Standard,* 9 Nov. 1957. pp. 1. 4: 11 Nov. 1957, pp. 1. 5: 12 Nov. 3957, p. 5; 14 Nov. 1957, n. 5; 20 Nov. 1957, p. 5: 12 Dec 1957, p. 5. 'Resolutions... 4-6 Apr. 1958'. file 'Kenya Indian Congress: Presidential Addresses and Resolutions. 1932-62'. Congress supplemental records, reel 1. 'Report by Congress President S.G. Amin. 11 Apr. 1958', *Ibid.,* Seidenberg, *Uhuru,* p. 135.

25. 'Press Office Handout No. 706: First Asian Combat Group In Operational Area'. 12 Nov. 1953. *ibid.* Nairobi Press Office. Press Office Handout No. 151: Asian Manpower Call up, 22 May 1953,file Position of the Asian Community in Kenya during the Emergency, 1952-53. C.O. 822/465. See also Baring to High Commissioner, 29 Dec. 1952.

26. Psychology of a Revolutionary', biography in Ambu H. Patel, compiler, *Struggle for Release Jomo Kenyatta and His Colleagues* (Nairobi: New Kenya, 1963), pp. 209-10.

27. Indian *Review* (Madras), Oct. 1957, p. 362. See also Mar. 1937, p. 183. C.O. draft by Swinton, 17 Apr. 1953, file Position of the Asian Community in Kenya during the Emergency, 1952-53', C.O. 822/465.

28. In 1952 Nazareth complained to Nehru personally about the term 'guests', and the Congress in 1953 sent Nehru a letter of protest. Nazareth, Broiun Man, pp. 170-1.

29. Apa Pant, *Mandala: an. Awakening* [Bombay: Orient Longman. 1978). ch. 2. For an excellent short biography, see Pandit, *Asians,* p. 205.

30. Pandit, *Asians,* p. 205.

31. B.G Vaghela, *East Africa Today: Comprehensive—Directory of British East Africa with* Who's *Who* (Bombay: Overseas Information, 1959), p. 511; and Pandit. Asians, p. 124. J.M. Desai, intv. by Gregory, 31 Jan. and 5Feb. 1973, Nairobi. Vinay J. Inamdar, intv. by Gregory, 31 Jan. 1972. Nairobi. J.S. Karmali, intv. by Gregory, 13 June 1985. Nairobi; see also his biography in Wilson, Who's Who, p. 52.

32. Apa B. Pant, *Undiplomatic Incidents,* pp. 20-2. J.M. Desai and Pant Interviews. Oginga Odinga is the only African who has left a record of his stay in India: *Two Months in India,* Nairobi: New Kenya, 1965.

33. The KIC... Presidenial Address by Mr. N. S. Mangat....31st July, 1st and 2nd Aug.. 1954. with the Resolutions', p. 10, file 'KIC: Presidential Addresses and Resolutions.' 1932-62'. Congress supplemental records, reel 1.

34. 'An Appeal by the Kenya Africans to the Nations of the World through the Government of India', 3 July 1953. file '1953. July-Sep.' EAINC records, reel 13.

35. *East African Standard,* 19 Jan. 1959, pp. 1. 3; 30 Jan. 1959, p. 3: 13 Apr. 1959, p. 3, 29 Apr. 1959, p. 7.

36. Times (London). 11 Nov. 1959, p. 12. George Bennett. *Kenya, A Political History* (London: Oxford University Press, 1963), p. 147. George Bennett and Carl G. Rosberg. *Kenyatta Election: Kenya, 1960-61* (Oxford: University Press, 1961), p. 16. Rosberg and Nottingham, Myth, pp. 317-8.

37. Nazareth, *Brown Man,* p. 363. Nazareth presents a revealing description of the 'jerky pathetic, somewhat sickening history' of the KNP, pp.350-66.

38. East *African Standard,* 24 Dec. 1959, p. 7. Nazareth, *Brown Man,* pp. 370, 380, 382-3. 389. 521.

39. Nazareth. *Brown Man,* pp. 370, 380, 521.

40. *Report of the Kenya Constitutional. Conference* (Chairman: Rt. Hon. lain Macleod, M.P.) held in. London in Jan, & *Feb., 1*960, Cmnd. 960 (London. 1960). Nazareth has a full account of the proceedings. *Brown Man,* ch. 17. See also Bennett and Rosberg, *Kenyatta Election,* p. 20; and. Rothchild. *Racial Bargaining in Independent Kernya: a Study of Minorities and Decolonisation* (London: Oxford University Press, 1973), p. 136. Although, the press was not admitted, the proceedings were well reported in the *Times* between 18 Jan. and 26 Feb. 1960. East *African Standard,* 3 Mar. 1960, p. 5.

41. KFP Secretary's Report, 18 Apr. 1960; and 'Statement of the Thirty-One'. n.d.. K.P. Shah Papers, SU microfilm 2174, reel 5. For an informative description of the KFP, see Seidenberg. *Uhuru,* ch. 6.

42. *Kenya: New Constitutional Arrangements,* Cmnd. 960 (London: HMSO, 1960). Seidenberg, Uhuru, p 153.

43. Bennett and Rosberg, *Kenyatta Election,* pp. 38-44. ''Statement to the Press', 11 Dec. 1960. K. P. Shah Papers.

44. Patel. 'Secretary's Report', in Patel, *Struggle,* p. 32.

45. Bennett and Resberg. *Kenyatta Election,* ch. VI and App. I.

46. Joseph Murumbi, 'An Appreciation', ch. *Ibid.,,* p. 11. See also Ramogi Achieng Oneko, Detention Days', ch. *Ibid.,,* pp. 17-20.

47. D.S. Pearson, Industrial *Development in East Africa* [Nairobi: Oxford University Press. 1969). pp. 288-9. Kenya, *Development Plan. 1966-70* (Nairobi: Government Printer, 1966), p. 241.

48. Peter Man-is and Anthony Somerset, *African Businessmen: a Study of Entrepreneurs hip and Development in Kenya* (London: Rou fledge & Kegan Paul, 1971), pp. 10-1.

49. The pertinent legislation was the Immigration Act, No. 25 of 1967, *Kenya Gazette Supplement: Acts, 1967,* No. 68, 25 Aug. 1967, pp. 159-77. It came into operation 1 Dec. 1967 and was augmented by Legal Notices Nos. 234, 235, 244, and 253. *Ibid.,.* Nos. 88, 94, and 97. Enforcement continued into the 1970s. In Jan. 1973. e.g., 418 traders were served four-month quit notices. *East African Standard,* 11 Jan. 1973. pp. 1, 3. *Sunday Nation* (Nairobi), 14 Jan. 1973, p. 4.

50. The pertinent minutes of the Federation are in file 7, 'Federation 3. Minutes. Circulars, etc.', Mombasa Indian Merchants' Chamber records, SU microfilm 1922, reel 3.

51. The relevant correspondence among the chambers and numerous clippings from the major newspapers are in file 38. 'Kenya Association of Chambers of Commerce', Mombasa Indian Merchants' Chamber records. SU microfilm 1922. reel 3. G.M. Motala (Honorary Secretary, KNCCI) to Chairman. Mombasa Merchants' Chamber. 14 June 1965; KNCCI. Minutes of the Conference Held in Nairobi... 7 July, 1965—file 'Kenya National Chamber of Commerce and Industry', said. *East African Standard,* 1 June 1965. pp. 1, 4. *Daily Nation,* 1 June 1965, p. 1.

BIBLIOGRAPHY

I. Primary Sources

A. Official Archives

A 1. India Office Records, London, and the Indian National Archives, New Delhi

(*a*) Proceedings of the Emigration Department of the Government of India

(b) Proceedings of the Foreign Department of the Government of India

A 2. Foreign Office Records, London

(*a*) Dispatches

(*b*) Foreign Office Confidential Prints

A 3. Colonial Office Archives, London

(*a*) Dispatches

(*b*) Colonial Office Confidential Prints

A 4. Records of the Bombay Government, Bombay

A 5. National Archives of Tanzania

(*a*) Zanzibar

(*b*) Dar es Salaam

A 6. Kenya National Archives, Nairobi

(*a*), (*b*) Lands Department, Nairobi

(c) Mombasa Provincial Archives

A 7. Uganda National Archives, Entebbe (referred to as Entebbe Archives in the text).

B. Non-Official Archives

B 1. Records of the East African Indian National Congress, Nairobi

B 2. Sidney Webb (Lord Passfield) Papers, London

B 3. International Missionary Council, London: Papers of Dr. J. H. Oldham

B 4. Lord Francis Scott Papers, Nairobi

B 5. Minutes of the Uganda Chamber of Commerce, Makerere

C. Official Publications

C 1. Parliamentary Papers

C 2. Official Reports and other publications

C 3. Proceedings of the Legislative Councils:

- *(a)* Proceedings of the Kenya Legislative Council
- *(b)* Proceedings of the Uganda Legislative Council
- (c) Proceedings of the Zanzibar Legislative Council

D. Non-Official Publications

D 1. Newspapers

D 2. Contemporary Publication

E. Oral Information

II Secondary Material

1. Books
2. Articles
3. Unpublished Theses

I. Primary Sources

Each reference to the sources listed below is accompanied by a brief note indicating the subject-matter.

A. Official Archives

A I. India Office Records, London, and The Indian National Archives, New Delhi

(a) Proceedings of the Emigration Department of the Government of India

These Proceedings have a common reference in both the above Archives, but for the period after 1922 only the material in the Indian National Archives has been seen.

June 1895—Proceedings no. 7, file 38, part B: Recruitment of Indian labour for German East Africa.

August 1895—Pros. I, 3-4, file 38, part A: Indian labour for G.E.A.

December 1895—Pros. 11-12, file 64 of 1890, part A: Emigration to E.A.

January 1896—Pros. 7-8, file 63 of 1895 and 8 of 1896, part A: Emigration to Zanzibar.

July 1896—Pros. 9-17, file 38 of 1895, part A: Emigration for Uganda Railway.

July 1896—Pros. 18-55, file 2, part A: Emigration for Uganda Railway.

September 1896—Pros. 2-4, file 66, part A: Emigration to Africa.

September 1896—Pros. 12-23, file 2, part A: Emigration for U. Railway.

October 1896—Pros. I, file 8, part A: Emigration to Zanzibar.

October 1896—Pros. 15-16, file 66, part A: Increased emigration to E.A.

January 1897—Pros. 3-4, file 18 of 1896, part A: Emigration to Zanzibar.

January 1897—Pros. 13-14, file 79 of 1896, part A: Indians in G.E.A.

February 1897—Pros. 8-14, file 5, part A: Indian labour for E.A.

March 1897—Pros. 1-6, file 5, part A: Indian labour for E.A.

March 1897—Pros. 7-11, file 10, part A: Form of agreement for Emigrants.

April 1897—Pros. 5-8, file 10, part A: Form of agreement for Emigrants.

May 1897—Pros. 10-39, file 10, part A: Emigration to E.A.

July 1897—Pros. 35-7, file 10, part A: Emigration to E.A.

August 1897—Pros. 4-6, file 37, part A: 'Free' Emigration to E.A.

September 1897—Pros. 1-2, file 5, part C: Emigration from Bombay.

September 1897—Pros. 8-14, file 10, part A: Emigration to U. Railway.

October 1897—Pros. 6-9, file 10, part A: Railway Agency at Karachi.

October 1897—Pros. 8-10, file 37, part B: Emigration from Bombay.

December 1897—Pros. 4-7, file 37, part B: 'Free' Emigration to E.A.

January 1898—Pros. 5, file 5, part B: Emigration to Zanzibar.

January 1898—Pros. 39-43, file 10, part A: Coolie emigration from Karachi.

February 1898—Pros. 7, file 21, part A: Coolie emigration.

April 1898—Pros. 6-n, file 21, part B: Coolie emigration.

June 1898—Pros. 7-8, file 7, part B: Openings for Indian artisans in E.A.

July 1898—Pros. 5-12, file 21, part A: Coolie emigration.

April 1899—Pros. 3-8, file 24, part A: Emigration to E.A.

April 1899—Pros. 9-14, file 27, part A: Emigration Agent in India for E.A.

July 1899—Pros. 17-21, file 27, part A: Emigration Agents in India for E.A.

November 1899—Pros. 3-8, file 54, part A: Clerks and artisans for E.A.

March 1900—Pros. 13-18, file 7, part A: Legalising of emigration to E.A. May 1900—Pros. 1-2, file 7, part A: Legalising of emigration to E.A.

June 1900—Pros. 9-10, file 47, part B: Indian agricultural scheme for G.E.A.

October 1900—Pros. 2-3, file 71, part B: Emigration Agents in India for E.A.

February 1901—Pros. 3-7, file 7 of 1900, part A: Legalising emigration.

March 1901—Pros. 1-9, file 20, part A: Legalising of emigration to E.A.

March 1901—Pros. 16-17, file 19, part A: Emigration to G.E.A.

May 1901—Pros. 12, file 41, part A: Indian agricultural settlement in E.A.

May 1901—Pros. I, file 39, part B: Immigration restriction in Zanzibar.

September 1901—Pros. 5-6, file 20, part A: Legalising of emigration.

September 1901—Pros. 12, file 41, part A: Indian agricultural settlement.

January 1902—Pros. 16, file 11, part B: Indian agricultural settlement.

April 1902—Pros. 5-8, file 19 of 1901, part A: Emigration to G.E.A.

September 1902—Pros. 2, file 93, part B: Emigration to G.E.A.

November 1902—Pros. 15-17, file 103, part A: Coolie emigration.

February 1903—Pros. 4, file 8, part A: Coolie emigration.

February 1904—Pros. n, file 19, part A: Indian agricultural settlement.

April 1904—Pros. I, file 19, part B: Indian settlement at Kibos.

December 1905—Pros. 5-6, file 99, part B: Emigration of artisans.

February 1906—Pros. 4-5, 15-16, file 5, part A: Immigration into Zanzibar.

May 1906—Pros. 9, file 5, part A: Immigration regulation in Zanzibar.

August 1906—Pros. 13-16, file 73, part A: Indian settlement in E.A.

November 1906—Pros. 12-18, file 73, part A: Indian settlement in E.A.

April 1907—Pros. 2-4, file 44, part A: Administration of coolie affairs at Karachi.

July 1908—Pros. 23-4, file 70, part B: U. Railway agents at Bombay.

September 1908—Pros. I, file 79, part C: Position of Indians in E.A.

September 1908—Pros. 5-6, file 79, part A: Indian representation.

December 1908—Pros. 23-5, file 110, part A: Voluntary emigration to E.A.

February 1910—Pros. 11-17, file 10, part B: Representations on behalf of Indians in East Africa.

March 1910—Pros. 1-2, file 20, part A: Recruitment of Indian artisans.

May 1910—Pros. 19-26, file 10, part B: Indian representations.

June 1910—Pros. 6-8, file 52, part A: Memorial of Indians in Zanzibar.

August 1910—Pros. 43, file 84, part B: Indian representation on Legco.

January 1911—Pros. 1-2, file 95, part A: Indian immigration to Zanzibar.

January 1911—Pros. 19, file 126, part B: Indian representation.

February 1911—Pros. 6-7, file 52, part A: Indian grievances in Zanzibar.

March 1911—Pros. 1-3, file 14, part A: Immigration to Zanzibar.

May 1911—Pros. 1-2, file 48, part A: Petition on behalf of Indians in E.A.

August 1911—Pros. I, file 76, part A: Indian grievances in Zanzibar.

June 1912—Pros. 25, file 77, part B: Indians in G.E.A.

October 1912—Pros. 11-13, file in, part A: Memorial on behalf of Indians in E.A.

May 1913—Pros. 2, file 60, part A: Uganda Licensing Ordinance, 1912.

June 1913—Pros. 13-15, file 45, part A: Representation on behalf of Indians in E.A.

February 1914—Pros. 34, filed: Position of Indians in E.A.

August 1914—Pros. 22, file 34, part A: Position of Indians in E.A.

April 1918—Pros. 11, filed: Position of Indians in E.A.

January 1919—Pros. I, part B: Indian settlement in G.E.A.

April 1919—Pros. 32, filed: Future of G.E.A.

May 1919—Pros. 15, filed: Future of G.E.A.

June 1919—Pros. 35-40, part A: Indian representations re Uganda Cotton Rules.

October 1919—Pros. 1-8, part A: Indian Question.

August 1920—Pros. 7-35, part A: Uganda Cotton Rules, 1918.

October 1920—Pros. 4-5, filed: Resolutions of Kampala Indian Assdc.

November 1920—Pros. 1-116, part A: Indian Question.

February 1921—Pros. 4, file 36, part A: Indian Question.

March 1921—Pros. 3, 16-47, part A: Indian Question.

March 1921—Pros. 48-51, part A: Indian Question.

July 1921—Pros. 1-8, part A: Indian Question.

August 1921—Pros. 10-28, part A: Indian Question.

August 1921—Pros. 1-2, part B: Indian Question.

September 1921—Pros. 30-41, 43-64, 73-4, filed: Indian Question in Tanganyika.

October 1921—Pros. 16-19, filed: Indian Question in Zanzibar.

November 1921—Pros. 19-20, 39, 49, filed: Indian Question.

December 1921—Pros. 10, 14, 17-17A, 42, filed: Indian Question.

January 1922—Pros. I, 11, filed: Indian Question.

June 1922—Pros. 20-6, 28-32, part B: Indian Question.

July 1922—Pros. 53, part B: Indian Question.

September 1922—Pros. 16-45, part A: Indian Question.

October 1922—Pros. 1-55, part A: Indian Question.

March 1923—Pros. 14-17, 29-33, part B: Indian Question.

June 1923—Pros. 26-73, part A: Indian Question.

June 1923—Pros. 21, 42, part B: Indian Question.

July 1923—Pros. 18, dep.: Indian Question.

November 1923—Pros. 73-157, part B: Indian Question.

July 1924—Pros. 1-65, part A: Position of Indians in E.A.

February 1925—Pros. 184-9, part B: Indians in Kenya.

September 1925—Pros. 1-92, part A: Departmental memo. on Indians in E.A.

May 1926—Pros. 23-6, part B: Indians in Tanganyika.

July 1927—Pros. 13-17, part A: Indians in Kenya.

February 1929—Pros. 1-31, part A: Position of Indians in E.A.

October 1929—Pros. 1-12, part A: Position of Indians in E.A.

December 1930—Pros. 123-4, part B: Indians in Tanganyika.

January 1931—Pros. 41-3, part B: Position of Indians in E.A.

March 1931—Pros. 108-9, part B: Indians in Tanganyika.

October 1931—Pros. l-n, part A: The E.A.I.N.C. split.

1932—file 289/32, L and O: Position of Indians in E.A.

1933—file 214/33, L and O: Position of Indians in E.A.

1933—file 344/33, L and O: Controversy re Marketing legislation in E.A.

1934—file 78/34, L and O: Indians in Zanzibar.

1934—file 130/34, L and O: Position of Indians in E.A.

1934—file 169-8134, 169-9/34, L and O: Marketing legislation.

1934—file 362/33, L and O: Controversy re Marketing legislation in E.A.

1934—file 370/34, L and O: E.A. Indian representation to Government of India.

1935—file 62-44/35, L and O: Position of Indians in E.A.

(b) Proceedings of the Foreign Department of the Government of India

November 1866—Pros. 45-7, Pol. A: Slavery in Zanzibar.

May 1867—Pros. 141-3, Pol. A: Slavery in Zanzibar.

April 1868—Pros. 144-6, Pol. A: Slavery in Zanzibar.

June 1868—Pros. 54-7, Pol. A: Slavery in Zanzibar.

December 1868—Pros. 45-51, Pol. A: Slavery in Zanzibar.

1870—Pros. 57, 214, S.I: Control of Zanzibar Agency by Government of India.

January 1873—Pros. 226-31, Sec.: Control of Zanzibar Agency.

February 1873—Pros. 119-21, Sec.: Frere Mission to Zanzibar.

February 1873—Pros. 338-44, Pol. A: Zanzibar Slave Market. June 1873—Pros. 334-5, Sec.: Memorandum by Frere.

July 1873—Pros. 23, Sec.: Proclamation by Rao of Kutch re Slave Trade.

July 1873—Pros. 235-6, Pol. A: Payment of Muscat subsidy by India.

August 1873—Pros. 116-116A, Pol. A: Control of Zanzibar Agency by India.

October 1873—Pros. 225, Pol. A: Closing of Zanzibar Slave Market.

October 1874—Pros. 48-9, Pol. A: Indians and Slave Trade.

December 1874—Pros. 61-4, Pol. A: Status of Indians at Zanzibar.

January 1877—Pros. 2-3, Genl. A: Status of Indians.

September 1880—Pros. 207, Pol. A: Zanzibar Customs.

July 1882—Pros. 532-54, Pol. A: Control of Zanzibar Agency by H.M.G

May 1883—Pros. 70-5, A Genl. E: H.M.G. to control Zanzibar Agency.

February 1883—Pros. 264, A Pol. E: Status of Indians at Zanzibar.

September 1883—Pros. 349-50, A Pol. E: Indian traders at Mombasa.

April 1884—Pros. 26-8, B Genl. E: Zanzibar trade reports.

May 1884—Pros. 29-71, A Pol. E: H.M.G. to control Zanzibar Agency.

July 1884—Pros. 161-2, A Pol. E: Indian Post Office at Zanzibar.

November 1884—Pros. 520-5, Ext. A: Indian Post Office.

October 1886—Pros. 25-33, Extl. A: Endowments in Zanzibar by Topan.

February 1889—Pros. 100-1. Extl. A: Recruitment of Indian labour by the I.B.E.A. Company.

October 1889—Pros. 10-15, Extl. A: Indian labour for I.B.E.A.

September 1890—Pros. 18, Extl. B: I.B.E.A. Company report.

November 1890—Pros. 94-5, Extl. A: Indian School at Zanzibar.

April 1891—Pros. 33-4, Extl. A: Indian school.

July 1895—Pros. 119, 159-70, Extl. A: Indians in G.E.A.

June 1900—Pros. 196, Extl. B: Indians in G.E.A. See also: India Office, Political Department, Political and Secret Letters Received, Zanzibar and Aden: Letters from Zanzibar, 1875-83.

2. Foreign Office Records, Public Record Office, London

(a) Dispatches

F.O. 84/425, Hamerton to Aberdeen, 21 May 1842 (Trade in Zanzibar).

F.O. 84/540, Hamerton to Aberdeen, 2 January 1844 (Indians in Zanzibar).

F.O. 84/1357, Kirk to Bombay, 24 August 1871 (Jairam Sewji).

F.O. 84/1344, Kirk to Granville, 28 September 1871 (Firm of Jairam Sewji).

F.O. 84/1357, Livingstone to Kirk, 30 October and 17 November 1871 (Activities of Indian traders).

F.O. 84/1344, Kirk to Bombay, 24 November 1871 (Jairam Sewji).

F.O. 84/1357, Kirk to Granville, 25 and 27 January 1872 (Jairam Sewji).

F.O. 84/1357, Kirk to Bombay, 10 April and 17 December 1872 (Indian traders in Zanzibar).

F.O. 84/1357, Kirk to Granville, 22 May and 6 August 1872 (Indian traders in E.A.).

F.O. 84/1357, Kirk to Bombay, 13 September 1872 (Rebuts Livingstone's allegations). F.O. 84/1391, Frere to Granville, 2 May 1873, enclosed 'Memorandum on the subject of the Muscat subsidy'. F.O. 84/1391, Frere to Granville, 7 May 1873, enclosed 'Memorandum on Banians or natives of India in East Africa', and 'Memorandum on the position and authority of the Sultan of Zanzibar'.

F.O. 84/1391, Frere to Granville, 10 May 1873, enclosed 'Memorandum on instructions and suggestions'.

F.O. 84/1391, Frere to Granville, 29 May 1873 (Indians in Zanzibar).

F.O. 84/1773, Kirk to Salisbury; March 1886 (Indian traders).

F.O. 84/1773, Kirk to Salisbury, I May 1886 (Tarya Topan).

F.O. 84/1773, Kirk to Salisbury, 10 May 1886 (Indian currency).

F.O. 84/1774, Kirk to Salisbury, 4 June 1886 (Indians in German sphere).

F.O. 84/1774, Kirk to Salisbury, 5 June 1886 (Indians in German sphere).

F.O. 84/1774, Holmwood to Salisbury, 25 July 1886 (Customs).

F.O. 84/1775, Holmwood to Salisbury, 23 September 1886 (Customs).

F.O. 84/1910, Euan Smith to Salisbury, 22 October 1888 (Peera Devji).

F.O. 84/2084, India Office to Foreign Office, 14 June 1890 (Indian Post Office at Zanzibar).

F.O. 84/2062, Euan Smith to Salisbury, 30 July 1890 (Indian School at *Zanzibar).*

F.O. 2/117, Employment of Indian troops in the Protectorates, 1889-96

F.O. 2/143, Employment of Indian troops in the Protectorates, 1897.

F.O. 2/170, Employment of Indian troops in the Protectorates, January to August 1898.

F.O. 2/171, Employment of Indian troops in the Protectorates, September to December 1898.

F.O. 2/204, Johoston to Salisbury, n and 13 October 1899 (Indians and the Uganda Railway).

F.O. 2,256, Employment of Indian troops in the Protectorates, January to June 1899.

F.O. 2/257, Employment of Indian troops in the Protectorates, July to December 1899.

F.O. 2/297, Johnston to Salisbury, 18 February 1900 (Indian precedents for E.A.).

F.O. 2/299, Johnston to Salisbury, 5 May 1900 (Indian contingent in Uganda).

F.O. 2/428, Employment of Indian troops in the Protectorates, January to July 1900.

F.O. 2/429, Employment of Indian troops in the Protectorates, August to December 1900.

F.O. 2/431, Agency in India for African Protectorates, 1896-1900. F.O. 2/443, Lansdowne to Eliot, 3 and 27 August 1902 (Indian settlement in E.A.).

F.O. 2/550, Employment of Indian troops in the Protectorates, January to May 1901.

F.O. 2/552, Agency in India for African Protectorates, 1901.

F.O. 2/569, Eliot to Lansdowne, 5 January 1902, enclosures, and minute by Hill, 25 February 1902 (Indian settlement).

F.O. 2/571, Eliot to Lansdowne, 25 April and 8 May 1902 (Indian settlement).

F.O. 2/576, Whitehouse to O'Callaghan, 13 February 1902, enclosures (Indians and the Uganda Railway).

F.O. 2/576, Eliot to Lansdowne, 31 March 1902 (European Settlers' opposition to the Indians).

F.O. 2/671, Coolie Emigration from India to African Protectorates, 1895-1902.

F.O. 2/788, Employment of Indian troops in. the Protectorates, 1902-3. F.O. 2/791, Agency in India for African Protectorates, 1902-3.

F.O. 2/795, Nairobi buildings, 1900-3.

F.O. 2/805, Eliot to Lansdowne, 21 January 1902, enclosed petition of the European colonists dated 4 January 1902, and comments thereon.

F.O. 2/894, Agency in India for African Protectorates, 1904.

F.O. 2/914, Stewart to Lansdowne, 16 January 1905, enclosed report on cotton growing in the E.A.P.

F.O. 2/916, Stewart to Lansdowne, 7 March 1905, enclosed report on Ukamba Province by Ainsworth.

F.O. 2/956, Coinage and currency in E.A. and Uganda, 1900-5.

(b) Foreign Office Confidential Prints

F.O.C.P. no. 2314 (Slave-dealing and slave-holding by Kutchees in

Zanzibar, 1819-70).

F.O.C.P. no. 1936, pp. 17-22 (Report on Zanzibar, 1870-1, by Kirk). F.O.C.P. no. 4637, p. 59 (Zanzibar Customs, 1880).

F.O.C.P. no. 6454, pp. 201, 207 (Sewa Hajee).

F.O.C.P. no. 7040, pp. 10-12 (Indian labour for Uganda Railway, 1897).

F.O.C.P. no. 7212, p. 227 (Indian traders along the Railway, 1898).

F.O.C.P. no. 7400, pp. 108-12 (Indian troops).

F.O.C.P. no. 7400, p. 269 (Influx of Indians into Ukamba, 1899).

F.O.C.P. no. 7402, p. 40 (Role of Indian troops in Uganda, 1899).

F.O.C.P. no. 7403, pp. 54-5 (Report on G.E.A. by the Aga Khan, *1899).*

F.O.C.P. no. 7422, pp. 116-19 (Indian traders along the Railway, 1899).

F.O.C.P. no. 7422, pp. 245-7, 268-9 (Importation of coolies for the Railway, 1899).

F.O.C.P. no. 7675, p. 32 (Report on G.E.A., 1900). F.O.C.P. no. 7690, pp. 16-17 (Johnston's support for Indian settlement, 1901).

F.O.C.P. no. 7690, pp. 65-87 (Report on G.E.A., 1901, by Hollis). F.O.C.P. no. 7732, pp. 253-6, 440 (Affairs of A. M. Jeevanjee, 1901).

F.O.C.P. no. 7732, pp. 312, 369 B and C (Support for Indian settlement in E.A.).

F.O.C.P. no. 7823, pp. 161-2 (Indian caravan traders, 1901).

F.O.C.P. no. 7823, p. 174 (Report by D. 0. Rabat, 1901).

F.O.C.P. no. 7823, p. 198 (Johnston on Indian traders and the circulation of currency in Uganda, 1901).

F.O.C.P. no. 7867, pp. 7-15 (Eliot's report on the E.A.P., June 1901).

F.O.C.P. no. 7922, p. 200 (Chief Engineer's report on Uganda Railway, June 1902).

F.O.C.P. no. 7946, pp. 28, 197 (Allidina Visram, 1902). F.O.C.P. no. 7946, pp. 96-9 (Scheme for Indian settlement, 1902). F.O.C.P. no. 7946, pp. 133, 156-7 (Memorandum by European settlers and official views thereon, 1902).

F.O.C.P. no. 7953, p. 108 (Indians in G.E.A., 1902).

F.O.C.P. no. 7953, pp. 187-8 (Scheme to settle Indian soldiers in East Africa, 1902).

F.O.C.P. no. 8438, pp. 121-2 (Report regarding Indian settlement, 1905).

F.O.C.P. no. 8438, pp. 255-71 (Ainsworth's report on Ukamba Province, 1905).

F.O.C.P. no. 8691, pp. 30-3 (Decline of Zanzibar as a commercial entrepot, 1905).

A3. Colonial Office Archives, Public Record Office, London

(a) Dispatches

C.O. 533/1, Stewart to Lansdowne, 14 March 1905, enclosed report on the financial position and trade of the E.A.P. by Bowring and Marsden.

CO. 533/2, Stewart to Lyttelton, 6 July 1905, enclosed report on the Uganda Railway for 1904-5 by H. A. F. Currie.

C.O. 533/3, Stewart to Lyttelton, 9 August 1905, enclosed memorandum on prospects for traders by Ainsworth and Marsden.

C.O. 533/3, Stewart to Lyttelton, 14 August 1905 (Opposes settlement of Indians in the Highlands).

C.O. 533/3, Jackson to Lyttelton, 26 August 1905, enclosed report of the Treasurer, E.A.P.

C.O. 533/4, Jackson to Lyttelton, 7 October 1905 (British Indian methods of Government).

C.O. 533/4, Jackson to Lyttelton, Telegram, 12 October 1905 (Indian Immigration, attached minute paper gives details of the Kibos scheme).

C.O. 533/4, Jackson to Lyttelton, 18 October 1905, enclosed petition of the European Colonists' Association, 23 August 1905.

C.O. 533/4, Lyttelton to Jackson, 25 October 1905 (Indian Immigration).

C.O. 533/5, Jackson to Lyttelton, n November 1905, enclosed minutes by Hobley, Ainsworth, and Jackson on the European Petition.

C.O. 533/6,1.0. to C.O., 8 July 1905, and enclosure (Administration of the affairs of Uganda Railway Coolies by Protector of Emigrants, Karachi).

C.O. 533/7, Bombay Agent Simson to C.O., 3 August 1905, and enclosures (Recruitment of Indian postal clerks for E.A.).

C.O. 533/19, Sadler to Elgin, 5 December 1906, enclosed report on Indian immigration.

C.O. 533/19, Jackson to Elgin, 20 and 22 December 1906, and enclosures (Subordinate Indian staff).

C.O. 533/59, Sadler to Crewe, Telegram, 12 April 1909 (Sanderson Committee).

C.O. 533/59, Jackson to Crewe, 20 May 1909 (Appointment of Jeevanjee to Legco).

C.O. 533/59, Jackson to Crewe, 21 May 1909 (Indian immigration).

C.O. 533/62, Girouard to Crewe, Telegram, 23 September 1909 (Opposes Indian agricultural settlement and Jeevanjee's appointment).

C.O. 533/63, Girouard to Crewe, 13 November 1909 (Interim report on the E.A.P.).

C.O. 533/102, Girouard to Harcourt, 19 February 1912 (Replacement of Jeevanjee).

C.O. 533/160, LO. to C.O., 13 January 1915, 8 June 1915, C.O. to LO., 21 January 1915, and minute of 10 June 1915 (Importation of Indian labour for Kilindini Harbour works).

CO. 533/160, W.O. to CO., 24 January 1915 (Indian Expeditionary Force for East Africa).

C.O. 536/74, Jeevanjee to C.O., Telegram, 14 January 1914 (Protest regarding Uganda Cotton Rules).

C.O. 536/79, Confidential report on Uganda Cotton Industry by S. Simpson, 31 July 1912, and memorandum thereon.

C.O. 537/402, Belfield to Harcourt, 27 August 1914 (Strike of Indian subordinate staff).

(b) Colonial Office Confidential Prints

C.O.C.P. 879/87/771, pp. 88-114 (Details regarding European Colonists' Petition, 1905).

C.O.C.P. 879/87/772, p. 165 (Memorandum on Traders in East Africa).

C.O.C.P. 879/87/772, p. 188 (Buildings leased by Government from *Jeevanjee).*

C.O.C.P. 879/92/844, p. 169 (Indian role in E.A.P., 1906).

C.O.C.P. 879/105/954, pp. 57-140, 146-53 (Girouard's Reports on the E.A.P., 1910).

A 4. Records of The Bombay Government, Maharashtra State Archives, Bombay

Bombay Government Archives, Political Department (hereafter referred to as P.D.), vol. no. 316, Muscat 1841/2, Compilation no. 101 (Establishment of British Agency in Zanzibar).

P.D. vol. Muscat 1842, Compilation nos. 59 and 145 (Establishment of British Agency in Zanzibar).

P.D. vol. 43 of 1842, Compilation no. 350 (Establishment of British Agency in Zanzibar).

P.D. vol. 59 of 1844, Compilation no. 289 (Firm of Jairam Sewji).

P.D. vol. 33 of 1861, Compilation no. 15 (Muscat-Zanzibar dispute).

P.D. vol. 135 of 1868, Compilation no. 478 (Emancipation of slaves in Zanzibar).

P.D. vol. 144 of 1870, Compilation no. 1198 (Firm of Jairam Sewji).

P.D. vol. 143 of 1871, Compilation no. 1659 (Zanzibar Customs).

P.D. vol. 145 of 1871 (Unfriendly attitude of Bhargash). P.D. vol. 230 of 1873, Compilation no. 88 (Zanzibar Slave Market).

P.D. vol. 280 of 1874, Compilation no. 1963 (Status of Indians in Zanzibar).

P.D. vol. 185 of 1887, Compilation no. 453 (Torya Topan).

P.D. vol. 281 of 1877, Compilation no. 62 (Indian School in Zanzibar) and Compilation no. 309 (Status of Indians at Zanzibar).

P.D. vol. 220 A of 1889, Compilation no. 873 (Peera Dewji).

P.D. vol. 174 of 1891, Compilation nos. 279 and 1063 (Indian School in Zanzibar).

P.D. vol. 134 of 1895, Compilation nos. 107 and 356 (Recruitment of Indians for service in G.E.A. and Congo).

Bombay Government Judicial Department, vol. 96 of 1896, Compilation no. 1170 (Emigration of artisans to E.A.).

Bombay Government, General Department (hereafter referred to as G.D.), vol. 119 C of 1896, Compilation no. 671, Part I (Coolie emigration to *E.A.)*.

G.D. vol. 120 C of 1896, Compilation no. 671, Part II (Coolie emigration).

P.D. vol. 137 of 1896, Compilation no. 795 (Emigration Agents at Bombay for the Uganda Railway).

P.D. vol. 143 of 1896, Compilation nos. 307 and 902 (Coolie Emigration to E.A.).

G.D. vol. 142 C of 1897, Compilation no. 671, Part I (Coolie emigration).

G.D. vol. 143 C of 1897, Compilation no. 671, Part III (Coolie emigration).

G.D. vol. 178 C of 1898, Compilation no. 671 (Coolie emigration).

G.D. vol. 179 C of 1898, Compilation no. 671, Parts II and III (Coolie emigration).

P.D. vol. 23 of 1899, Compilation no. 1140 (Agent in Bombay for the African Protectorates).

P.D. vol. 63 of 1900, Compilation no. 1097 (Indian artisans for G.E.A.).

G.D. vol. 245 C of 1900, Compilation nos. 94,103,120 (Coolie emigration).

G.D. vol. 277 C of 1901, Compilation no. 40 (Legalising emigration to E.A.).

G.D. vol. 278 C of 1901, Compilation nos. 91, 106, 120 (Emigration to E.A.).

G.D. vol. 279 C of 1901, Compilation nos. 141,159 (Emigration to E.A.).

G.D. vol. 280 C of 1901, Compilation no. 181 (Emigration to E.A.).

G.D. vol. 323 C of 1902, Compilation no. 54 (Emigration to E.A.).

G.D. vol. 340 C of 1903, Compilation no. 82 (Emigration to E.A.).

Judicial Department, vol. 88 of 1904, Compilation no. 49 (Emigration to E.A.).

G.D. vol. 394 C of 1906, Compilation no. 55 (Indian settlement in E.A.).

G.D. vol. 5 C of 1907, Compilation no. 64 (Illegal emigration to E.A.).

G.D. vol. 8 C of 1909, Compilation no. 9 (Voluntary emigration to E.A.).

G.D. vol. 59 of 1910, Compilation no. 417 (Illegal emigration to E.A.).

G.D. vol. 71 of 1911, Compilation no. 1199 (Emigration to E.A.).

P.D. vol. 122 of 1912, Compilation no. 1541 (Memorial to Government of India on behalf of Indians in E.A.).

P.D. vol. 113 of 1913, Compilation 1282 (Memorial to Government of India on behalf of Indians in E.A.).

P.D. 1914, Compilation no. 1335 (Emigration to G.E.A.).

These were consulted before the National Archives were established. References to relevant material in the records in Zanzibar and Dar es Salaam are, therefore, provided separately.

(a) Zanzibar

Serial no. E n, Hamerton to Bombay, Outward Letters no. 13 of 1848 and no. 12 of 1849 (Firm of Jairam Sewji).

Serial no. E. 19, Hamerton to Bombay, Outward Letters no. 9 and 13 of 1854 (British Indians in Zanzibar).

Serial no. E. 26, Rigby to Bombay, Outward Letter no. 23 of 1858 (Trade between Zanzibar and Bombay).

Serial no. E. 26, Rigby to Bombay, Outward Letter no. 46 of 1859 (Report on Zanzibar).

Serial no. E. 28, Rigby to Bombay, Outward Letter no. 3 of 1860 (Report on Zanzibar).

Serial no. E. 41, Churchill to Bombay, Outward Letter no. 50/193 of 1868 (Jairam Sewji).

(b) Dar es Salaam

File no. 3150 (1920) (Segregation of Races).

File no. 3033/3 (1920-2) (Sale of ex-enemy property).

File no. 7235 (1923) (Indian Question).

File no. 7596 (1924-5) (Controversy re the Profits Tax).

File no. 7092, vol. I (1922) and vol. ii (1926) (Trading Licensing Ordinance, 1923).

File no. 7017 (1925) (Indian education).

File no. 7652 (1925) (Sewa Hajee).

A 6. Kenya National Archives, Nairobi

The Mombasa Provincial records are quoted separately as a part of them were consulted in Mombasa before they were moved to the National Archives in Nairobi.

(a)

PC/CP. 1/1/2: Machakos District Political Record Book, 1889-1912.

PC/NZA. 3/22, I/I to 1/16 and 3/22/1, 3: Indian settlement at Kibos.

PC/NZA. 1/2: Nyanza Province Annual Reports, 1905-45.

MKS/I: Machakos District Annual Reports, 1909-16.

PC/CP. 9/3/I: Land Settlement, 1909.

MKS/57: Machakos District Political Record Book, vol. ii, 1910-11.

KBU/2, 3, 4: Kiambu District Annual Reports, 1910, 1911, and 1912.

TTA/5: Political Record Book, Taita District, vol. I, 1913-25.

PC/RVP. 2/8/2-21: Uasin Gishu District Annual Reports, 1913-45.

PC/CP. 1/3/4: Machakos District Political Record Book, 1914-21.

NFD. II: Annual Reports, Samburu District, 1914-28.

ELGM/10: Elgeyo-Marakwet District Misc. Correspondence, 1914-30.

DC/KAJ. 9/1/1: Political Record Book, Kajiado District.

PC/CP. 4/3/1: Central Province Annual Reports, 1934-8.

PC/CP. 15/1/2: Political Record Book, Central Province, 1921-9.

PC/CP. 4/2/3: Ukamba Province Annual Reports, 1925-32.

ARC/(GH)—103: Indian Education, 1929-48.

ARC(GH)—141 I: Federation of Indian Chambers of Commerce and Industry of Eastern Africa.

PC/CP. 4/1/2: Kikuyu Province Annual Reports, 1920-32.

ARC(GH)—77: A. M. Jeevanjee.

(b) Lands Department, Nairobi

File no. 15993: General Question of Policy re Indians in E.A.P.

(c) *Mombasa Provincial Archives* (i) Material seen at Mombasa:

Shelf 65, file 6: 'Uganda Railway, Outward, 1898-1900.'

Shelf 66, file 10: 'Inward Uganda Administration 1896-99.'

Shelf 66, file ii: 'Uganda Railway, Inward, 1898-1900.'

Shelf 76, file 50: ' Ukamba Outward 1899.'

Shelf 88, file 138: 'Inward H.M. Commissioner 1906.'

Shelf 64, file 260 of 1912: Annual Reports 1911-12 from Districts.

Shelf I, file 37 of 1912: Quarterly Reports 1911 from Districts.

Shelf 8, file 177: Correspondence with Agents in India.

Shelf 12, file 204: Legal Status of Indians in E.A., 1914.

Shelf 30, file 404: Indian School, Mombasa, 1915-21.

Shelf 50, file 1215: Indian Association in E.A., 1916-21.

(ii) Material seen at Nairobi:

Mombasa file no. 103/7: Allidina Visram Soap Factory, 1907.

Mombasa file no. 2/126: Township property in Mombasa.

Mombasa file no. 3/286: Abolition of Bombay Agency.

Mombasa file no. 38/605: Visram's goods at Kisumu, 1915-16.

Mombasa file no. 37/576: Permits to open shops, 1915-16.

Mombasa file no. 42/797: Indian mills on alienated lands, 1917.

Mombasa file no. 43/902: Segregation of races, 1918.

Mombasa file no. 64/10: Political unrest, 1923.

Mombasa file no. 2/253: Closer Union Commission. 1927-31.

Mombasa file no. 2/1/2: Municipal Government Mombasa, 1930-2.

Mombasa file no. 2/241: Financial Inquiry, Lord Moyne, 1932.

Mombasa file no. 2/283: Kenya Highlands League, 1938-9.

Mombasa file no. 106/58: Evidence, Mombasa Labour Commission of Inquiry, 1939.

A 7. Uganda National Archives, Entebbe

Class A29, item I: Correspondence with Government of India, 1900-6.

Class A27, item 4: Indian surveyors for Uganda, 1901-5.

File no. 1703/1909: Artisans from India.

File no. 386 of 1909: Emigration from India to Crown Colonies.

Secretariat Minute Papers, nos. 1608, 2115, 2974: Indian Contingent in Uganda.

File no. 1827/1909: Report on Cotton by H. Bell.

File no. 1323/1909: Ivory trading in Karamoja.

File no. 409/1906: Busoga trade prospects.

File no. 5426, Part I and II: Policy of Concentration in petty townships and trading centres.

File no. 661: Regulation of cotton buying in Eastern Province.

File no. 8629: Federation of Indian Chambers of Commerce and Industry.

File no. 5387: Cotton Ginners Association.

File no. C. 585: Visit of Revd. C. F. Andrews.

File no. 5550: Indian Association, Kampala.

File no. 539, Part I and II: Indian education in Uganda.

File no. 7401: Sugar mill at Lugazi.

File no. 141: Residence by Non-European on Land.

File no. 6024: Report on the E.A.I.N.C. for 1919.

File no. 4092: Indian newspapers in E.A., 1920.

File no. 1138: Buganda Province Annual Reports from 1909.

File no. 2135: Northern Province Annual Reports from 1909.

File no. 703: Eastern Province Annual Reports from 1909.

File no. 925: Eastern Province Annual Reports from 1908-9.

File no. 1972 C: Buganda Province Monthly Reports, 1914.

File no. 4832: Allidina Visram (contains comprehensive information).

File no. 1330: Allidina Visram's agents in Eastern Province and Abyssinia.

File no. 1145/1909: Allidina Visram and the Oil Industry in Bukedi.

File no. 831/1907: Allidina Visram and Toro Produce.

File no. 6520: Miscellaneous: Allidina Visram.

File nos. 57 and 72: Allidina Visram's Agents in Congo, 1908-9.

File no. 4303: Allidina Visram and trade in hoes.

File nos. 553, 756, and 4699: Allidina Visram and porters.

File no. 5677: Allidina Visram and war with Germany.

File no. 1207: Allidina Visram and Agent at Mbale, 1907.

File nos.46.87,262,579,671,990, 10106,1322, and 5075: Allidina Visram's land.

File no. 806: Allidina Visram, Leather Tannery, Entebbe, 1907.

File no. 131: Allidina Visram, Erection of ginnery and oil factory at Entebbe, 1910.

File no. 1208: Allidina Visram and coffee, 1907.

File no. 569: Allidina Visram and timber industry, 1908.

File nos. 146, 409, 483: Allidina Visram and timber industry, 1909.

B. Non-Official Archives

B I. Records of The East African Indian National Congress (now the Kenya Indian Congress) Nairobi Files marked:

"Correspondence and Proceedings of the Indian Association Nairobi, 1917-1922.'

'Correspondence 1918.'

'East Africa Indian Deputation to London 1920.'

'Outward 1920-23.'

'Indian Association Nairobi: Report for the Year 1921.' 'Correspondence 1922.'

'Correspondence with Kenya and Uganda Governments 1921.'

'Correspondence with Indians Overseas Association.' no. 43:

'Correspondence with Kenya Government re Poll Tax 1924.' no. 26: 'Correspondence 1925-27.'

'Resolutions 1931 Congress.'

'Miscellaneous Correspondence 1931-33.'

'Outward 1933.'

'Secretary's Report 1933-34.'

'Correspondence 1935.'

'Secretary's Report 1938.'

1939 Correspondence.'

'Inter-temtorial Conference 1946.'

In addition, the following printed material in the Congress records provides valuable information (some of this material can now also be found in the History Department Archives, University College, Nairobi):

(i) *Presidential Addresses* (including Resolutions of Sessions), by T. M. Jeevanjee (1914)' Sarojini Naidu (1924), Tyeb Alt (1927), H. N. Kunzru (1929), A. D. Sheth (1932), J. B. Pandya (1934), A. H. Kaderbhoy (1935). A. B. Patel (1938, 1942, and 1945), S. G. Amin (1946), Shamsud-Deen (1944), D. D. Puri (1948), and S. Gautama (1960).

(ii) Memorandum on the Federation of British East African Territories and Constitutional Changes in Kenya submitted by the E.A.I.N.C. to the Hilton Young Commission.'

(iii) 'Supplement to the Memorandum submitted by the E.A.I.N.C. to the Hilton Young Commission.'

(iv) 'Memorandum submitted by the Executive Committee of the E.A.I.N.C. to the Secretary of State for the Colonies on the "Reservation of Highlands of Kenya for Europeans", 7 October 1938.'

(v) 'Petition of the E.A.I.N.C. to the King to Disallow Religious Separate Electorates, 10 January 1952."

B 2. Sidney Webb (Lord Passfield) Papers, London School of Economics

Vol. iv, file E, item 108 (d): Boycott of the Joint Select Committee by the Tanganyika Indians.

Vol. v, file F, item 123, 128, and 134 (i): E.A.I.N.C. Split 1931.

B 3. International Missionary Council, Edinburgh House, London, *Papers of Dr. J. H. Oldham*

Box marked: 'Kenya Indians.'

File marked: 'Kenya Indians: Colonial Office.

File 'Kenya Indians: General Correspondence.'

File ' Kenya Indians: Indian Delegation and Correspondence with India.'

File 'India, C. F. Andrews.'

File 'East Africa: Indians in East Africa.'

File 'Kenya Indians: Archbishop of Canterbury.'

File 'Native Unrest (1922): Harry Thuku.'

B 4. Lord Francis Scott Papers, University College, Nairobi

File no. D/37: Resolutions passed at Conference on Constitutional

Advance, July 1933. File no. E/25-6: Resolutions passed by the Convention of Associations, September 1935.

File no. E/io: Statement of the Settlers' Case 1935.

B 5. Minutes of The Uganda Chamber of Commerce, Makerere University College Library, Kampala

These minutes, especially for the decade after 1905, provide useful information about the early Indian traders in Uganda.

C. Official Publications

C I. Parliamentary Papers

Report by Sir A. Hardinge on the condition and progress of the East African Protectorate from its establishment to the 20th July 1897, C. 8683 (1897).

Report by Sir A. Hardinge on the British East Africa Protectorate for the year 1897-98, C. 9125 (1899).

Report on the Uganda Railway by Sir G. Molesworth, C. 9331 (1899).

Despatch from H.M. Special Commissioner in Uganda relating to travellers in the Protectorate, *Cd. 590 (1901).*

Report by H.M. Special Commissioner on the Protectorate of Uganda, *Cd. 671 (1901).*

Final Report of the Uganda Railway Committee, *Cd. 2164 (1904).*

Reports relating to the administration of the East African Protectorate, Cd. 2740 (1905).

Correspondence relating to affairs in the E.A.P., *Cd. 4122 (1908).*

Correspondence relating to the tenure of land in the E.A.P., *Cd. 4117 (1908).*

Report of the Committee on Emigration from India to the Crown Colonies *and Protectorates, Part I, Cd. 5192 (1910).*

Ibid.,, Part II, Minutes of Evidence, Cd. 5193 (1910).

Ibid.,, Part III, Papers laid before the Committee, Cd. 5194 (1910).

Correspondence regarding the position of Indians in East Africa, Cmd. 1311 (1921).

Report by Sir Benjamin Robertson, dated 4 August 1020 regarding the proposed settlement of Indian agriculturists in Tanganyika Territory Cmd. 1312 (1921). Indians in Kenya, Cmd. 1922 (1923);

Report of the East Africa Commission, *Cmd. 2387 (1925).*

Future policy in regard to Eastern Africa, *Cmd. 2904 (1927).*

Report of the Commission on Closer Union of the Dependencies in Eastern and Central Africa, Cmd. 3234 (1929).

Report of Sir Samuel Wilson on his visit to East Africa, *Cmd. 3378 (1929).* Memorandum on native policy in East Africa, *Cmd. 3573 (1930).* Statement of the conclusions of H.M.'s Government in the U.K. as regards Closer Union in East Africa, *Cmd. 3574 (1930).*

Report by the Financial Commissioner (Lord Moyne) on certain questions in Kenya, *Cmd. 4093 (1932).*

East Africa Royal Commission 1953-1955 report, Cmd. 9475 (1955).

C 2. Official Reports

C P. Rigby, *Report on the Zanzibar Dominions* (Bombay, 1861). *Handbook for East Africa, Uganda and Zanzibar* (Mombasa, 1904). E.A.P.

Report of the Land Committee (Nairobi, 1905). W. J. Simpson, *Report on sanitary matters in the E.A.P., Uganda and Zanzibar* (Colonial Office, 1915). E.A.P., *Economic Commission report* (Nairobi, 1919).

T. Sleith, Report on trade conditions in British East Africa Uganda and

Zanzibar *(Cape Town, 1919).*

Uganda, Report of the Uganda Development Commission (Entebbe, 1920). Proceedings of the Standing Joint Committee on Indian affairs (London, 1921).

Zanzibar, Report of the Commission on Agriculture *(Zanzibar, 1923). Kenya,* Report of the Local Government Commission *(Nairobi, 1927).*

Uganda, Report of the Commission of Enquiry into the cotton industry of Uganda *(Entebbe, 1929).*

Uganda, Report of the Local Government Committee (Entebbe, 1930). Report by the Rt, Hon. V. S. S. Sastri, regarding his Mission to East Africa (Delhi, 1930). Joint Select Committee on Closer Union in East Africa, vol. I, Report (London, 1931).

Ibid., vol. ii, Minutes of Evidence.

Ibid., vol. iii. Appendices. Papers relating to the question of Closer Union of Kenya, Uganda and Tanganyika Territory, *Colonial no. 57 (1931).*

C. A. Bartlett and J. S. Last, Report on the indebtedness of the Agricultural Classes, 1933 (Zanzibar, 1934).

Kenya, Land Commission, Evidence, *vol. iii (Nairobi, 1934).*

Report by K. P. S. Menon on marketing legislation in Tanganyika, Uganda and Kenya, 1935.

C.O. Pamphlet no. 274. Zanzibar, Report of a sub-committee of Zanzibar Advisory Council on Education, on grants-in-aid and on the reorganisation of Indian education *(Zanzibar, 1935).*

Report of the Commission appointed to enquire into and report on the financial position and system of taxation of Kenya, *Colonial no. 116 (1936).*

B. H. Binder, Report on the Zanzibar clove industry *(Zanzibar, 1936). A. A. Kazimi,* An Enquiry into Indian education in East Africa *(Nairobi, 1948).*

Report of the Commission on the Civil Services of Kenya, Tanganyika, Uganda and Zanzibar *(London, 1948).*

Kenya, Report of the Committee on Educational Expenditure (European and Asian) (Nairobi, 1948).

Kenya, Report of the Select Committee on Indian education (Nairobi, 1949). Tanganyika, Department of Education'. Triennial Survey 1955-57 (Dar es *Salaam, 1958).*

Kenya, Report on Asian and European education in Kenya *(Nairobi, 1958).*

Uganda, Annual Report of the Education Department 1060 *(Entebbe, 1960).*

India, Gazette of India Extraordinary, *24 June 1935, refers to the marketing legislation in East Africa.*

Kenya, *Official Gazette* (see especially the issue of 18 August 1920 and 17 August 1923).

Zanzibar, *Official Gazette* (the various issues during the 1890s are particularly useful).

Census Reports for Kenya, Uganda, Tanganyika, and Zanzibar and *Annual Reports* for Kenya, Uganda, Tanganyika, and Zanzibar.

C 3. Proceedings of The Legislative Councils

(a) Proceedings of the Kenya Legislative Council

31 October 1910: Jeevanjee's allegations in London.

18 January 1915, pp. 11-12: Objects of the Crown Lands Ordinance.

19 June 1917, pp. 19, 21: Indian demands for elective representation.

9 December 1918, pp. 44-8: Indian Question.

24 February 1919, p. 3: Northey's views on the Indian Question.

29 November 1920, p. 6: The Milner 'solution'.

10 February 1921, pp. 85-6: Segregation.

8 March 1927, p. 27: Indian elections.

30 August 1927, pp. 300-1: Grigg's views on the Indian Question.

25 April 1934, p. 97: L Dass.

9 May 1934, pp. 185-210: Separate European and Asian Civil Service.

28 June 1935, pp. 69, 73:1. Dass. I

July 1935, pp. 110-II: I. Dass.

3 July 1935, pp. 188-231: J. B. Pandya's opposition to marketing legislation.

5 November 1936, pp. 392-406: J. B. Pandya.

12 November 1936, pp. 545-59: Indian representation on municipal councils.

16 November 1936, pp. 610-11: Indian representation on municipal councils.

10 November 1937, p. 189: Opposition to Transport Licensing Bill.

12 November 1937, p. 261: Opposition to Transport Licensing Bill.

17 November 1937, pp. 387-8. 406:1. Dass.

9 August 1938, pp. 67-72:1. Dass speaks on behalf of Kikuyu Central Association.

10 August 1938, pp. 116-23: I. Dass on behalf of K.C.A.

17 August 1938, pp. 226-41:1. Dass speaks on behalf of the Kamba Protest Movement.

9 November 1938, p. 205: Indian representation on municipal councils.

21 April 1939, pp. 255-71: A. B. Patel's motion against the Highlands Order-in-Council.

21 April 1939, pp. 284-9: I. Dass reads African petition regarding Highlands.

14 December 1939, p. 361: Shamsud-Deen on racial discrimination in Civil Service.

14 December 1939, p. 389:1. Dass.

26 November 1946, p. 371: Indian views on Government expenditure.

29 November 1946, pp. 479-91: A. B. Patel. 23 October 1953, pp. 107-8: E. Mathu's views on Asians.

(b) Proceedings of the Uganda Legislative Council

3 March 1921, Appendix B: Indian Question.

10 June 1921, Appendix A and p. 15: Indian Question.

20 August 1921, Appendix A and p. 15: Indian Question.

28 May 1926, Appendix B: Indians in Uganda.

5 December 1932: Marketing legislation.

(c) *Proceedings of the Zanzibar Legislative Council*

10 December 1936: Address by the British Resident re the clove controversy.

30 September 1937: Address by the British Resident re the clove controversy.

2 December 1937: Address by the British Resident re the clove controversy.

Sessional Paper no. 5 of 1935: Report of the Commission on Agricultural Indebtedness.

Sessional Paper no. 10 of 1935: Indian education.

Sessional Paper no. 13 of 1937: Regulation of the clove industry.

Sessional Paper no. 14 of 1937: Regulation of the clove industry.

Sessional Paper no. 6 of 1938: Regulation of the clove industry.

D. Non-Official Publications

D I. Newspapers

(i) East African Standard (Nairobi)

6 January and 22 December 1906: Sadler's relations with the Indians.

13 January 1906: Indian traders supplying 'rebels' at Kilwa.

17 February 1906: Indian traders supplying 'rebels' at Kilwa.

7 April 1906: Indian mass meeting at Mombasa.

15 December 1906: Indian delegation to London.

25 January, 3 May, and 21 June 1919: Indian Question.

18 and 20 August and 11 December 1920: Indian Question.

17 July 1926: Obituary on M. A. Desai.

20 January, 21 and 28 April, and 5 May 1934: Political controversy in Kenya and Uganda.

11 January 1960: Joint statement by Indian Congress and Muslim League.

13 December 1962, 25 April 1963, I October 1964, and 18 March 1966: Information about four leading Asian businessmen.

16 November 1962,31 December 1965, and I January 1966: A. M. Jeevanjee as founder of the *Standard.*

(ii) The Leader of B.E.A. *(Nairobi}*

27 June 1908: Indian petition for representation.

2 April, 7 and 21 May, 3 and 17 September and particularly I October 1910, and 17 April 1915: for information about Jeevanjee.

8 and 15 July 1916: for information about Allidina Visram.

The Leader Annual and Gazetteer of British East Africa 1914.

D 2. Contemporary Publications: Books, Pamphlets and Articles

Under this category only those works are mentioned which have provided valuable Primary information. Other contemporary publications have been listed as secondary sources. The list is arranged chronologically:

J. H. SPEKE, Journal of the discovery of the source of the Nile *(London, 1863).*

—— What led to the discovery of the source of the Nile *(London, 1864).*

R. F. Burton, *Zanzibar, city, island and coast,* 2 vols. (London, 1872).

The Last Journals of David Livingstone, 2 vols. (London, 1874).

J. Christie, *Cholera epidemics in East Africa* (London, 1876).

V. L. Cameron, *Across Africa,* 2 vols. (London, 1877).

H. M. Stanley, *Through the Dark Continent,* 2 vols. (London, 1878).

J. F. Elton, *Travels and researches among the lakes and mountains of East and Central Africa* (London, 1879).

P. L. Mcdermott, *British East Africa or IBEA* (London, 1893).

F. D. Lugard, The rise of our East African Empire, *2 vols. (London, 1893).*

J. R. J. Macdonald, Soldiering and surveying in B.E.A., 18 1-04 (London, 1897).

J. Ainsworth, 'A description of the Ukamba Province, E.A.P. 1900'. | CO. Pamphlet no. 6.

F. L. O'callaghan, 'Uganda Railway', *Professional papers of the Corps of Royal Engineers 1900,* xxvi, Paper viii, C.O. Pamphlet no. 7.

H. Samuel, "The Uganda of today', *Journal of the Society of Arts,* ii, no. 2626 (20 March 1903), C.O. Pamphlet no. 15.

H. H. Johnston, *The Uganda Protectorate, 2* vols. (London, 1902).

R. N. Lyne, Zanzibar in contemporary times *(London, 1905).*

J. H. Patterson, *The man-eaters of savo* (London, 1907).

W. S. Churchill, My African journey *(London, 1908).*

A. M. Jeevanjee, An appeal on behalf of Indians in East Africa (Bombay, 1912).

Koloniale Monatsblatter, Berlin (1913).

A. M. Jeevanjee, *Sanitation in Nairobi* (Bombay, 1915), C.O. Pamphlet no. 214.

Deutsches Koloniale Lexicon, vol. ii (Berlin, 1920).

C. F. Andrews, *The Indian Question in East Africa* (Nairobi, 1921),

C.O. Pamphlet no. 61. Lord Delamere and C. K. Archer, *Memorandum on the case against the claims of Indians in Kenya* (Nairobi, 1921).

East African Standard, The Indian problem in Kenya, April-October 1921 (Nairobi, 1922).

Indians Abroad: *Kenya* (Bulletin of the Imperial Indian Citizenship Association, Bombay, 1923).

W. M. Ross, *Kenya from within* (London, 1927).

A. H. Hardinge, *A diplomatist in the East* (London, 1928). Indians abroad: *East Africa: Royal Commission on the Union of East Africa* (Bulletin of the Imperial Indian Citizenship Association, Bombay, 1928).

C. W. Hobley, Kenya from chartered company to Crown Colony (London, 1929).

Speeches by H.E. Sir Edward Grigg, 1925-30 (Nairobi, 1930).

F. J. Jackson, *Early days in East Africa* (London, 1930).

P. D. Master, *Segregation of Indians in Kenya* (Mombasa, 1931).

Memorandum by the Indian National Association, Zanzibar, *25 February 1935, C.O. Pamphlet no. 270.*

T. J. Mboya, *Freedom and after* (London, 1963).

M. Blundell, *So rough a wind* (London, 1964).

II Secondary Material

G. Bennett and C. Rosberg, *The Kenyatta election: Kenya 1960-61* (London, 1961).

G. Bennett, *Kenya: A political history* (London, 1963).

N. R. Bennett, *Studies in East African history* (Boston, 1963).

H. Brode, *Tippoo Tib* (London, 1907).

—— *British and German East Africa* (London, 1911).

R. L. Buell, *The native problem in Africa, 2* vols. (New York, 1928).

V. Chanan Singh, *The Indian case against the Immigration Bill* (Nairobi, 1947).

F. D. Corfield, The origins and growth of Mau Mau: an historical survey*(Nairobi, 1960).*

R. Coupland, *East Africa and its Oxford,* 1938).

The exploitation of East Africa, 1856-1890 (London, 1939).

Lord Cranworth, *Kenya Chronicles* (London, 1939).

I. M. Cumpston, Indians overseas in British territories, 1834-54 *(Oxford)*

G. Delf, *Asians in East Africa* (London, 1963).

M. R. Dilley, *British policy in Kenya Colony* (New York, 1937).

Y. S. A. Drumkey, *Drumkey's Year Book of East Africa* (Bombay, 1908).

C. Euot, *The East Africa Protectorate* (London, 1905).

G. S. P. Freeman-Grenville, medieval history of the coast o Tanganyika (London, 1962). N. GANGULEE, Indians in the Empire overseas (London, 1947).

D. Ghai (ed.). *Portrait of a minority: Asians in East Africa* (Nairobi, 1965).

J. Gray, *History of Zanzibar* (London, 1962).

R. G. Gregory, *Sidney Webb and East Africa* (Berkeley, 1962).

Lord Hailey, *An African survey* (London, rev. ed. 1957).

W. K. Hancock, *Survey of British Commonwealth affairs,* 2 vols. (London, 1938). V. Harlow and Mrs. E. M. CHILVER (eds.). *History of East Africa* vol. ii (Oxford, 1965).

M. F. Hill, *Permanent way,* vol. I (Nairobi, 1949).

L. W. Holungsworth, *The Asians of East Africa* (London, 1960).

C. Horden, Military operations in East Africa, *vol. I (London, 1941).*

G. Hunter, *The New societies of tropical Africa* (London, 1962).

E. Huxley, *The sorcerer's apprentice* (London, 1951).

K. Ingham, *The making of Modern Uganda* (London, 1958).

—— *A history of East Africa* (London, 1962).

W. Junker, *Travels in Africa,* Tr. A. H. Keane (London, 1892).

Kenya Indian Congress, *A spotlight on the Asians of Kenya* (Nairobi, 1963).

C. Kondapi, *Indians overseas, 18 39-49* (New Delhi, 1951).

C. Legum, *Must we lose Africa* (London, 1954).

N. Leys, *Kenya* (London, 1924).

W. R. Louis, *Ruanda Urundi 1884- IOJa* (Oxford, 1963).

D. A. Low and R. C. Pratt, *Buganda and British overrule* (London, 1960).

F. D. Lugard, *The dual mandate in British Tropical Africa* (London, 1922).

P. Mitchell, *African afterthoughts* (London, 1954).

H. Moyse-Bartlett, *The King's African Rifles* (Aldershot, 1956).

G. H. Mungeam, *British Rule in Kenya, 1886-1012* (Oxford, 1966).

R. Oliver, *The missionary factor in East Africa* (London, 1952).

—— *Sir Harry Johnston and the scramble for Africa* (London, 1959).

—— and G. Mathew (eds.). *History of East Africa,* vol. I (Oxford, 1963).

S. Pandit, *Asians in East Africa: who's who* (Nairobi, 1963).

H. R. A. Philp, *A new day in Kenya* (London, 1936).

S. Playne and F. H. Gale, *East Africa (British)* (London, 1908-9).

J. B. Purvis, *Through Uganda to Mount Elgon (London, 1909).*

N. V. Rajkumar, Indians outside India *(New Delhi, 1951).*

K. Robinson and F. Madden, *Essays in Imperial Government presented to Margery Per-ham* (Oxford, 1963).

R. Robinson and J. Gallagher, *Africa and the Victorians* (London, 1961).

J. Roscoe, *The soul of Central Africa* (London, 1922).

C. E. B. Russell, General Rigby, Zanzibar and the slave trade (London, 1935). Sobers Commercial Directory and Handbook of Uganda 1947-48 (Kampala, 1948).

G. F. Sayers, *The handbook of Tanganyika* (London, 1930).

J. Strandes, *The Portuguese period in East Africa,* tr. Jean F. Wallwork (Nairobi, 1961).

H. M. Stanley, *In darkest Africa*, 2 vols. (London, 1890).

S. Wood, *Kenya: The tensions of progress* (London, 1960).

2. Articles

G. Bennett, "The development of political organisation in Kenya', *Political studies,* v, no. 2 (June 1957), 113-30.

N. R. Bennett, "Americans in Zanzibar 1825-45', *Tanganyika notes and records,* no. 56 (March 1961), 101-6.

—— 'Americans in Zanzibar 1845-65', *Tanganyika notes and records,* no. 57 (September 1961), 121-31.

E. Ehruch, "Some social and economic implications of paternalism in Uganda', *Journal of African history,* iv, no. 2 (1963), 275-85.

J. Gray, 'Early connections between the U.S. and East Africa", *Tanganyika notes and records,* no. 22 (December 1946), 55-86.

H. S. Morris, 'Indians in East Africa: a study in a plural society', *British journal of sociology,* vii, no. 3 (1956).

D. F. Pocock, '"Difference" in East Africa: A study of caste and religion in modem Indian society'. *Southwestern journal of anthropology,* 13, no. 4 (Winter 1957), 289-300.

G.C. Whitehouse, 'The building of the Kenya and Uganda Railway', *Uganda journal,* 12, no. I (March 1948), 1-15.

INDEX

A

B

C

K

L

M

N

O

P

Q

R

S

[illegible] Guiana, West Indies, Fiji Islands [illegible] Africa. It [illegible] to be [illegible] East Africa [illegible] of the Asian community [illegible] it is important to [illegible] the [illegible] political, economic and social [illegible] of the [illegible] population in [illegible] for the [illegible] [illegible] closely [illegible] on some [illegible] the fact that many businessmen, [illegible] doctors, accountants and other professional men [illegible] proportion of their earnings from the Asian [illegible] reinforce [illegible] propensity to [illegible] needs and aspirations.

Economically Active Population

[illegible] of the Asian [illegible] [illegible] reports indicate that the economically active population constituted about 25-27 per cent of the entire Asian population in the three East African countries. This is a much lower proportion than among the European community, the main reasons for this are, of course, the higher proportion of European women in employment, as well as a lower proportion of children and retired persons in the European population of East Africa. Another remarkable feature of the Asian community, again in sharp contrast to the European, is the relatively small proportion of the economically active population working as employees. However, the [illegible] patterns in this respect are sufficiently divergent for us to consider each country separately.